ATHENA VRETTOS

Somatic Fictions

Imagining Illness in
Victorian Culture

STANFORD UNIVERSITY PRESS
STANFORD, CALIFORNIA
1995

Stanford University Press
Stanford, California
©1995 by the Board of Trustees of the Leland Stanford Junior University
Printed in the United States of America

CIP data are at the end of the book

Stanford University Press publications are distributed exclusively by
Stanford University Press within the United States, Canada, and Mexico;
they are distributed exclusively by Cambridge University Press
throughout the rest of the world.

For my mother,
Margaret Vrettos Gannon,
and in memory of
Thomas E. Yingling,
May 3, 1951 to July 28, 1992

Acknowledgments

I have accumulated numerous debts in the writing of this book, and I wish to express my gratitude to the following individuals and institutions. A fellowship from the American Council of Learned Societies allowed me a year's sabbatical to write and research, and a Horace H. Rackham Faculty Recognition Award from the University of Michigan provided extra funding for research expenses during that year and beyond. The Department of English at the University of Michigan granted me a one-semester leave and provided less tangible but equally sustaining intellectual support from my colleagues there over the past five years. The Women's Studies Program at the University of Michigan provided funding for my research assistant Erin O'Connor, who has contributed substantially to this book's production. Without her creative discoveries in library holdings and her tireless dedication in proofreading, this book could never have been finished. The Summer Research Opportunities Program and the Honors Program at the University of Michigan sponsored two undergraduate researchers, Upjeet Chandan and Miriam Cohen, to study advice about women's reading habits and exercise in popular nineteenth-century health manuals. Their careful work in the summer of 1991 helped provide crucial background for the first and last chapters. I also thank Kathleen Marien for her help in the research and translation of nineteenth-century crowd theory for Chapter 3.

I am fortunate to have had Helen Tartar as editor, Jan Spauschus Johnson as associate editor, and Janet Mowery as copy editor at Stanford University Press. They have been consistently supportive and meticulous in the book's preparation. I also thank Dianne Sadoff for her careful reading of the manuscript and advice about the conclusion. A version of Chapter 2 originally appeared in *Victorian Studies* 33: 4 (Summer 1990), 551–79; I am grateful to Patrick Brantlinger and the editorial board for their encouragement and advice.

I have benefited from the insight and critical judgment of a number of friends and colleagues at Michigan who have read portions or all of the manuscript in its various incarnations. Jonathan Freedman, Anne Herrmann, Marjorie Levinson, Anita Norich, and Martha Vicinus provided crucial input at different stages. John Kucich patiently read more versions of the manuscript than anyone should have been expected to, offering consistently helpful and intelligent commentary. Adela Pinch generously offered her time, ideas, friendship, and support, reading drafts, frequently at odd hours, with unusual care and insight. Over the years she has become the reader I most often imagine while I write.

The book has also been enriched by a network of friendships that date back to my years in Philadelphia. My greatest intellectual debt is to Elaine Scarry, whose ability to see through a tangled web of ideas, usually over the telephone, will always seem miraculous to me. Her example, her sympathy, and her generosity of vision have consistently enriched my thinking and enabled my writing. Nina Auerbach's rigorous skepticism about "murky" language and the example of her inventive mind and prose established a standard I have carried with me through the years. I am also thankful to David McWhirter for his cogent criticism, especially on *Wings of the Dove*. Among many friends from Philadelphia, Michael Awkward, Steve Goldsmith, Colleen Lamos, Celeste Langan, Joe Valente, and most of all Tom Yingling provided me with models of scholarly excellence and a supportive community in which to grow. This book is dedicated to Tom, who helped me in more ways than I can ever express, and whose combination of kindness, intelligence, and joy in life enriched us all. Steve Goldsmith deserves thanks for his consistently probing questions and demanding intellectual standards during our many summer discussions over coffee in Berkeley. My appreciation also to Samuel Palmer Goldsmith for his concentrated attention to mud puddles during one particularly productive and clarifying discussion with his father during an afternoon walk in the park.

My mother, Margaret Vrettos Gannon, to whom this book is also dedicated, has demonstrated unfailing support and the utmost patience with all the foibles of an academic daughter. I thank her for always believing in me, and for giving me the freedom to grow in directions she might not always have anticipated.

Finally, my most important and most intangible debt is to Christopher Flint, who cheered and sustained me through the bleakest moments, listened patiently to the most incoherent ramblings, and still subjected my prose to the most rigorous criticism in the face of often petulant opposition. Without his nurturing, both intellectual and emotional, this book could not have been completed.

A.V.

Contents

⁊

SOMATIC FICTIONS

Introduction

To talk of diseases is a sort of Arabian Nights' entertainment.

—Sir William Osler

૪

The attraction of the "medical" body, its diseases and diagnoses, as a subject of narrative interest is, as the celebrated nineteenth-century physician Sir William Osler recognized, seemingly endless. Like the mythical "wandering womb" of the hysteric, fictions of illness make their appearance in multiple and shifting areas of Victorian thought. It is difficult to find many Victorian novels that do not participate in a general dialogue about sickness and health, whether through sustained representations of physical affliction and exertion or passing metaphors of bodily sensitivity and threat. Equally pervasive are the narrative maneuvers of Victorian medical texts in their attempts to define medicine as a philosophical as well as a scientific endeavor determined, like the Victorian novel, to answer questions about the material, social, and spiritual nature of human relations.

Yet amidst this compelling desire to "talk of diseases" in the nineteenth century lies a competing urge to define both the appropriate and potentially inappropriate forms these narratives should take.[1] When William Osler contemplates the seductive entrance of disease into language, he includes an important caveat: "To talk of diseases is a sort of Arabian Nights' entertainment *to which no discreet nurse will lend her talents*" (94, my emphasis). Simultaneously invoking and revoking expectations of narrative pleasure through the specter of professional discretion, Osler's recognition of the ludic function of talking about diseases (as testified in his own extensive writings) appears not as a celebration of medical narrative, but as a caution to nurses to resist the temptations of playing Scheherazade. By enjoining nurses to maintain silence amidst the narrative possibilities of the sickroom, Osler suggests that to talk of diseases is not only ethically inappropriate, but potentially and dangerously transformative. In effect, to speak of illness is to replicate, linguistically, the process of its transmission from one subject to another. Once disease enters into language, its transmissive potential multiplies; the nurse who describes one patient's symptoms may discover other patients, carried away by the imaginative potential of disease, incorporating those symptoms. The somatic consequences of narrative place the literary or medical "text" in a mediatory position not only between teller and audience, but between imaginative and corporeal categories of experience. To respond to a narrative emotionally or physically may produce illness; conversely, to be ill is to produce narrative.

The central project of this book is to examine what it meant to "talk of diseases" in the second half of the nineteenth century. I am interested in how the Victorian middle classes attempted to understand and control their world through a process of physiological and pathological definition, and the problems they encountered in doing so. In exploring the historical assumptions and systems of belief that invested sickness and health with social meaning, this book treats narrative as a crucial component of cultural history.[2] It seeks to identify some of the figurative and ideological spaces the human body occupied in Victorian cultural narratives and the ways in which conceptions of illness structured popular assumptions about individual and social identities.[3] Narratives of illness, whether in medical case histories, advice manuals, or literary texts, could shape individual experiences of suffering. They could also shape how people perceived relationships between mind and body, self and other, private and public spheres. As Sharon Cameron has argued, in the absence of any certain knowledge of the world outside, to anatomize the self and explore the boundaries of one's physical existence may provide our only access to knowledge (5–6).[4] Yet the power of illness to make one's own body seem alien, to transgress somatic and psychic boundaries, or to link disparate groups of people through the process of contagion suggested the potential instability of human identity. In the process of exploring this instability through medical and literary narratives, Victorian culture confronted the otherness of disease and its capacity to reconfigure conceptions of the self.

It may seem counterintuitive to discuss a subject as palpably real and materially immediate as physical illness in terms of medical fictions and narrative paradigms. Yet to the extent that language has the power to shape and filter human experience and to invest individual practices with historically specific meanings, such narratives chart the available categories through which people came to understand themselves and the structures of social interaction.[5] The title of this book thus underscores my belief that the ways in which people talked about health and disease are not only issues of medical history, but also forms of cultural fiction making, providing a set of collective stories middle-class Victorians told about their social and material relations. These representational structures provide us with important access to cultural patterns of perception, fantasy, and belief. I am thus more concerned with the imaginative configurations through which Victorian culture understood illness than with the historical reality of individual symptoms or the retrospective accuracy of medical diagnoses. By focusing on literary and medical representations of illness, by assessing their common structures, conflicts, and shifting ideological assumptions, we can identify what Fredric Jameson would call the "master narratives" that helped shape Victorian thought.[6] These stories, I argue, served to inscribe cultural values on the most basic physiological level. They addressed the human need to transform the abstract into the concrete—to see the physical body as a reflection of the social body—which is, according to Mary Douglas, one of our most basic symbolic gestures (115–16, 162). In this context, I argue that the persistent attempts by Victorian writers and physicians to define the terms of human physicality, to locate in the body the source of sexual and social divisions, to create a physiological blueprint that would explain the meaning of racial difference and restore a sense of social and material order provided a means of controlling potentially disturbing cultural issues by relocating them in questions of physiology.

I take this entanglement between bodies and narratives—both in the sickroom and in the literary text—as my starting point, beginning the book with a series of questions Victorian writers posed about the relationships between language, embodiment, and subjectivity: What are the effects of speech or silence—that is, our sense of control over language or language's control over us—on physical well-being? To what extent do people use their bodies to communicate emotions that lack other forms of expression? Or, alternatively, how does physical distress shape the powers of imagination or emotional experience? Is spirituality thought to be shaped by or perceived through bodily pain? From questions of narrative and imaginative production I move to questions of consumption, identifying how many Victorians perceived the act of reading as potentially transgressive, challenging the boundaries between mind and body, self and world: What is the relationship between what a person reads and how that person feels? How do emotions generated by reading translate into bodily experiences or illnesses? To what extent is reading an experience shaped by gender? All of these questions, which are essentially framed in terms of individual experience—exploring my body rather than the world's bodies—in turn generate questions about collectivity that occupy the later chapters: To what extent were pain and emotion perceived as collective rather than merely individual experiences? Could emotions and impressions as well as diseases be contagious? What, if any, physical consequences arise from acts of sympathy? When we look at the problem of collective experience—which Victorian culture did through mediums such as hypnosis, theatrical performance, hysterical suggestibility, and crowd psychology—we can see how interactions between self and other and between self and world presuppose political contexts. Group experiences necessitate defining what constitutes a group, and it is the categories through which groups of people were defined physiologically in the nineteenth century that generates my final series of questions: To what extent were people defined by what they took into their bodies, whether food or ideas? Was civilization measured through the individual or collective body? What was the status of pain, and why were different people or groups of people thought to feel pain differently? How was physical well-being connected to evolutionary progress? Victorian culture frequently expressed these and other questions through distinctions of gender, class, nationality, or race—as in assumptions about the appropriateness of different reading habits and nervous responses in men and women, or contrasting levels of sensitivity to pain in different racial groups—thereby connecting biological and social identities.

This particular set of questions is intended to convey a larger sequence of conceptual links from the politics of the individual body to the politics of collective bodies. Despite repeated attempts to make the individual and the social coalesce, nineteenth-century representations of illness reveal a persistent sense of disjunction between individual physical experience and the cultural discourses through which that experience was shaped or defined. On the one hand, the human body was perceived as a private domain, a concrete foundation for the self that preceded the violence of cultural and linguistic appropriation. On the other hand, the body seemed unable to sustain this fiction of self-sufficiency. The permeability of its boundaries (implicit in actions such as eating, copulating, or giving birth) were made explicit in the presence of disease, for disease constituted a breakdown in corporeal integrity, wholeness, or control. The condition of physical illness highlighted the essential dependence and necessary publicity of the body—that is, the extent to which individual physical experience was made up of a series of interactions with the surrounding world. Both the conformity and the contradictions between self-image (what Freud called "body-ego") and social image were made manifest in the face of disease.

Here we might regard Krook's famous "spontaneous combustion" in *Bleak House*—the dispersal of his body over the bricks and alleyways of London—as Dickens's metaphor for the workings of all disease; that is, an explosion of the private body into the public domain. Historically, this corporeal explosion took a variety of forms. The proliferation of medical writings in the nineteenth century—which included lectures, textbooks, journals, essays, advice manuals, case studies, photographic comparisons and analyses—and their role in establishing physiological, behavioral, and cultural norms served to highlight the body and its potential for disease. One of the consequences of this attention was the reshaping of gender

categories. Michel Foucault has noted how this "discursive explosion" (*History of Sexuality*, 17), which he traces over the past three
centuries, formed a means of codifying and containing human sexuality through the institutionalization of medicine and science.[7] Subsequent works such as Thomas Laqueur's comparative history of reproductive biology, Londa Schiebinger's study of skeletal illustra-
tion, and Ludmilla Jordanova's analysis of medical vision and the
gendering of scientific knowledge have identified the ways in which
nineteenth-century science sought to define sexual difference in the
most basic structures of human anatomy.[8]

In addition to the sheer bulk of published writings on the human
body in Victorian medicine and science, we can see how the training physicians underwent promoted an association between the interpretation of disease and participation in a public spectacle. Taught
in classrooms that resembled theaters, nineteenth-century medicine
exhibited the bodies (both alive and dead) of impoverished patients
in ways that could seem disturbingly public to a culture deeply invested in ideals of corporeal and domestic privacy.[9] This tendency
toward medical spectacle was perhaps most pronounced in France,
where the ecstatic performances of Jean-Martin Charcot's hysterics
at the Salpêtrière pushed the equation between medicine and theater
to its logical extreme. The renowned neurologist and his patients
played to packed audiences that included, according to one contemporary medical observer, not only Parisian medical students, but
also "authors, journalists, leading actors and actresses, fashionable
demimondaines, all full of morbid curiosity to witness the startling
phenomena of hypnotism almost forgotten since the days of Mesmer and Braid" (Munthe, 296).[10] The hysterical postures of Charcot's patients were further recorded in the famous collection of photographs *Iconographie photographique de la Salpêtrière*, which provided an additional layer of spectacle and, as Peter Stallybrass and
Allon White have suggested, identified hysteria as the ultimate trope
of carnivalesque display (189).[11]

Although the Victorian bourgeoisie were notoriously self-conscious about the intrusions of medicine upon individual (and particularly female) privacy, formulating elaborate techniques for preserving female modesty during gynecological examinations, the

working-class patient entering a charity or teaching hospital encountered a different set of assumptions about visual and tactile accessibility (Sadoff, 42). Scenes of medical instruction, and the cultural anxieties about class exploitation and bodily privacy they encoded, became available for public scrutiny as much through literature as through performances like Charcot's. To take one example, George Moore's 1894 novel *Esther Waters* describes the admission of the impoverished young heroine into a London charity hospital to find "a room full of people, eight or nine young men and women" eating sweets, discussing the latest plays and shilling novels (115). The very routinization of the patient's treatment in this scene may provide a measure of the body's successful "explosion" into public spaces: in the carnivalesque atmosphere of Moore's delivery room, Esther's labor must compete with other forms of entertainment for the attention of the medical audience. Only at the moment when her body becomes a medical problem, necessitating the administration of chloroform, does Esther's childbirth displace the attractions of the shilling novel with more compelling narrative possibilities. We can see this scene as a structural counterpart to the spectacle of Charcot's hysterics: each reveals the dramatic capacity of medical instruction to make public the inner life of the patient; each positions the female body in the midst of medical spectacle.[12]

In a parallel model of medical publicity, we find doctors' testimony entering the nineteenth-century courtroom (and the popular press) in order to identify and explain the physiological bases of behavior. By emphasizing the need to "interpret" the defendant's body, or in some cases that of the victim, these legal debates provided a public forum for the display of medical knowledge and, in some cases, for confrontations between competing schools of medical thought (Harris, 198). At the same time, increasingly necessary urban health reforms were challenging the Victorian ideal of domestic sanctity, invading the family shrine to inspect its drainage, ventilation, and waste removal (Wohl, 67–69). By the end of the century, fears of contagion that originated in repeated fever epidemics (we might think here of the trajectory of Jo's smallpox from Tom-All-Alone's to Esther Summerson's bedroom in rural *Bleak House*) and outbreaks of syphilis in the middle-class family had been extended to theories of moral contagion arising from the proximity of different classes in the midst of a crowd.

Ultimately, these combined efforts to organize, sanitize, and explain the workings of disease can be seen as attempts to incorporate—literally, unite—bodies in an orderly system of belief. This incorporation, in turn, served to establish guidelines for political and social action. If the individual human body could register signs of cultural distress—whether through patterns of mental alienation or racial deterioration, depleted nerves or muscular atrophy, to mention just a few focuses of medical anxiety—then the interpretation of bodies became an important form of social cartography. This desire was instituted in "sciences" such as physiognomy, phrenology, and anthropometry, each of which measured the contours of the human body in an attempt to provide predictive knowledge of interior identity or, alternatively, comparative social progress.[13] The idea that a body contained stories about an individual's life, habits, heredity, or emotions, and that doctors served as privileged interpreters of those stories provided the medical profession with a narrative structure for the revelation of social and scientific "truths."[14] In this way, the human body became one of the central, and most contested, icons for cultural definition.

As I have suggested, the bodies that this book examines are primarily discursive—bodies constructed through the mediums of medical and scientific theory, political rhetoric, and literary imagination. The most seemingly objective case history is still a form of narrative, a verbal fiction that recreates the diseased body in the process of diagnosing the causes of its symptoms. Even an intimate diary entry signals a body already transformed into language and therefore shaped by its epistemological limits. The "meaning" of these bodies is not so much passively reflected in language as produced by it. In characterizing my focus as a discursive one, I draw in part upon the work of Michel Foucault, whose historical analyses of complexly interwoven and decentered power relations have made it possible for scholars to think about how the body and definitions of disease were produced through discourse. My emphasis on the narrative repre-

sentation of illness in Victorian culture has been enabled and ener-
gized by Foucault's studies of medicine, madness, sexuality, and discipline in the eighteenth and nineteenth centuries, though as many
recent feminists have pointed out, the role that gender plays in configurations of language and power is noticeably absent from most
of Foucault's writings.[15] In my discussions of gender, race, and imperialism, for example, which connect the micropolitics of the body
to issues of national and global power, I am influenced by Foucault's
concept of discourse as a diffuse network of power relations that
shapes human lives. However, because this study is most centrally
concerned with gender and tends to read patterns of cultural narrative in terms of their incoherences and displacements, I am more
methodologically indebted to materialist-feminist approaches to history, ideology, and narrative than to Foucault's analyses of the structures of power. For example, Judith Newton and Deborah Rosenfelt have discussed how materialist-feminist criticism tends to view
ideology not as a direct or monolithic enforcement of dominant interests, but rather as "a complex and contradictory system of representations (discourses, images, myths) through which we experience ourselves in relation to each other and to the social structures in
which we live" (xix).[16]

My approach departs as well, however, from those feminist studies of women's illness in the nineteenth century that have emphasized the debilitating ways in which medicine, psychiatry, and the
biological sciences constructed definitions of womanhood and
pathologized female reproductive processes. While critics and historians such as Elaine Showalter, Barbara Ehrenreich, Deirdre English, and most recently Diane Price Herndl have provided important groundwork for feminist analyses of women's illnesses in the
nineteenth century, they tend to view the construction of gender
identity as a static component of Victorian ideology.[17] By locating
how narratives of illness could be employed under specific circumstances for conflicting ideological purposes, and how conceptions of
illness could simultaneously reinforce and disrupt definitions of gender, my emphasis is on the particular and changing uses of somatic
fictions in shaping the relationships among cultural, class, and gender identities. It is this view of the instability of cultural construc-

tions, their inability to remain confined by the explanatory and disciplinary purposes for which they originally emerge, that distinguishes this book from many feminist critiques of the Victorian medical establishment.

By addressing literary and medical narratives as specific genres, overlapping in many of the stories they tell, but with their own sets of ideological and aesthetic tensions, I chart the circumstances in which narratives of sickness and health enter the social field and take on both personal and cultural meanings. To the extent that these meanings are unstable, contested, and continually renegotiated, they reveal the underlying historical tensions that make up cultural practices and systems of belief. Foucauldian studies of power and many feminist analyses of gender have tended to ignore such instabilities and contradictions in order to construct a coherent account of cultural practices. In one of the most ambitious feminist arguments drawing upon Foucault, Nancy Armstrong has discussed the power of discourse to shape conceptions of human psychology and subjectivity, arguing that both "conduct literature" and the eighteenth- and nineteenth-century domestic novel produced the modern bourgeois subject as female. This new gendering of subjectivity was, in Armstrong's view, stripped away from more material conceptions of self. Thus in discussing one of the attempted rapes in Richardson's *Pamela*, Armstrong argues that "it is not a creature of flesh and blood that Mr. B. encounters in the body naked and supine upon the bed, but a proliferation of female words and feelings" (116). In Armstrong's account, the middle-class domestic woman, as the prototype of modern subjectivity, was not only depoliticized but effectively disembodied. This representation of subjectivity, Armstrong claims, "would eventually hollow out the material body of the woman in order to fill it with the materials of a gender-based self, or female psychology" (71). Although I find Armstrong's theory of female subjectivity as bodily erasure a compelling way of thinking about the economies of body and mind, it fails to account for the wide variety of relationships between gender, embodiment, and psychology in the nineteenth-century novel (as well as in medical discourse and middle-class culture). That is, Armstrong's gendering of subjectivity, with its consequent disembodying of the domestic woman, offers only one of a number of possible ways nineteenth-century British culture came to understand the psychological and somatic components of gender identity. In presenting the female subject as a coherent product of an emerging bourgeois ideology, Armstrong collapses the instabilities inherent in the production of cultural meaning.

Ultimately, then, I am interested in the inability of Victorian culture to tell a coherent story of itself, or more specifically of its social and material relations, despite a strong desire to do so. The contradictions, retellings, and conflicting epistemological models and means of incorporating difference that appear in Victorian literature and medicine offer important sites of ideological dispute. In defining my approach to nineteenth-century culture through the repetitions and contradictions of narrative, I have borrowed loosely from Freud's conceptualization of hysteria as an incoherent or interrupted narrative history (*Dora*, 31). Although my methodology is not psychoanalytic, and I do not intend to suggest that Victorian culture can somehow be diagnosed as collectively hysterical in Freudian terms, I find that some of the categories Freud used to frame his understanding of hysteria—narrative contradiction, incoherence, repetition, displacement, impediment, amnesia, and conflict—offer ways of understanding cultural processes at work. Mary Poovey's study of the formulation of gender ideology in the mid-Victorian period provides a useful way of thinking about the study of contradiction in cultural and historical rather than psychoanalytic terms. Poovey has argued that what appears to be a superficially coherent and complete system of beliefs about sexual differences, gender roles, and relations was, upon closer scrutiny, "fissured by competing emphases and interests." Ideological formulations could be contested and their instabilities revealed through what Poovey calls the "ideological work of gender" (3–4). In focusing on these "fissures" Poovey explores both the interstices of the cultural process at work and the Herculean efforts that went into producing and fortifying that tenuous historical veneer of coherence. However, if Foucault is guilty of ignoring gender, Poovey may be overestimating its powers of disruption. By identifying gender as the primary means of challenging the coherence of social ideologies, Poovey risks reinscribing it as a totalizing channel of opposition. Insofar as gender conflict was incorporated into medical subjects, it was inconsistent in its ability to challenge or disperse cultural beliefs. Furthermore, it is not always the case that ideological "fissures" were unselfconscious in the ways that Poovey's argument implies. In certain circumstances, contradictions could function as ideological release points, paradoxically enabling dominant social paradigms to retain their boundaries of authority by licensing and containing superficial ideological divisions.[18] I would argue, then, that patterns of contradiction can themselves function in multiple contexts, offering a layered excavation of social, institutional, and imaginative practices. Narrative disruptions offer shifting sites of resistance that are subject to the threat of co-optation. In this book, I assume that the discovery of various forms of disruption in the narratives I address can signal underlying ideological coherences as well as areas of unresolved tensions and incoherence in the social field.

To take just one example of how this process might take shape around the subject of illness, we can see how competing cultural "meanings" of nervous sensitivity (one of the somatic fictions that this book is most interested in) were used to define a surprisingly wide range of experiences and beliefs. Nervousness could signal spirituality as well as sexuality, imaginative expression or incipient insanity. It was used to describe emotional exhaustion as well as unexplained physical pain and to define evolutionary progress as well as the debilitating effects of modern civilization. In their very attempts to stabilize the meaning of the human nervous system, many Victorian accounts of nervous sensitivity—both medical and literary—reveal a fundamentally unstable conceptual framework. They virtually map out the sites where ideological tensions were most volatile. We might, then, think about these accounts and the roles they played in Victorian culture as a form of ideological conversion hysteria—a collective somaticization of areas of social conflict. The narratives I discuss are consistent only in their inconsistencies—that is, in their capacity to contain and reveal their own unstable cultural meanings. And in the competing and often contradictory uses of these narratives in literature, medicine, and pre-Freudian psychology (among other discourses), as well as in their adaptations and transformations for different purposes at different times, we can see both cultural tensions and moments of ideological consolidation at work.

Through this process of narrative production and appropriation, the Victorian middle classes negotiated their relationship to a changing society, converting cultural anxieties into somatic categories of self- and social definition. By attempting to reconstruct the cultural codes and narrative structures that shaped nineteenth-century conceptions of sickness and health, we can better understand the vexed relationship between the human body and the act of figuration.

My methodology maintains, then, a distinct place for the "literary." Rather than reading nineteenth-century medicine as merely a context for the novels or merging the medical treatise and the novel into a unified notion of cultural text, I treat "fiction" or "narrative" as the necessary and pervasive means by which relations between the individual and the social body are negotiated. I claim, further, that the narrative of *illness* took on an imaginative centrality for Victorian culture precisely because it invoked the most basic material reality—sensory and corporeal experience. In effect, somatic fictions mystified that reality and rendered it abstract by shaping how the material conditions of life could be understood. My strategy throughout the book is to identify sites of struggle over hermeneutic control of the narratives on which cultural identity is supposed to be based. But neither the structures that make up cultural identity, nor the control of how they are produced, is stable. Fissured, elastic, and insistently mobile, they are as often marked by logical incoherence and categorical confusion as they are by an underlying ideological consistency. This is not to empty out ideology as a category of analysis or to deny the presence of social norms, determining interests, or dominant cultural motives. Rather, it is to challenge the notion that these norms, interests, and motives functioned as part of a consistent and monolithic social framework. Thus, we cannot assume that, despite their terminological expediency, either "ideology" or "Victorian culture" describes a unified field. Although both may contain coherent intentions that arise from particular circumstances, the interaction of these intentions can destabilize social norms, assumptions, and values, even as they are articulated.

My project here is thus twofold: to analyze the complex interaction between nineteenth-century medical theory and narrative discourse, and to determine how Victorian fictions of sickness and health functioned as imaginative by-products of these spheres, both challenging and reinforcing stereotypes of gender, class, and race. The chapters that follow alternate readings of medical and literary materials, exploring different sets of interlocking social tensions and beliefs. Each addresses a different cluster of medical and literary narratives that share a common structure, theme, or ideological framework. The questions they address frequently overlap—that is, one chapter may double back to pick up the loose threads of an earlier argument—but I have avoided employing a strictly chronological trajectory. Although my focus is predominantly on middle-class Victorian cultural practices, and the literature I examine is primarily British (with periodic intrusions of American texts), my discussion of nineteenth-century medical theory and advice literature includes a wide range of British, American, and continental sources. The reasons for this lie in the widespread exchange of knowledge within the medical community, the rapid translation and publication of influential medical treatises, and the practice, particularly common among British physicians, of completing some portion of their medical training in Europe. In addition, my use of medical materials is more concerned with the emerging fields of neurology, psychiatry, and psychology than with any other branches of medicine, partly because of their rich development during the second half of the nineteenth century, and partly because they sought to articulate modes of interaction between body and mind that figure so prominently in Victorian literature.[19] My choices of literary texts are intended to be similarly wide-ranging. I am interested not only in how texts move back and forth between disciplines but also in how they traverse the fluctuating boundaries of high and low culture. By situating familiar literary texts in new frameworks and opening up some less familiar ones to critical discussion, I seek to demonstrate the engagement of both canonical and more marginal nineteenth-century authors in a cultural dialogue about health and disease.[20]

Chapter 1 focuses on the gendering of body language, exploring disputes over the legibility or illegibility of the female body and women's ability to produce and interpret somatic texts. It situates these disputes in the Victorian ambivalence about the uncertain effects of emotion and reading, which, as John Mullan has pointed out, were inherited from eighteenth-century assumptions about sensibility. Exploring the linguistic positioning and gendering of the ailing body, I identify a pervasive tendency in Victorian culture to read the human body—and particularly the female body—as a text that offers privileged access to the emotional life of the subject. In both medical-advice literature and Victorian novels, illnesses frequently appear as indirect expressions of emotional meaning. They constitute an immediately recognizable and conventional language that was subject to a complex set of interpretive codes. These codes were shaped, at least in part, by medical assumptions about women's nervous susceptibility. I argue that in Louisa May Alcott's *Hospital Sketches* and *Little Women*, Elizabeth Gaskell's *Cousin Phillis*, and Charlotte Brontë's *Shirley*, these codes are highlighted as part of the texts' own poetics of illness. They provide models for reading the patient's silence by identifying certain kinds of illnesses (consumption, chlorosis, anorexia, brain fever) as strategies of communication that effectively renounce or circumvent spoken language in favor of the more immediate, material reality of the heroine's ailing body. They thereby construct both a semiotics of emotional distress and an affective hermeneutics in which the nurse becomes the privileged interpreter of embodied emotions. The very familiarity of these conventions was signaled, in turn, by parodies of affective nursing in later Victorian sensation fiction. By addressing the ways in which illness was perceived as both a form of and a substitute for language, we can see how illness became a privileged signifier for examining the conditions of women's discursive authority.

Chapter 2 examines the opposite relationship between body and voice, tracing acts of narrative inscription that attempt to relocate and reshape a threatened corporeal experience in a linguistic artifact. While Chapter 1 addresses how perceived failures of language highlighted the role of the body in the development and expression of female identity, Chapter 2 examines how perceived disjunctions between body and mind (as in the case of nervous disease) inspired a renewed faith in language as a means of reconstructing the self.[21] Using Alice James's *Diary*, Charlotte Brontë's *Villette*, and George Eliot's *Daniel Deronda*, I demonstrate how both real and fictional nervous sufferers confronted the ambiguity of their illnesses through acts of narrative refiguration, symbolically transforming their tenuous physical status into more concrete narrative forms. Just as Alice James used her diary to affirm a private sense of self when faced with conflicting medical diagnoses, Brontë and Eliot employed nervous illness as part of an emerging psychological realism in order to denote physical, emotional, and spiritual experience. Ultimately, these texts attempt to contain the visionary energy of their heroines, to explain their psychic force through the symptoms and structures of disease. In this they reproduce one of the central projects of nineteenth-century neurology: the attempt to find scientific explanations for what had previously been seen as spiritual or supernatural events.

Chapter 3 begins the transition from individual to collective embodiments, examining specular and mimetic theories of disease. It focuses on a condition Victorian physicians diagnosed as "neuromimesis"—neurotic imitation of disease—and identifies the relationship between this specific form of hysteria and cultural anxieties about physical and emotional contagion, gender identity, and medical authority. I argue that the association of neuromimesis with sympathetic forms of spectatorship and, by extension, feminized forms of viewing, served as a means of excluding women from the medical profession. By showing how the medical establishment defined its own specular authority in opposition to this particular functional disease, I suggest that the professional investment in "objective" medical vision was crucial to the gender identity of the physician, as was the need to distance the gazing subject from the object of examination. The chapter demonstrates how the gender economies of these viewing relationships were part of a wider cultural dialogue about the consequences of sympathetic identification. This dialogue was played out most extensively in the construction of the audience in Victorian sickroom scenes. Using texts such as Harriet Beecher Stowe's *Uncle Tom's Cabin*, George du Maurier's *Trilby*, George Eliot's *Middlemarch*, and Henry James's *Wings of the Dove*, I argue for a Victorian theory of spectatorship that negotiates between sympathetic participation and clinical detachment, thereby manipulating and disrupting the reader's sense of gender identification.

Chapter 4 moves from disease to health, addressing the politics of fitness and its relation to imperialist ideology. It examines how the precepts of social Darwinism led to an emphasis on health as a physical and moral imperative and a crucial tool for assessing the comparative fitness of populations. It traces a widespread movement among nineteenth-century physicians, scientists, anthropologists, and educators to promote the health of the middle and upper classes while at the same time leaving myths about the physical insensibility of laborers, criminals, and "savage races" intact. By examining how nineteenth-century studies of pain, mortality, reproductive capacity, and nutrition were used to establish biological bases of inferiority and to justify the need for imperialist expansion, this chapter demonstrates the imaginative link between the healthy body and gender, racial, and class identities. However, at the same time that health was being promoted as a national duty, a number of Victorian authors were displaying both a distrust of biological imperatives and an ambivalence about fitness as a category of human value. This dynamic relation between health and disease informs many late Victorian texts about empire; for example, both H. Rider Haggard's *She* and Bram Stoker's *Dracula* can be read as nightmare visions of impervious health and racial superiority. By viewing these texts as the logical outcome of Victorian mythologies of sickness and health, and as commentaries on the tangled politics of imperialism, this final chapter charts some of the broader cultural implications of Victorian fictions of disease.

Ultimately, I see the book as tracing not only a series of cultural obsessions through the pages of literary and medical texts, but also a series of literary paradigms that place bodies and texts in theoretical or substitutional relationships with each other. Thus certain patterns are repeated in the structure of the chapters: The opening chapters, for example, address the relationship between material and linguistic embodiment, examining the tensions between two characteristic, and opposing, paradigms for thinking about language, illness, and gender identity. In the first paradigm, the human body functions as a form of narrative; in the second, the narrative functions as a form of bodily substitution. Subsequent chapters extend these paradigms to address both interactive issues (relations between bodies) and collective social identities (relations of difference). Thus, in a rough schematic form, the first chapter is about the body as a text; the second chapter is about the text as a body, or more precisely, the production of narrative as an act of embodiment; the third chapter is about the embodiment of the reader and about the act of reading as a form of emotional and gender transgression; and the fourth chapter is about popular fiction as a form of collective social embodiment and a symbolic substitute for national identity. By focusing on the processes through which bodies were transformed into narratives, this book addresses the reasons why health and disease seemed compelling subjects for fiction making in the nineteenth century, outlining patterns of medical and literary storytelling and the competing ideological purposes these stories could serve in the culture at large. These processes are not, however, systematic; their incoherences do not resolve themselves into tidy or unified conclusions about the workings of power or the formulation of ideology. The introduction of literature into the study of Victorian cultural practices multiplies the axes of imaginative production, often calling into question the very narrative maneuvers and structures of meaning that the text invokes. In the transcoding of literary and medical narratives, then, we find densely textured confrontations with the problems of somatic representation.

CHAPTER I

Body Language and the Poetics of Illness

If we trace the genesis of human character, by considering the conditions of existence through which the human race passed in early barbaric times and during civilization, we shall see that the weaker sex has naturally acquired certain mental traits by its dealings with the stronger. . . . The wives of merciless savages must, other things equal, have prospered in proportion to their powers of disguising their feelings. Women who betrayed the state of antagonism produced in them by ill-treatment, would be less likely to survive and leave offspring than those who con- cealed their antagonism; and hence, by inheritance and selection, a growth of this trait proportionate to the requirement. In some cases, again, the arts of persuasion enabled women to protect themselves, and by implication their offspring; where, in the ab- sence of such arts, they would have disappeared early, or would have reared fewer children. One further ability may be named as likely to be cultivated and established—the ability to distinguish quickly the passing feelings of those around. In barbarous times a woman who could from a movement, tone of voice, or expres- sion of face, instantly detect in her savage husband the passion that was rising, would be likely to escape dangers run into by a woman less skilled in interpreting the natural language of feeling. Hence, from the perpetual exercise of this power, and the survival of those having most of it, we may infer its establishment as a feminine faculty.

—Herbert Spencer, *The Study of Sociology*

ʄ

Herbert Spencer's discussion of gender differences in social and linguistic behavior is notable for its emphasis on suppression, disguise, and the reading of bodily signs as women's natural legacies from primitive human culture. To censor or transmute the expression of one's own feelings and to decipher the subtle emotional gestures of others are, in Spencer's formulation, complementary feminine faculties. For Spencer, the human body becomes both the source and the aim of women's hermeneutic activity: it offers a "natural language of feeling" that is both more primitive and more essential to women's survival than spoken language. Because they provided crucial adaptations to the conditions of primitive human culture, these alternative semiotic systems helped to shape female identity and social roles in the process of species survival, becoming, according to Spencer's formula, part of the necessary biological programming of modern femininity.[1] As a result of this programming, women would presumably be more adept than men at disguising their feelings and would thus be better adapted to interpreting indirect forms of communication. Spencer's social-Darwinian explanation of women's linguistic and hermeneutic behaviors naturalizes social practices while providing what is essentially a unidirectional epistemology: What women must discover, decode, and be acutely sensitive to in men is precisely the emotional iterability (and readability) that they must suppress in themselves. At the same time that women must become good readers of men, they must prevent themselves from being well-read. But the very notion of women as unreadable made them subject to increased scrutiny. Their strategies of emotional disguise produce Spencer's desire to interpret them. Furthermore, as strategies for survival, women's acts of emotional and linguistic indirection constitute an aggressive mechanism of defense at the same time that they suggest a severe degree of self-effacement. Spencer thus makes a virtue out of female necessity. In the paradigm he constructs, women function as complacent participants in Victorian ideology— in the inscription of their own "meaning"—by encoding their own bodies, and reading others, as texts.

Spencer's explanation of social and linguistic practices demonstrates some common assumptions about gender and body language that characterized Victorian culture. Although there was no systematic psychological theory that explored the relationship between emotional repression and somatic expression until Freud's early studies of hysteria and his development of "the talking cure," there was, nevertheless, a widespread Victorian belief in the expressive or communicative potential of the human—and particularly female—body. Like Sherlock Holmes, many Victorians were deeply interested in reading bodies as texts. They developed elaborate theories for decoding physical details, symptoms, and gestures—theories that assumed that people spoke through their bodies and interpreted the bodies of others in particularly structured, usually gendered, ways.[2] This communicative potential is most explicitly, and extravagantly, present in Victorian representations of illness. What Spencer describes as women's special "aptitude for guessing the state of mind through the external signs" is, in effect, the basis for a feminine hermeneutics that Victorian fiction repeatedly manifests (343). In this chapter I argue that the interpretation of both physical signs and medical symptoms as part of Spencer's "natural language of feeling" was a crucial aspect of how Victorians defined and understood the affective structures of gender identity. In particular, I address how literary and medical representations of illness contributed to a hermeneutics of bodily detail that assumed a direct correspondence between emotion and symptom, charting the physical consequences of feelings in order, ultimately, to channel and control them. In this fashion, we can see Spencer's account of women's behavioral legacy as part of a larger cultural project that sought to explain the relationship between language, gender, and emotion. Spencer applauds the mystery of female emotion at the same time that he classifies it out of existence by turning it into a language that men can finally "read" in the form of an evolutionary narrative.

It is not, of course, my intention to claim that Spencer's account of women's discursive practices is linguistically or historically accurate, or that it describes the nonverbal ways women communicated in the nineteenth century.[3] Rather, my interest lies in the extent to which Victorian culture *believed* that women communicated and interpreted more somatically than men and how this belief shaped perceptions of social behavior and gender identity in the nineteenth century. Recently, feminist critics have tended to dismiss the terms in which nineteenth-century culture understood women's illnesses, particularly hysteria, by portraying them as monolithic assertions of medical and patriarchal power. This portrayal has resulted in interpretations of the female sufferer as either a transgressive feminist heroine who challenges cultural norms of behavior with her perplexing and metamorphic array of symptoms, or a passive victim of medical tyranny.[4] Neither of these perspectives provides a completely effective way of studying the competing and often contradictory cultural meanings of illness in the nineteenth century. Elaine Showalter, for example, dismisses as merely "traditional" Victorian theories of hysteria that explained it in terms of sexual repression: "It was much simpler to blame sexual frustration, to continue to see hysterical women as lovelorn Ophelias, than to investigate women's intellectual frustration, lack of mobility, or needs for autonomy and control" (*Female Malady*, 132). In rightly complicating the contributing factors of hysteria, Showalter ignores complex implications of apparently "simple" nineteenth-century explanations of female maladies. What exactly did it mean to see hysterical women as lovelorn Ophelias? What link between fiction, emotion, and medical symptom did this imply? How did this model shape the way early and mid-Victorian culture understood women's emotional lives, sexual needs, and discursive possibilities? Although nineteenth-century women's nervous illnesses undoubtedly arose from complex and imperfectly understood causes that contemporaries chose to ignore, we must nevertheless consider the terms through which Victorians understood such illnesses and explore their links to the formation of gender identities and ideologies.[5]

One of the central paradigms of nineteenth-century somatic ideology did, in fact, attempt to relate psychosomatic states to complex internal relations. In explaining early-nineteenth-century therapeutics, Charles Rosenberg has emphasized how a conceptualization of the human body as a system of dynamic exchange dominated both the medical and the popular imagination. This conceptualization was guided by two fundamental principles of bodily economy: First, "every part of the body was related inevitably and inextricably with every other. A distracted mind could curdle the stomach; a dyspeptic stomach could agitate the mind." Second, "the body was seen as a system of intake and outgo—a system which had, necessarily, to remain in balance if the individual were to remain healthy. . . . Equilibrium was synonymous with health, disequilibrium with illness" (40). As Rosenberg suggests, this way of viewing the relationship between mental and bodily functions was not limited to the field of medicine, but rather was part of a larger system of belief that shaped cultural behavior and understanding (40). Although Rosenberg writes about the early nineteenth century, his explanation of both an internal paradigm of bodily economy and an external one that emphasized the body's "dynamic interactions with its environment" (40) form the basis for many later therapeutic suppositions. While diagnostic categories and therapeutic techniques underwent important transformations during the course of the century, medical and cultural beliefs about bodily economy, relationships of depletion and exchange maintained their importance (if not always in a consistent form) as conceptual frameworks. The discovery of the first law of thermodynamics (the conservation of energy) in the 1840's made economic theories of body and mind increasingly prominent after mid-century.[6] These accounts of mind/body economies help to explain the prevalent role "feelings" played in nineteenth-century discussions of illness. Insofar as physiological effects could be attributed to the emotional life of the subject, learning to read the physical signs of emotion formed a crucial medical and literary project.

If emotions could produce somatic effects, the heightened sensitivity of female emotions could magnify the production of physical symptoms. Physicians generally held that "the whole vasomotor system of the female was far more excitable than that of the male, marking her with a tendency to greater tension, irritability, and emotionalism. Laughing, crying, blushing and quickened heart beat were all marks of her peculiar mental state" (Haller and Haller, 73–74). Conditions including chronic headaches, brain fever, chlorosis, consumption, anorexia, hysteria, and eventually neurasthenia were all attributed (at least in part) to the emotional and mental state of the patient, and particularly the female patient, thereby reinforcing the idea that women's emotions were more somatic, and their diseases more complicated by emotions, than men's. Yet in attributing the heightened potential for female emotionalism to physiological causes, nineteenth-century physicians implied that excitability was a natural component of women's biological identity. If women were *naturally* prone to displays of emotion, there would seemingly be no need for the parental surveillance and medical interventions that doctors and advice manuals routinely recommended. While attempting to naturalize feminine affect, doctors defined this ostensibly normal condition as the source of women's dysfunctional behavior. By instructing mothers in the emotional meanings of their adolescent daughters' bodily symptoms and warning them to watch out for dangerous signs of ill health that could arise from various affective traumas, nineteenth-century advice literature participated in the pathologization of female emotion. It furthermore gave women an occupation suited to their hermeneutic proclivities, teaching them to become narcissistic watchdogs of their own symptoms while suggesting that they lacked (because of their constitutional susceptibility to heightened emotion) the capacity to solve the problems their own bodies "naturally" created.

The extent of this proliferation of causes and symptoms can be seen in the ever-widening inclusion of direct and indirect triggers of female maladies. Thus while women were both instructed and assumed to be privileged readers of the "natural language of feeling," their actual literary reading practices became the focus of medical scrutiny. This emphasis on the deleterious effects of reading dates back to eighteenth-century discussions of sensibility. As both Michel Foucault and John Mullan have indicated, eighteenth-century medical treatises frequently asserted that imaginary emotions and desires contracted through reading sentimental poetry and novels had the power to provoke nervous illness, particularly in susceptible young women.[7] Thomas Trotter's 1807 *View of the Nervous Temperament*, for example, warned that "the love-sick trash of most modern compositions" posed a threat to health. "To the female mind, in particular, as being endued with finer feeling, this species of literary poison has been often fatal; and some of the most unfortunate of the sex have imputed their ruin chiefly to reading novels" (88). As a result, many advice manuals cautioned mothers to censor their daughters' reading matter, particularly avoiding fictions that offered models of sentimental suffering. This form of emotional and literary censorship lasted well into the Victorian period, appropriated in the service of changing conceptions of illness and femininity during the course of the century. In 1808 Samuel Jennings listed "idleness" and "reading novels and romances" as two primary causes of female illness (18–19). Lydia Maria Child's 1831 *Mother's Book* stresses the "unhealthy influence" and "intellectual intemperance" of gothic and sentimental fiction, its tendency to produce "weakness and delirium" (93–94). An 1853 manual contends that young ladies' wounded affections form the "secret cause of much ill health, insanity, and even death" (Abell, 199). And a manual published as late as 1907 warns that "music, literature, and art, imaginative works of all sorts mix themselves up with sex feelings, so that the two help to form the emotional nature. . . . The falling in love and the disappointments connected therewith during early adolescence often lead to hysteria, to attacks of depression, and changes in character and conduct. In such cases there is usually hereditary nervousness or weakness of some sort" (Clouston, 51, 72). The significant differences between Jennings's and Child's advice and Clouston's are the latter's inclusion of heredity in his analysis of hysterical tendencies and his explicit emphasis on adolescent sexuality as the foundation of an emotional nature. These changes reflect the greater emphasis on hereditary causes of nervous illness in the latter decades of the nineteenth century and an increasing recognition of "sex feelings" in women's psychological and emotional development. Despite these important transformations in the conception of female sexuality, however, there is a striking diachronic consistency in the anxiety about reading as an intensifying and destabilizing external influence on women's most private emotional lives. There is also a significant parallel between concern about female reading habits and concern about (primarily male) masturbation in Victorian advice manuals. Medical and social proscriptions against women's reading of sentimental, gothic, or sensational fiction constructed a female version of the dangers of "solitary practices." In both cases, the entrance of the imagination into unlicensed channels created a state of imbalance, potentially depleting nervous resources and thereby threatening physical health.

Ultimately, reading inculcated the very affective and responsive behaviors women would come to regard as the diagnosable (and natural) results of their disorders. Doctors reproduced this structure of assumptions in their own case studies, emphasizing the somatic effects of emotional fluctuation and interpreting women according to the literary conventions of the very sentimental fiction that supposedly contributed to their medical conditions. In an 1847 case study published in *The Lancet*, one doctor described the treatment of an unmarried, physically deformed woman who died after childbirth under medical care. Although the doctor suggested that her physical handicaps and small size added to the complications of her pregnancy, and he acknowledged that she suffered considerable pain both before and after the birth of her child by caesarean operation without anesthesia, he nevertheless attributed the cause of her death to her shame in being an unmarried mother (*The Lancet*, February 6, 1847, 139–40). In interpreting the deterioration of his patient's physical condition as an expression of her emotional trauma, the attending doctor assumed a direct correspondence and causal relationship between mind and body that outweighed the evidence of medical complications. In effect, he diagnosed the patient's illness according to the generic conventions of the sentimental novel in its portrayal of the fallen woman: the patient's dying body communicated, more than anything else, her state of emotional distress.

The role that literary conventions sometimes played in medical diagnoses was thus to explain the influence of the patient's emotional life on the progress of his (and more particularly her) condition. Emotional distress constituted a medical complication, and the doctor could recognize emotional distress by its similarity to fictional paradigms. This same interpretive correlation could, in turn, be applied to acts of emotional control. If distress could disrupt the healing process, the containment or rechanneling of distress could facilitate recovery. This correlation between emotional control and the recovery of health is perhaps most clearly enacted in the physician Samuel Warren's popularized descriptions of case studies published in *Blackwood's Edinburgh Magazine* in the 1830's. Warren describes the case of a well-bred young lady suffering from breast cancer, who is able to maintain a state of emotional stability and stoic resistance to pain throughout an operation to remove the tumor in her breast. Mrs. St. ——— spends the entire operation, performed before the discovery of anesthesia, with her eyes focused on a letter from her husband that she has requested the physician to hold before her. By channeling her emotions into their proper sphere, she is able to withstand the shock to her system. The sustaining (or anesthetizing) force of marital correspondence effectively contains the patient's dangerous emotional energies, thus preventing them from disrupting both operation and recovery. Only when the operation has been successfully completed and she has been conveyed upstairs to her own bed, does Mrs. St. ——— faint. Yet the focus of her affective containment is itself the most sentimental of objects. One could reasonably expect the love letter from an absent spouse to generate emotional excess rather than control. Warren's emphasis suggests that it is the letter's status as both a sentimental keepsake and a symbol of marital fidelity that makes it the proper container for a young wife's feelings. But rather than resolving the letter's contradictions, this alliance merely highlights the contested nature of sentimentality, sensibility, and affect in medical discussions of female nature. We find the cultural meaning of female sickness codified through a medical rhetoric that sought to diagnose and treat women's illnesses as products of their emotional instability or, conversely, to attribute the recovery of health to proper emotional balance, while still defining emotional fluctuation and excess as woman's most natural, biological inheritance. In stressing the links between emotionalism and illness, physicians implied that a woman's most natural channel for emotional communication was physiological, yet the translation of emotion into symptom constituted a source of dysfunctional health.

Ultimately, when doctors complained about women's tendency toward emotional excess and problematic reading habits, they identified the very qualities that made women ideal subjects, producing the need for medical advice and treatment. The embodied "nature" of female emotions created the very mystery that Victorian medicine sought to demystify and explain away. It is in this combined (and contradictory) attempt to naturalize, pathologize, and decode the semiotics of bodily communication that we can see Victorian anxieties about gender ideology at work. Women's symptoms took on multiple and coded meanings for Victorian medicine, providing the skilled diagnostician with a privileged access to the emotional life of the subject. Yet women's own presumed access to this inner life, through the intuitive reading of bodily signs, placed them in competition with the very practitioners who sought to "read" them. It is this hermeneutic paradox—that the most adept female interpreter of bodily signs might be the patient most in need of medical interpretation and intervention—that we find played out repeatedly in literary representations of female maladies. As nineteenth-century authors explored the conditions of women's discursive practices, they produced models for decoding the poetics of illness.

Doctors frequently exploited novels as both a contributing cause of female illness and a paradigm for interpreting the symptoms of emotional distress; but Victorian novels were no less absorbed by the links between fiction and illness, gender and emotion. Victorian authors cautioned about the somatic effects of emotional engagement while simultaneously seeking to produce sympathetic emotional responses in the reader. Harriet Martineau's novel *Deerbrook*, in its numerous portrayals of female illness, is a virtual handbook on the ways in which "looks and tones" may communicate "what words and acts had been forbidden to convey" (287). Functioning as a companion piece to her advice books, Martineau's novel provides an extended meditation on the medical consequences of women's disguised speech and emotions. The narrative voice laments at one point, "There are sad tales sung and told everywhere of brains crazed, and graves dug by hopeless love: and I fear that many more sink down into disease and death from this cause, than are at all suspected to be its victims" (163–64). According to Martineau's formula, illness or even death could constitute an elaborate form of body language that she instructs her readers to interpret. As I suggest in Chapter 3, the profusion of ailing heroines and sentimental deathbed scenes in Victorian fiction provided important training ground for both real and implied readers. Victorian writers routinely assumed the reader's fluency in the interpretation of body language; at the same time they provided lessons in somatic decoding for those less attuned to "the language of nature." Despite the overwhelmingly male control of the medical profession in the nineteenth century, expertise in reading the emotional language of the sickroom was constructed as a distinctly feminine (or potentially feminizing) practice.

As I have suggested, insofar as women's hermeneutic skills and their powers of emotional disguise were believed to be complementary attributes, women's intuitive relationship to body language took two forms: interpreting the physical symptoms of emotion and producing them. These twin gestures correspond, in turn, to the figures of nurse and patient in Victorian fiction. Representations of illness in nineteenth-century novels manifest many of the same contradictions about emotional iterability and readability that we find in the medical literature of the period. In particular, the figure of the nurse—as either an idealized enactment of feminine hermeneutics or a sensational spectacle of feminine emotion gone astray—highlights some of the tensions within Victorian culture over the proper interpretation of affect. Insofar as women's emotional lives were perceived as both somatically encoded and medically or intuitively legible, as mysterious texts that defied interpretation at the same time they demanded it, they could assume radically different ideological meanings and literary forms. The conflict between medical constructions of emotional susceptibility as a normal function of the female nervous system (and part of women's natural biological inheritance), and the pathologization of female emotional excess is perhaps most clearly enacted in Victorian fictions that highlight the interpretive (and in some cases narrative) skills of the nurse who makes the patient's body legible to the reader through a privileged access to unspoken feelings. In texts such as Alcott's *Hospital Sketches* and *Little Women*, Gaskell's *Cousin Phillis*, and Charlotte Brontë's *Shirley*, we find an emphasis on somatic communication that illuminates the network of cultural assumptions about gender, illness, and language that I have described.[8] Each highlights the failure of spoken language to provide adequate channels for the expression of intense feelings; each demonstrates a different way in which illness functions to communicate the inner life of the patient; and each posits the ailing body as simultaneously legible and illegible. Ultimately, these texts idealize the affective hermeneutics of nursing and the semiotics of emotional and somatic distress in ways that are later challenged by dangerous confrontations with affective excess in works such as Mrs. Henry Wood's *East Lynne* and Wilkie Collins's *Dead Secret*. Although a common cultural narrative about the "natural language of feeling" seems to emerge from these texts (and many others, such as Henry James's *Wings of the Dove*, which I take up in Chapter 3), the conflicting meanings ascribed to that narrative suggest that the relationship between gender, illness, and emotion was both formally and ideologically unstable.

Emotional Ventriloquism

Alcott is perhaps the most explicit of the three writers in outlining the strengths of an intuitive feminine hermeneutics, seeing it as a necessary skill for nursing the sick and wounded. In her autobiographical *Hospital Sketches* (1863), recounting her experiences nursing Civil War soldiers, Alcott makes a claim for women's somatic literacy, describing the "sympathetic encouragement which women give, in look, touch, and tone more effectually than in words" (7). She demonstrates how this faculty can assist women in the field of nursing, recounting her own nonverbal communications with and interpretations of wounded soldiers. She describes staring at unconscious faces that "almost seemed to speak," claiming, "though they made no confidences in words, I read their lives" (44). In one detailed account of a soldier's death, Alcott interprets her patient's bodily movements as a language that provides access to his emotional experience:

The strong body rebelled against death, and fought every inch of the way, forcing him to draw each breath with a spasm, and clench his hands with an imploring look, as if he asked, "How long must I endure this, and be still!" For hours he suffered dumbly, without a moment's respite, or a moment's murmuring; his limbs grew cold, his face damp, his lips white, and, again and again, he tore the covering off his breast, as if the lightest weight added to his agony; yet through it all, his eyes never lost their perfect serenity, and the man's soul seemed to sit therein, undaunted by the ills that vexed his flesh. (56)

Despite its grounding in the reality of a soldier's pain, the scene appears elaborately staged. The act of reading the patient's body involves Alcott's participation in a series of generic conventions that include the expansive physical gestures of melodrama (the "clenched hands," the "imploring look," the covering torn from his breast) and the pathos of sentimental fiction (the silent suffering and "perfect serenity" of the dying hero's soul). Alcott even provides hypothetical dialogue, substituting her own imaginative speech for the patient's silence. Ventriloquism becomes one of the defining gestures of *Hospital Sketches*, as Alcott describes her own "sympathizing murmur[s]" in response to the soldiers and her longing "to groan for them, when pride kept their white lips shut" (37). Alcott frames the scene in such a way that the reader is simultaneously encouraged to interpret the dying soldier's body and instructed in the hermeneutic conventions of nursing. These conventions are, Alcott stresses, quite different from those practiced by the doctor (and particularly the surgeon), whose sole concern is with interpreting the bodies of his patients *as* bodies.[9] She translates the efficiency of the surgeon's work into metaphors of domestic duty, describing how one surgeon who had served in the Crimea "seemed to regard a dilapidated body very much as I should have regarded a damaged garment; and, turning up his cuffs, whipped out a very unpleasant looking housewife, cutting, sawing, patching and piecing, with the enthusiasm of an accomplished surgical seamstress" (36). The surgeon's proper work is the patching of flesh, just as the housewife's is the patching of clothing, and "The more intricate the wound, the better he liked it" (36). Yet this relentless materialism leads Alcott to criticize the tendency of the medical profession to fragment body and soul, "regarding a man and his wound as separate institutions" (91). It is the nurse's job to reconstruct the patient's fragmented identity, reading his soul through his body and thus reaffirming their dynamic relationship. In observing some of the traumatic emotional effects of battle on Civil War soldiers—the same debilitating symptoms that first led Silas Weir Mitchell to develop his "rest cure"—Alcott finds that in some cases the patient's "mind had suffered more than his body" (45), thus necessitating the interpretive (and narrative) skills of a good nurse.[10]

Ultimately, nursing and femininity become interchangeable concepts in Alcott's *Sketches*. In learning to read the emotional language of the body, the nurse uses the skills of sympathy that are most closely associated with a distinctly feminine "nature." Yet the underlying gender ideology of this association involves a more complex definition of femininity than at first it seems, for as Alcott points out, not all women make good nurses; the more delicate ones' proper "sphere" is that of "a comfortable bandbox on a high shelf" (91). The femininity of the nurse is predicated first and foremost on her capacity for emotional bonding with the patient:

You ask if nurses are obliged to witness amputations and such matters, as a part of their duty? I think not, unless they wish; for the patient is under the effects of ether, and needs no care but such as the surgeons can best give. Our work begins afterward, when the poor soul comes to himself, sick, faint, and wandering; full of strange pains and confused visions, of disagreeable sensations and sights. Then we must sooth and sustain, tend and watch; preaching and practicing patience, till sleep and time have restored courage and self-control. (90)

When Alcott is invited to attend a dissection she refuses, claiming, "my nerves belonged to the living, not to the dead, and I had better finish my education as a nurse before I began that of a surgeon" (91). Here Alcott implies that it is one's nervous system, rather than a strong stomach, medical expertise, or any other defining physical or intellectual qualities, that is most crucial for effective nursing practices. To participate in a dissection is to channel one's nervous energies away from an engagement with the living patient, and Alcott is vaguely disturbed by the transgression of the personal bond that dissection implies. She finds it "trying" to think of doctors cutting into "some person whom I had nursed and cared for," because to conceive of the body in such starkly material terms is to risk becoming like the doctor who "feared his profession blunted his sensibilities" (91).[11] Yet Alcott resists making a strictly biological distinction between the nurse's and doctor's roles, instead demonstrating a preference for the feminizing characteristics of intuition and empathy in both genders and professions. Thus she prefers the doctor "who suffered more in giving pain than did his patients in enduring it" to a more brutally efficient one who expected his patients to assist him in operations and who was capable of "whipping off legs like an animated guillotine" (92–93).[12] She admits, however, that this preference, and her "desire to insinuate a few of [the efficient doctor's] own disagreeable knives and scissors into him," amounts to little better than a "prejudice" (92). In *Sketches*, then, Alcott places the feminine interpretation of emotion at the center of the medical project at the same time that she constructs practical gender distinctions between doctors tending to bodies and nurses tending to souls. Alcott carves out a spiritual role for the nurse that asserts her unique capacity for reading silences and transforming them into narratives; she finds even (or perhaps especially) the unconscious body or the body convulsed with pain in pressing need of interpretation. Through these acts of emotional ventriloquism Alcott authorizes her own narrative voice, asserting her role as the chronicler of wounded bodies as they manifest wounded minds.

We can see the same emphasis on the translation of body into soul in Alcott's fictional work, particularly *Little Women* (1868), which in a limited way takes up the subject of nursing where *Hospital Sketches* leaves off. Here too Alcott poses the patient's emotional life as an interpretive problem that necessitates the skilled decoding of physical symptoms. Beth March's lingering illness confuses her sister Jo, who is more adept at reading literary texts than she is at reading bodies. Although Alcott was prone to interpret the embodied emotions of male invalids in the language of sentiment and melodrama, she parodies this formulaic mode of reading when Jo mistakes Beth's pallor for the conventional signs of unrequited love. Jo's first response is to try to write a new ending to Beth's story as she might for her own heroines, thereby transforming the deathbed drama into a narrative of miraculous recovery. But in this instance literature misleads Jo in reading bodily signs. When her efforts fail to produce the expected transformation, Jo slowly learns to interpret Beth's symptoms by intuition rather than generic literary design, as individual to Beth rather than conventional to heroines. Like Alcott's own response to nursing the wounded, Jo's response to Beth's illness teaches her to reaffirm the relationship between emotional and bodily experience. Jo's initiation into somatic interpretation is simultaneously an initiation into femininity. Outspoken and male-identified, Jo is forced to study the more nuanced gestures of Beth's life, gestures that draw on traditional codes of feminine domestic virtue. In this way, Jo becomes the end result of a dialectic in which linguistic and intuitive body hermeneutics coalesce; she becomes an "accurate" reader of somatic texts, as well as a producer of narratives about them.

If Jo's role in *Little Women* highlights the interpretation of body language, Beth's role explores its modes of production. In the textual economy of Alcott's novel, Beth's silences stand out from the surrounding narratives that her sisters construct. Beth's and Jo's sharply contrasting gender roles explore the conflict between feminine identity and linguistic authority. Whereas the strong, masculine Jo is the family "scribbler," making her way in the world through the art of storytelling, Beth is associated with the passive virtues of domesticity and silence. Beth is incapable of refiguring the world in fiction. Her only dream is "to stay at home safe with father and mother, and help take care of the family" (129). During a storytelling game at Laurie's picnic, Beth "disappear[s] behind Jo" (118), leaving control of language to her more verbally dexterous sister. Whereas the other participants shape the interlocking stories to their own temperaments (Mr. Brooke fashions a tale of chivalrous knighthood; Meg a ghostly romance; Amy a fairy tale, and Jo a playful confusion of genres), Beth's life remains untransformed by linguistic play. In the world of *Little Women* progress to adulthood necessitates the power of self-transformation; even the selfish Amy learns to "mould her character as carefully as she moulds her little clay figures" (201). Beth never matures because she does not seek access to a self-authorizing discourse. Her inability to construct a narrative identity parallels her inability to leave the home, and invalidism becomes the logical extension of her domesticity. Beth tells Jo, "I never made any plans about what I'd do when I grew up; I never thought of being married as you all did. I couldn't seem to imagine myself anything but stupid little Beth, trotting about at home" (338–39). The fact that Beth's lingering death comes at the onset of adolescence allows her to retain her childhood identity amidst the changing structure of the March family. Volume 2 of *Little Women*, which Alcott titled *Good Wives*, charts the three sisters' assimilation into the adult world, their transformation from independent children into wives and mothers. Beth's role is excluded from the title, yet her disease provides a commentary on it, for as Nina Auerbach has pointed out, "Beth's lingering death symbolizes the marriages of the remaining sisters" ("Afterword," 466). Alcott envisions Beth's illness as a distinctly feminine form of communication and the logical consequence of a domestic ideal. In this way, *Little Women* provides a companion piece to *Hospital Sketches*, for in each the ailing body is both the source and the aim of narrative production and feminine hermeneutics; Alcott displays her literacy in both languages, using the genre of sentimental fiction and the nursing chronicle to reconnect material and spiritual definitions of the self.

Eloquent Deceptions and Somatic Truth

Alcott, like Showalter, critiques the conventional interpretation of female illness as a sign of unrequited love, suggesting a more complex reading of emotional causation and feminine speechlessness. Both Elizabeth Gaskell's novella *Cousin Phillis* (1865) and Charlotte Brontë's novel *Shirley* (1849) examine the somatic consequences of repressed desire and linguistic betrayal in their portrayals of illness. Each explores the psychological processes at work in the transformation of feelings into symptoms, and each charts the semiotic structures of women's body language in order to provide a commentary on acts of narrative production. Whereas Beth March's illness provides a substitute for the absence of a self-authorizing narrative, the illnesses of Gaskell's and Brontë's heroines mark attempts to assert control over romantic narratives that have effectively eluded, betrayed, or erased their capacity for speech.

Gaskell's novella examines how illness functions as a response to the ambiguity of spoken and written language. In *Cousin Phillis*, the heroine's illness accentuates her inability to reconcile speech and action, identifying the indirect language of bodily symptom as the most powerful assertion of a material "truth." Questions of language—written, spoken, corporeal—and questions of interpretation—translation, multivalence, reader response—are at the center of Gaskell's story. In the course of the narrative we learn that the heroine, Phillis Holman, has been brought up by her father to believe in the unity of word and meaning and to treat her parents' speech with biblical reverence, "as if they had been St Peter and St Paul" (250). An Independent minister and a stern proponent of clear, straightforward words and deeds, Ebenezer Holman instructs his daughter in classical languages, teaching her a literal mode of translation. When the more worldly hero, Edward Holdsworth, enters the world of Hope Farm, he introduces Phillis to the possibility of double meanings, teasing her with "a style of half-joking talk that Phillis was not accustomed to" (259). Phillis's father believes Holdsworth's mode of speech to be a temptation akin to "dram-drinking" (266), because it manifests the storyteller's power to intoxicate his audience. In contrast, Holdsworth finds the minister's linguistic rigor to be a "very wholesome exercise, this trying to make one's words represent one's thoughts, instead of merely looking to their effect on others." Holdsworth attempts to curb his "random assertions and exaggerated expressions, such as one always uses" (264), but he is finally unable to embrace the family's moralistic fervor about language and complains, "Why make a bugbear of a word?" (265).

Holdsworth expresses his desire for Phillis indirectly, through marginalia in Phillis's Italian texts. Paul, Phillis's cousin and Gaskell's narrator, questions the propriety of Holdsworth's tactics, feeling that his friend's intrusion into Phillis's textual notes is "taking a liberty" (262) with her intellectual (and, implicitly, her sexual) privacy, transforming literary translation into a powerful medium for romantic expression.[13] Ultimately, Phillis and Edward's mediated dialogue is not congruent with the household's religious standards of linguistic honesty. Holdsworth's intrusion into female marginalia, like Lockwood's perusal of Cathy's diary in *Wuthering Heights*, generates sexually charged consequences. Phillis falls in love with Holdsworth before he has declared his intentions openly, and Holdsworth's subsequent transfer to work in Canada and marriage to a French-Canadian woman precipitate Phillis's case of brain fever.

Phillis's decline actually takes place in two stages that are shaped by Paul's attempts to read Phillis's bodily signs. Upon observing that Phillis has become pale, quiet, and listless in response to Holdsworth's departure, Paul tries to cure her by telling her that Holdsworth had spoken of his love for Phillis and his desire to marry her when he returned. Upon hearing that Holdsworth's spoken words, written messages, and physical gestures demonstrated a unity of emotional intentions, Phillis temporarily recovers and shows all the transformative physical signs of requited love. When Holdsworth then writes that he has met a woman who reminds him of Phillis, and later that he has married her (thereby suggesting the interchangeability, rather than uniqueness, of female identity), Phillis becomes ill with brain fever and almost dies. Here Paul's role as mediator parallels that of the textual marginalia. He is implicated in Holdsworth's betrayal of emotional truth by his own attempts at mediation; at the same time, Paul demonstrates his faith in these confidences as accurate reflections of Holdsworth's feelings and lasting expressions of his intentions. Paul subscribes, in effect, to the same interpretive values that Phillis and her family do, and is indirectly betrayed by this faith.

Gaskell is quite explicit about the relationship between textual ambiguity, emotional trauma, and the onset of illness. Because Phillis has no direct access to Holdsworth's emotional life, she has relied not only on Paul's testimony but also on the "language of nature" to provide a gloss on Holdsworth's marginalia. As her servant and nursemaid, Betty, notes, "there's eyes, and there's hands, as well as tongues" (298).[14] But in Holdsworth's case, neither physical signs nor marginal notations predict subsequent actions. Phillis's attempt to "read" Holdsworth according to an interpretive theory that would unify words and gestures as signs of an objective inner truth proves to be unreliable in a polyvalent world of human motives and interactions. Clinging to her faith in objective meaning, and seeking to repair the rift made by Holdsworth's indirect communications, Phillis responds to linguistic indeterminacy by offering her own body as the ultimate unified text. She thereby appropriates her father's biblical hermeneutics to the service of feminine somatic expression. As a gesture of protest, Phillis's wasted frame links emotions and actions; it proclaims her faith in a self unmediated by language. By asserting her insistently material presence (and her equally insistent refusal to translate emotions into speech), Phillis's symptoms force those around her to "read" her unspoken version of the romantic narrative as the true one.[15] Thus in becoming the author of her own illness, she simultaneously authorizes her own (silent) narrative, converting both the household and the extended community to an interpretive paradigm that places gestures above words. In the face of Phillis's illness the household is forced into a stance of mute sympathy that demands the careful reading of one another's facial expressions and bodily gestures. Paul describes how "in *these silent days* our very lives had been an *unspoken prayer*. Now we met in the house-place, and *looked at each other* with strange recognition of the *thankfulness on all our faces*." When he tries to speak, Reverend Holman's words come out only as sobs, and an aged farmhand declares, "I reckon we have blessed the Lord wi' all our souls, though *we've ne'er talked about it*; and maybe *He'll not need spoken words* this night" (315, emphases mine). The household becomes silent in response to Phillis's silence; they refuse to speak falsely in response to her refusal. Thus when asked by his fellow ministers to resign himself to giving his daughter up to God, the Reverend Holman declines to speak the words demanded of him, declaring, "What I do not feel I will not express; using words as if they were a charm" (313). Gaskell's narrative interrogates (and genders) the conditions of discursive authority, staging a confrontation between the desire for a unified, objective, and self-controlled meaning and the inevitable ambiguities, exaggerations, and falsehoods of the fictional project. In the disjunction between private (feminine, emotional, somatic) truth and public language, Gaskell identifies the ambiguity of her own project, an ambiguity that resonates in the unresolved ending of the story. The narrative ends soon after Phillis's recovery from brain fever, without her having regained either energy or good spirits. Phillis's final desire for a "change of thought and scene" as a way of going "back to the peace of the old days" (317) corresponds to the advice offered by many nineteenth-century health manuals but leaves the state of her health, like the narrative, unresolved. The very ability to write (rather than somatize) the narrative presupposes a relationship to language that the text identifies with the public realm of Holdsworth's verbal dexterity. As a narrator who is simultaneously complicitous in, confused by, and acutely attuned to his cousin's illness, Paul is poised between the position of a nurse who reads the patient's body and transforms it into narrative and the role of one who uses language for effect.[16] In the terms proposed by

Gaskell's story, the literary text, unlike the heroine's body, is too implicated in the deceptions and mediations of fiction to control the
production of meaning or claim the status of truth.[17]

Maternal Nursing and the Dangers of Affect

Charlotte Brontë's *Shirley* combines what I have identified as the
affective hermeneutics of nursing with the construction of illness as
an expression of the emotional life of the patient.[18] Like Alcott,
Brontë instructs the reader in the accurate interpretation of bodily
symptoms, and like Gaskell, she associates the somatic with both
privacy and truth. But Brontë is more explicit than Gaskell in her
critique of linguistic authority and social practice, employing illness
to explore the ramifications of normative femininity on women's psychological development.

In many ways Caroline Helstone is one of Brontë's most conventional heroines; unlike the more passionately expressive Jane Eyre
or the more independent and aggressive Shirley Keeldar, Caroline
seems trapped in conduct book codes of proper feminine behavior.
Even her illness serves as a proof of her femininity, as she responds
to her lover's indifference through a process of self-starvation. Faced
with the choice of whether "to pursue him, or to turn upon herself"
(107), Caroline chooses a suitably maidenly decline. Brontë explicitly frames Caroline's dilemma as a linguistic one, observing, "A
lover masculine so disappointed can speak . . . a lover feminine can
say nothing. . . . Nature would brand such demonstration as a rebellion against her instincts, and would vindictively repay it afterwards by the thunderbolt of self-contempt smiting suddenly in secret" (105). This passage suggests that Caroline's illness arises out
of a cultural demand for feminine quiescence. Brontë goes on to
trace a tradition of silent, dying women through the Helstone family history; she describes Caroline's aunt, Mary Cave Helstone, as
"a girl with the face of a Madonna; a girl of living marble; stillness
personified" (52), whose "silent . . . lingering decline" (53) seems the
natural consequence of her passive femininity. By associating her
with both artistic stasis and silence, Brontë reveals Mary Cave's
deadly acquiescence in her own objectification; Caroline stares at

her aunt's framed portrait as she contemplates women's circum-scribed lives. Like Mary Cave, Caroline is frequently described in metaphors of silence. Her beauty, according to the Reverend Hall, is of "a very quiet order" (271), and even Caroline's ladylike cloth-ing conveys her restrained nature, for Caroline "never makes a bus-tle in moving" (157). Through these images Brontë explores Caro-line's participation in cultural codes of genteel femininity that pro-hibit self-assertive behavior and speech; at the same time, Brontë exposes the fatal consequences of women's self-erasure.

Illness, then, becomes the direct result of Caroline's silence, forc-ing others to read her corporeal transformation and interpret its un-derlying message. The neighborhood watches and comments as Car-oline grows paler, responding to her decline according to their own hermeneutic abilities. Her uncle, as baffled by Caroline's metamor-phosis as by the death of his wife, complains, "These women are in-comprehensible. . . . To-day you see them bouncing, buxom, red as cherries, and round as apples; to-morrow they exhibit themselves ef-fete as dead weeds, blanched and broken down. And the reason of it all? that's the puzzle" (189). In posing the mutability of the female body as a "puzzle" to be solved, the Reverend Helstone articulates a sense of diagnostic confusion similar to what many nineteenth-cen-tury doctors felt when confronted with the mysterious correspon-dence between emotional fluctuations and somatic symptoms. It is, predictably, the female population of the neighborhood who are able to read this "natural language of feeling." Caroline perceives that "young ladies looked at her in a way she understood, and from which she shrank. Their eyes said they knew she had been 'disap-pointed,' as custom phrases it" (192).

The intended audience of Caroline's fading body is her lover, Robert Moore. When Caroline's illness is most eloquent, however, Robert's ability to read it remains in question. Preoccupied with questions of labor and management in the public sphere, Robert is unskilled in interpreting the nuances of feminine emotion and seem-ingly oblivious to the existence of Caroline's psychosomatic distress: "As he looked up, the light of the candles on the mantelpiece fell full on her face: all its paleness, all its change, all its forlorn meaning were clearly revealed. Robert had good eyes, and might have seen it, if he would: whether he did see it, nothing indicated" (252). As the reader becomes progressively attuned to the semiotics of Caroline's illness, Robert seems to become increasingly insensitive. When he begins to make love to the heiress Shirley Keeldar, Robert ignores the signs of Caroline's jealousy and despair. Each time Caroline watches Robert and Shirley together, her pallor and silence increase. Eventually she becomes, like Mary Cave, a symbol of walking death, haunting Robert as a ghost from the past rather than a living woman. Robert tells her:

I walked into the cottage parlour. . . . There was no candle in the room . . . and broad moonbeams poured through the panes: there you were, Lina, at the casement, shrinking a little to one side in an attitude not unusual with you. You were dressed in white, as I have seen you dressed at an evening party. For half a second, your fresh, living face seemed turned towards me, looking at me. . . . Two steps forward broke the spell: the drapery of the dress changed outline; the tints of the complexion dissolved, and were formless: positively, as I reached the spot, there was nothing left but the sweep of a white muslin curtain. (255)

Robert's vision of the ghostly curtain parallels the progress of Caroline's disappearing body.[19] He watches as "the tints of the complexion dissolve" and become "formless," leaving only the clothing without the life. Brontë suggests that the real Caroline is dissolving herself in similarly haunting ways; like her habitual "shrinking . . . attitude," Caroline's shrinking body conveys her emotional trauma. Her illness simultaneously reveals the presence of a body beneath her ladylike clothing and causes its slow deterioration. Brontë implies that behind Robert's attempt to avoid recognizing his cousin's illness is buried the knowledge of his own participation in it. Though not yet dead, Caroline has already become a ghost in Robert's imagination, a manifestation of his own betrayal and guilt.

When Caroline's decline develops into a critical case of brain fever, Brontë indicates the serious consequences of Caroline's emotional constraint.[20] Not only a product of unrequited love, Caroline's disease also marks the conflict between realism and romanticism that divides the novel. Brontë implies that Caroline's despair arises from her continued feeling of displacement in the masculine world her uncle and Robert represent.[21] Torn between the romantic impulses of her nature and her lonely insignificance in the face of violent strikes and manufacturing crises, Caroline wearies of a life that has proved void of emotional fulfillment. Having tried "to see things as they were, and not to be romantic" (172), Caroline finds that the "real" world offers no place for her. She realizes, like Brontë, that "imagination" may be "a disease rather than a gift of the mind" (48), but finds she is unable to relinquish the imaginary romance that threatens her health.[22]

Brontë's interest in the emotional content of Caroline's illness is most explicit in the text's nursing scenes. Highlighting the connection between nursing a child and nursing a patient, Brontë makes nursing and maternity interchangeable occupations, revealing Caroline's nurse to be her long-absent mother.[23] This particular plot twist was reproduced in sentimental and sensational genres later in the century; as I suggest later, similar scenes occur in Mrs. Henry Wood's *East Lynne* and Wilkie Collins's *Dead Secret*; even *Bleak House* portrays a reunion between Esther and Lady Dedlock as Esther recovers from smallpox.[24] For Brontë, this mother-daughter reunion highlights the simultaneous recovery of health and identity, offering motherhood as the paradigmatic form of nursing that can provide privileged capacities for interpreting the external signs of internal emotions, thereby healing the patient. Finding that "she and her nurse coalesced in wondrous union" (424), Caroline experiences illness as a condition in which physical, rather than verbal, communication is paramount. When Mrs. Pryor finally reveals her "prior" relationship to her patient, Caroline exclaims, "But if you *are* my mother, the world is all changed to me. Surely I can live—I should like to recover—" (434). It is the nurse's (mother's) ability to read the emotional secrets and needs of her patient (daughter) that restores Caroline to health. In contrast, Caroline's uncle is only confused and alienated by the nuances of female illness and the mysteries of affect: "Let a woman ask me to give her an edible or a wearable . . . I can, at least, understand the demand: but when they pine for they know not what—sympathy—sentiment—some of these indefinite abstractions—I can't do it: I don't know it; I haven't got it" (440). Declaring himself master of the material world, Caroline's uncle relinquishes mental and emotional abstractions to the sphere of feminine knowledge. Brontë develops this correlation further when Mrs. Pryor declares her own property rights in the reproductive project: "Papa . . . gave you the oval of your face and the regularity of your lineaments: the outside *he* conferred; but the heart and the brain are *mine*: the germs are from *me*" (433). Reversing traditional accounts of reproduction, which saw the female as contributing matter for the development of the male "germ" or spirit, Caroline's mother stakes her unique claim to Caroline's internal organs of feeling and thought.

For Caroline, the effects of masculine denseness and duplicity are repaired by the union with maternal truth. Caroline's discovery of her origin symbolically reconnects signifier to signified through the unmediated communication between her own body and her mother's. The two women become virtually interchangeable during Caroline's illness: "And the child lulled the parent, as the parent had erst lulled the child" (436).[25] No longer entrapped in metaphors of silence, Caroline recovers both flesh and life:

Long before the emaciated outlines of her aspect began to fill, or its departed colour to return, a more subtle change took place: all grew softer and warmer. Instead of a marble mask and glassy eye, Mrs. Pryor saw laid on the pillow a face pale and wasted enough, perhaps more haggard than the other appearance, but less awful; for it was a sick, living girl—not a mere white mould, or rigid piece of statuary. (444)

Like Pygmalion's awakening statue, Caroline's body slowly comes to life. The references to a "marble mask," "glassy eye," "white mould," and "rigid piece of statuary" in this passage metaphorically recall Caroline's connection to the dead Mary Cave. But Brontë implies that Caroline has rejected her aunt's model of self-effacement and can now seek an identity and voice of her own. Once recovered, Caroline sheds her lassitude and begins to pursue her recalcitrant lover, arranging clandestine meetings and cheerfully braving freezing weather to visit him during his own recovery from a wound. Indeed, it is through Robert's own feminizing convalescence that the "romantic" half of the text emerges as the dominant genre; as Robert comes to terms with his own abstract feelings, the love story supersedes the narrative of labor unrest, educating the hero in the gestural nuances of emotional expression.

Brontë's idealized correlation between nursing, maternity, and the interpretation of emotion is challenged, however, in Victorian sensation novels such as *East Lynne* (1861) and *The Dead Secret* (1857), where the melodrama of maternal nursing produces its own pathologies. Both Wood and Collins construct the mother's act of nursing as dangerously overidentified with the child-patient; in these cases, interpretive capacities serve only to produce, rather than relieve, hysterical symptoms. Laurie Langbauer has noted the more general collapse between hysteria and maternity in *East Lynne*, arguing that the text not only makes hysteria natural to woman in the same ways that maternity is naturalized, but also makes maternity and hysteria virtually interchangeable conditions. Thus, rather than causing or curing hysteria, motherhood *is* a state of hysteria in Wood's text (Langbauer, 172). I would add that this collapse is most acute in the scenes of nursing precisely because of the interpretive engagement between illness and affect. When the heroine, Lady Isabel Vane, returns disguised as a governess and, ultimately, nurses one of her dying children, her nursing is, in effect, *too* sympathetic; she is *too* good at interpreting the emotional life of her patient because she is overinvolved in the illness of her child. As I argue in Chapter 3, this concern about excessive emotion in the sickroom marked a more widespread fear within the medical profession about the feminizing effects of medical sympathy. In Wood's novel, the nurse is endangered by her own hysterical maternity; Lady Isabel's agitation imperils her very access to the patient by threatening to expose her inappropriate identity. Alternately repressing her emotional and verbal outbursts and giving way to private expressions of emotional despair, Lady Isabel's fluctuating feelings are made acute in the face of her son's death, and they hasten her own death "from a broken heart."[26] In this way, Wood's likening of nursing to maternity becomes part of a cultural discourse about affective excess, which drew upon medical correlations between feminine excitability and somatic symptoms. Unable to restrain her emotions, the maternal nurse is condemned to die from them.

Like *East Lynne*, Wilkie Collins's *Dead Secret* pathologizes the threat of maternal overidentification, but Collins's spectacle of female emotion gone astray is even more acute than Wood's. In addition to endangering her own health, Collins's secretly maternal nurse endangers the health of her child. In *The Dead Secret* Sarah Leeson, a lady's maid turned housekeeper, is called in an emergency to nurse her own daughter, who was secretly given up at birth to be raised as the child of Sarah's former mistress. Upon meeting with her daughter, who is now recovering from the birth of her own child, Sarah, a.k.a. Mrs. Jazeph, suffers from a violent nervous agitation that leads the daughter to believe that her nurse is a madwoman. Collins transforms the idealized ministrations of the nurse into a disturbing parody of medical attendance:

Mrs. Jazeph's touch, light and tender as it was, had such a strangely disconcerting effect on her, that she could not succeed, for the moment, in collecting her thoughts so as to reply, except in the briefest manner. The careful hands of the nurse lingered with a stealthy gentleness among the locks of her hair; the pale, wasted face of the new nurse approached, every now and then, more closely to her own than appeared at all needful. A vague sensation of uneasiness, which she could not trace to any particular part of her—which she could hardly say that she really felt, in a bodily sense, at all—seemed to be floating about her, to be hanging around and over her, like the air she breathed. (115)

The smothering sense of discomfort and vaguely homophobic anxiety produced by the "stealthy gentleness" of Mrs. Jazeph's nursing technique collapses the very bodily distinctions that the daughter seeks to reassert when she attempts to identify a somatic source of her unease. Not only does the nurse intrude upon the patient's physical privacy, she also transmits her own emotional excitability in a process that reproduces the collapse of bodily boundaries between them. Mrs. Jazeph's nervous energy and anxiety extend into the very environment of the sickroom, and her patient breathes in air that is seemingly filled with the traces of her mother's emotional excess. The mother's hysterical symptoms thus reproduce the act of nursing as a disconcerting emotional spectacle, a nightmare of feminine affect. And in a further collapse of the boundaries between nurse and patient, Mrs. Jazeph refocuses attention from the interpretation of her patient's body to her own, commanding even the doctor's attention.

He longingly speculates that the nurse "would be an interesting case to treat" (102). Eventually, Mrs. Jazeph's barely repressed emotional outbursts produce a state of screaming terror in her patient:

The hot breath of the woman, as she spoke, beat on Rosamond's cheek, and seemed to fly in one fever-throb through every vein of her body. The nervous shock of that unutterable sensation burst the bonds of the terror that had hitherto held her motionless and speechless. She started up in bed with a scream, caught hold of the bell-rope, and pulled it violently. (125)

Collins's portrayal of maternity as madness, and of the maternal nurse as catalyst for her patient's hysteria, challenges sentimental portrayals of mother-daughter relationships and empathetic ideals of nursing. Here we find the affective hermeneutics naturalized by Spencer, and celebrated, albeit in quite different ways, by Alcott, Gaskell, and Brontë, revealed as a form of emotional monstrosity that threatens both health and identity. Maternity and emotional excess are revealed as coterminous, the source rather than the cure of illness. The somatization of emotion becomes another proof of women's (and perhaps society's) dangerous permeability—between self and other, body and mind. Collins thus plays upon cultural apprehensions about feminine affect that lie beneath sentimental idealizations of motherhood, nursing, and even illness. He identifies the "natural language of feeling" as unsettling precisely because of its association with femininity, its tendency to excess, and its causal correlation with disease.

Ultimately, Wood's and Collins's hysterical maternal nurse is not so much a refutation of Brontë's and Alcott's idealized one as she is her dark twin; she extends the intuitive vision of nursing to its logical affective extreme. If the ideal nurse is empathically attuned to her patient's body, the hysterical nurse has crossed into a state of hermeneutic excess that threatens the boundaries of identity. In the sensational economy of female emotion, the nurse who is most adept at reading the signs of bodily distress, and therefore most feminine in her intuitive (and reproductive) bond with the patient, is threatened by her own capacity for illness. Her skill in reading the patient's feelings is inseparable from her own equally natural tendency to somatize emotional experience. In this way, the nurse's interpretive acumen enters the realm of pathology; she becomes, for Wood and Collins at least, a prime candidate for medical scrutiny and an emblem of feminine identity in its most problematically "natural" state of emotional extremes. To the extent that nurses function as narrators of their patients' stories, acting as ventriloquists for patients' emotions by translating the language of the suffering body into a more legible form, they become emblematic of the linguistic contradictions inherent in Victorian definitions of femininity. To interpret what someone else feels is to participate in an economy of feminine affect that is continually threatened by a potential loss of control. Medical definitions of emotional excess as both paradigmatically feminine and precipitously pathological sought, ultimately, to control that which was dangerously uncontrollable in the human psyche, first by displacing it onto a definition of femininity and then by subjecting it to classification as a form of body language with its own rules of grammar and codes of meaning. Yet in the often contradictory forms this language could take, in the competing "readings" and interlocking rhetorics of illness and affect, we can see that the cultural significance of female illness in nineteenth-century literature, medicine, and popular understanding, was considerably more complex than either a model of rebellion or a model of victimization can account for. To the extent that a common cultural narrative about the "natural language of feeling" emerges from these texts, it reveals both the symbolic importance and the ideological instability of body language as a category of meaning. On the one hand, illness becomes both a form and a substitute for language, a strategy of feminine communication that posits the material body as having a privileged access to "truth." On the other hand, the interpretation of illness mobilized conflicting theories of somatic legibility and illegibility, competing definitions of the normal and the pathological, and cultural apprehensions about emotional repression and emotional excess. In this way, the cultural significance of illness consistently exceeded the medical categorizations that attempted to control it, providing multiple strategies for reading the human body and its languages.

CHAPTER 2

From Neurosis to Narrative
The Private Life of the Nerves

> To him who waits, all things come! My aspirations may have
> been eccentric, but I cannot complain now, that they have not
> been brilliantly fulfilled. Ever since I have been ill, I have longed
> and longed for some palpable disease, no matter how conven-
> tionally dreadful a label it might have, but I was always driven
> back to stagger alone under the monstrous mass of subjective
> sensations, which that sympathetic being "the medical man" had
> no higher inspiration than to assure me I was personally respon-
> sible for, washing his hands of me with a graceful complacency.
>
> —Alice James, *The Diary of Alice James*

Alice James's lifelong search for a disease palpable enough to be declared real delineates the problem posed by "subjective sensations"
for nervous sufferers in the nineteenth century. Insofar as nervous
illness was linked (albeit vaguely) to the emotional life of the subject and perceived as a form of body language, doctors presumed
that the sufferer's symptoms were subjective, and in some cases in-
tentional. Because they lacked organic causes, illnesses such as hysteria, hypochondria, and neurasthenia bore a problematic relationship to the body; they called attention to the dynamic connection
between the mind's power and the body's pain.[1] Their victims experienced the immediate physical effects of illness without corresponding physical causes and, as a result, were denied the validity
of their pain by the medical establishment. Thus Alice James could
express relief when, after a lifetime of mysterious nervous maladies

that baffled each successive doctor she consulted, she finally was diagnosed as having breast cancer (Strouse, 333). For Alice, the visible reality of a tumor provided an immediate and palpable focus for what was otherwise a subjective experience of pain. But Alice's dilemma reveals a contradiction implicit in Victorian attitudes toward the nervous body, for what is pain if not immediate, palpable, and real?[2] Faced with opposing views of her body, which was publicly denied (through the authorized language of medicine) and privately affirmed (through the unauthorized language of Alice's secret diary), Alice assumed a double existence. By taking control of her own story, Alice transformed an unsatisfactory medical narrative—her case history—into a personal narrative that affirmed her body's reality by projecting it onto the written page. In other words, through the act of inscribing her experience of illness (albeit in an often flippant and self-deprecatory manner), Alice was able to sustain a belief in the validity of her physical experience in the face of medical denials and doubts.[3]

The battle for narrative control of Alice James's life ended, in a sense, with a merging of the two competing narratives. Once diagnosed with cancer, Alice felt that her own narrative had triumphed and subsumed those of the unsympathetic "medical men." Her private body had achieved the public recognition she had long sought, and her cancer served as a way of "lifting us out of the formless vague and setting us within the very heart of the sustaining concrete" (James, 207). Alice's pressing need for the sustenance of the "concrete" indicates the debilitating process of physical self-alienation that could be effected by nervous disease. Her solution to this dilemma—reshaping the "formless vague" of her body into the form of her secret diary—suggests the way imaginative structures could symbolically reaffirm individual identity when it was threatened by the disorder of disease.

Many figurations of the nervous body in Victorian fiction reflect a dilemma and solution similar to Alice James's. Just as Alice used her diary symbolically to reconstruct her body in a more durable form, nervous sufferers in Victorian fiction are often portrayed in the act of projecting the "formless vague" of their own disordered physicality into more "concrete" narrative spaces. In such figurations the body is not so much represented in as replaced by a narrative act. In effect, I am arguing here for a relationship between body and voice opposite to that proposed by the texts in Chapter 1. Far from using the body as a substitute for language, the heroines I discuss in this chapter perceive their "bodies" as ambiguous in much the same ways that Phillis Holman perceived language to be. In these cases, the act of narration becomes the solution to corporeal uncertainty. To illustrate this intricate relationship between neurosis and narrative form I have chosen two Victorian novels that provide extended meditations on nervous illness but that present the problem from opposite narrative stances. The first, Charlotte Brontë's *Villette*, merges nervous sensibility and narrative sensibility by confronting the reader with the hysterical first-person narrator—Lucy Snowe—and by tracing how hysteria informs her acts of narration and, in turn, how narration expresses and embodies her hysteria.[4] The second example, George Eliot's *Daniel Deronda*, poses the problem of hysteria as a disruption of the text's formal narrative voice. Gwendolen Harleth's incipient neurosis takes the form of a secret spiritual life. Her unorthodox visions and premonitions function as an internal narrative that takes shape within the larger chronicle. Thus, while Gwendolen's story is told in the framework of Eliot's omniscient third-person narrative, Gwendolen seems to experience her life in terms of a private counternarrative that challenges the cultural and ideological presuppositions of the novel's dominant narrative voice. Together *Villette* and *Daniel Deronda* suggest the range of narrative signification offered by Victorian fictions of the nerves and the centrality of narrative paradigms in reconnecting public and private perceptions of the nervous body.

Nervous Spirituality

The problem of physicality posed by nervous illnesses became a critical issue in Victorian medical research and practice and spawned a variety of conflicting theories. The ambiguous status of the nervous body that Alice James experienced so keenly was implicit in nineteenth-century medical definitions of neuroses, for as I have already suggested, neuroses inserted a troublesome middle category in the comfortable duality of body and mind. On the one hand, neuroses did not correspond to diseases of the body such as cancer and tuberculosis because nervous disorders lacked a distinct pathology.[5] Their symptoms were often vague and changeable, rarely conforming to a clear definition or easy diagnosis. On the other hand, the various physical symptoms that often (though not always) accompanied neuroses separated such disorders from madness. Nervous sufferers could, for the most part, continue to function rationally even when their symptoms were acute and their nerves were most sensitized. Thus Alice James could claim, "The only difference between me and the insane was that I had not only all the horrors and suffering of insanity but the duties of doctor, nurse, and strait-jacket imposed upon me, too" (149).

The problems Victorian physicians encountered in classifying, diagnosing and treating nervous ailments were reflected in the changing definitions of neurosis throughout the century and the changing status of the body in these definitions. The Victorian word "nerves" was not, as we might assume, a synonym for psychological distress. George Frederick Drinka notes that "most 'neuroses' were thought to stem from weak and delicate nerves, literally stretched or lax, overworked or overexcited. It was only as the Victorian period waned that the question of psychological causation became more central to medical thinking" (12). In effect, the causal relationship between body and mind in Victorian theories of neurosis developed according to contradictory paradigms over the course of the century. Whereas earlier medical theories generally focused on the physical basis of the nerves, arguing that emotional excesses literally stretched nervous tissues beyond their normal capacities, thereby producing physical symptoms, later theories tended to view physical symptoms as the direct (and subjective) product of mental or emotional causes, abandoning the intermediary link of strained nervous tissues. At the same time, hereditary theories of nervous illness that stressed physiological and psychological degeneration became popular after Darwin. It would thus be a mistake to view Victorian medicine as a unified community of discourse, for despite a general movement toward recognizing the role of the psyche in nervous disease, at any given time competing physiological and psychological theories of causation could and did coexist.[6] Indeed, so entangled did the terminology of body and mind become that Victorians routinely collapsed physiological processes with emotional or psychological ones. Responding to this confusion, the British physician John Hughlings Jackson noted the meaninglessness of these categories even as he employed them, observing that "there is no physiology of the mind any more than there is psychology of the nervous system" (417).[7] These interpretive shifts and contradictory explanations attest to the precarious separation between mental and corporeal realms in Victorian medical thinking and suggest that in studying neuroses physicians were forced to develop new paradigms for defining health and disease.

The philosophical challenge implicit in Victorian medical theories—that is, the ability of nervous disease to disrupt received categories of experience—suggests that Victorian thinking about nervous disease reflected broader crises of class, gender, and religion in Victorian culture. As more became known about the nerves, new debates arose about the hereditary and environmental causes of neuroses and the relationship between nervous illness and such factors as work, education, intelligence, sexual development, and spirituality. Whereas Herbert Spencer and the American physician George Miller Beard both argued that increases in nervous disease were a result of evolutionary progress and arose from a new society of "brain-workers," thereby allying neurosis with the educated classes, others believed such disorders accompanied the hereditary taint of criminals, prostitutes, psychopaths, and homosexuals.[8] Furthermore, at a time when the first colleges for women were opening in England and America, theories of neurosis that addressed sexual difference also received considerable attention. Although, as I suggested in Chapter 1, throughout the century British and American doctors routinely blamed women's nervous symptoms on excessive reading and intellectual stimulation, these diagnoses were eventually codified into a theory that specifically linked a greater frequency of nervous illness to advances in female education. In 1867, Sir James Paget claimed in his *Clinical Lectures and Essays* that the higher education of women was "favorable to the development of the nervous constitution" (230–31), and in 1873 the American physician Edward

Clarke argued in a widely published and controversial treatise, *Sex in Education; Or, a Fair Chance for the Girls,* that the education of women, by rechanneling blood from the uterus to the brain during puberty, threatened their sexual development, which in turn led to nervous disease (17–18).[9]

In their elaborate search for the causes of nervous illness, Victorian physicians also explored a variety of spiritual connections between physical and mental conditions. Neuroses were associated with both the visionary experiences of saints and the relinquished will of the mesmerized.[10] For example, Robert Brudenell Carter's pioneering work on hysteria led him to speculate about its role in religious experience. We can see the triumphant energy with which Carter debunked saints and miracles in his 1855 diatribe against the gullibility of Catholics and the posturing of religious hysterics. He claims:

In Roman Catholic countries, where miracles find ready credence, women of this class play their parts upon a more prominent stage than is commonly accorded to them here; although even in England . . . cases of wonderful trance, and of supernatural abstinence, have not been altogether wanting. But the performances of the young ladies, whose history has been written by the Earl of Shrewsbury, far transcend those of their most distinguished Protestant rivals; and the Ecstatica and the Addolorata will be long remembered, not only as striking examples of the ingenuity of tertiary hysteria; but in consequence of the knavery of their accomplices, and the surpassing credulity of their dupes. (227)

It was not only Catholicism, however, that became the focus of medical attention. In 1863 Isaac Ray claimed that "religious excitement, beyond all other forms of excitement . . . derange[s] the healthy balance of the mental faculties" (189). Similarly, in his 1872 *Principles of Psychology,* Herbert Spencer noted that the same process of sympathetic identification took place in "hysterical subjects" and "religious enthusiasms" (574), thereby demystifying the expression of spirituality and reducing it to a psychological principle.[11]

These views were echoed in continental debates in which women such as Bernadette of Lourdes, whose childhood vision of the Virgin Mary directed her to a spring of healing waters, and the bleeding Belgian ecstatic Louise Lateau were subjected to competing scrutiny from medical and religious skeptics. Both their physical symptoms—in Louise Lateau's case continuously bleeding wounds that corresponded to Christ's—and their religious visions and hallucinations were cited as proof of either sainthood or hysteria (Drinka, 269–70). Each of these women expressed her physical reality in the form of a religious narrative, but the struggle for interpretive control of those narratives pitted the medical community against the Catholic church. To physicians like Carter and Jean-Martin Charcot, the physical manifestations and religious visions of women like Bernadette and Louise corresponded to the behavior and symptoms of hysterical patients. For example, when under hypnosis Charcot's hysterics at the Salpêtrière adopted exaggerated postures of religious and sexual ecstasy, which seemed to link their neuroses to those of other visionaries.[12] Their spiritual experiences suggested that all forms of ecstasy might be a function of neurosis and that the visions and miracles of saints could be subjected to rational, medical, and scientific explanation.

Practitioners of Victorian medicine were thus forced to confront spiritual and ontological issues that had formerly been the province of organized religion and philosophy, and their responses to this challenge were by no means consistent or unified. Although some scientists and physicians dismissed all forms of spirituality and spiritualism as either a remnant of the irrational past or a sign of contemporary charlatanism, others sought empirical answers to spiritual questions. As early as 1840 the British doctor Thomas Laycock observed that the study of nervous phenomena "stretch on the one side into the dim regions of metaphysics, on the other into the illimitable space of the physical sciences;—the investigation being entangled, in addition, with a hundred theological questions, themselves involved in doubt and obscurity" (86). Eventually, and amid much controversy, the study of neuroses expanded to include psychic phenomena. Victorian interest in the paranormal—mesmerism, telepathy, hallucination—was frequently linked to the study of the nerves, and both were increasingly subjected to scientific scrutiny throughout the century.[13]

According to Terry Castle, "The rationalists did not so much negate the traditional spirit world as displace it into the realm of psychology" ("Phantasmagoria," 52). For example, in 1844 Sir George LeFevre claimed that instances of faith healing were really a product of mesmerism. In his medical treatise, *An Apology for the Nerves*, LeFevre noted that mesmerism "represents a great power equal to a host or an army, exercising its influence over our moral and physical being." In attributing all acts of faith healing to the mysterious power of human will over physical experience, LeFevre insisted that such powers were "as paramount in the present day as in times gone by. . . . It is the same [power] that cured the woman of hemorrhagy, and the man at the pool of Bethesda" (69). In the process of demystifying miracles, LeFevre invests the human mind with all the power and authority of a heavenly host. Similarly, in an 1845 study entitled *The Philosophy of Mystery*, British surgeon and medical librarian Walter Cooper Dendy set out to examine a variety of spiritual phenomena and to incorporate them into a coherent scientific theory. Dendy produced a series of physical explanations for psychic events that attributed phenomena such as visions, demonic possessions, and religious ecstasies to anything from indigestion to hysteria (288, 328–29). Dendy, like many of his contemporaries, believed that by revealing the scientific bases behind spiritual mysteries he was actually clarifying and strengthening the role of religion by bringing it into harmony with modern science. Thus he claimed that "philosophy and *natural* theology mutually *confirm* each other. The latter teaches us that which it is our duty to believe; the former, to believe more firmly" (178). This rationale for turning the focus of medicine and science to religious subjects appears with some frequency in Victorian studies of psychic phenomena. Indeed, according to J. P. Williams, some Victorian scientists believed that in phenomena such as mesmerism and telepathy "lay the promise of an empirical account of the soul and its nature, and an objective proof of the reality of spiritual values" (237).[14]

Amidst a variety of inquiries into these subjects, mesmerism became the psychic experience most frequently associated with nervous disease, eventually taking a central place in Victorian studies of hysteria. Although originally derided by the medical establishment and associated with both quackery and sexual license, mesmerism (or hypnosis) came to play an increasingly important role in

the diagnosis and treatment of nervous disorders.[15] The distinctions
between trance states and certain nervous conditions were called into
question by their external similarity, and even while refuting the elaborate claims of popular mesmerists, Robert Brudenell Carter noted
that "the mesmeric phenomena and the nervous diseases fade into
each other by imperceptible transition" (230). At the same time, the
power of mesmerism to influence human will revealed that the
boundaries of identity were less stable than had formerly been assumed. Charcot's assertion that susceptibility to hypnosis was a sign
of incipient nervous disorder implied that neurosis involved a potential destabilization of the self. Other physicians recognized that
most people were susceptible to hypnosis (and thus they could not
all be neurotics), but this theory also posed potential challenges to
the concept of free will. Carter claimed that "in the production of . . .
hysteria, the power of emotion must act in direct opposition to that
of will; and must be strong in exact proportion to its weakness"
(219). Did the presence of disease or the power of a hypnotist over-
ride a person's ability to make moral choices? What was the effect
of weakened nerves on human behavior and individual conscience?
These vexed medical and philosophical questions were eventually
addressed in legal arenas when Victorian doctors were called on to
testify in the courtroom about the influence of neurosis and hypnosis on human behavior.[16] The conclusions that many doctors came
to as a result of such case studies raised disturbing possibilities about
the widespread nature and power of the nerves. Here, as elsewhere
in Victorian medical debates, questions raised by disease eventually
entered the realm of morality. The relationship between body and
mind, action and conscience, self and society were confronted in
medical and legal territories, and important social and psychological questions were addressed through the vehicle of nervous disease.

The sheer range of social inquiry that characterized Victorian
studies of the nerves attests to the imaginative power of nervous illness not only for the sufferer but also for the medical profession and
the Victorian writer. The status of the body as a cultural symbol was
emphasized with increasing vigor as its spatial boundaries seemed
to become more tenuous, and medical discourse offered a means of
containing and codifying what appeared to be the limitless energy

and ambiguity of nervous disease. This view of the nervous body as a reflection of cultural anxieties corresponds to what Anita and Michael Fellman have seen as a trend in nineteenth-century attitudes toward illness. Viewing the popular interest in medical questions as part of an attempt to situate the self in a rapidly changing world, the Fellmans note:

Perceived disorder in the outer world was paralleled by an assumption of bodily fragility within. By emphasizing the building of personal boundaries, fears were expressed that such boundaries might be disintegrating, that the self was threatened within a threatened society. Not only were the mind and body major symbolic regions and foci of general social anxieties, they seemed to offer the first and foremost potential ordering places. (15)[17]

It is this view of body and mind as frontiers on which to establish order that links prevailing medical attitudes to fictional portrayals of nervous disease. Both discourses display a common interest in neurological questions as they relate to cultural and spiritual domains, thereby participating in a widespread Victorian tendency to displace diffuse and chaotic social issues onto more immediate questions of physiology. A little like Freud's definition of hysterical symptoms as vessels into which various neurotic contents are poured, the trope of nervous disease was made to serve various social, ideological, and rhetorical ends.[18] On the one hand, figurations of neurosis such as Brontë's and Eliot's addressed the process by which the nervous body could be imaginatively refigured. On the other hand, fictions of the nerves were used to challenge traditional concepts of identity and to act out cultural and intellectual upheavals on the immediate and palpable terrain of the body.

Psychic Spaces: *Villette, Daniel Deronda*

Although much of the attention paid to nervous disorders by the medical profession occurred after the publication of *Villette* in 1853, Charlotte Brontë had some exposure to prevailing theories of neurosis through consultations about her own recurring nervous symptoms. In addition, her familiarity with materialist challenges to religious doctrine, through her friendship with Harriet Martineau, and her interest in mesmerism and popular debates about body and mind suggest that Brontë was both caught up in and skeptical about the popular enthusiasm for questions of scientific rationalism, mesmerism, and spiritualism around mid-century (Gaskell, *Life*, 438–41, 610). In her study of the relationship between nineteenth-century literature and theories of personality, *Eros and Psyche*, Karen Chase suggests that Brontë's fictional use of "heterodox theories of mind [such as phrenology and physiognomy] . . . reveals an impatience with prevailing notions of personality, and a desire for finer distinctions and deeper explanations than philosophy or medical science offered" (55).

Even more than Brontë, Eliot was writing at a time and within an intellectual atmosphere that made her keenly aware of innovations in Victorian medicine and psychology. Her familiarity with scientific and secular debates about psychic phenomena, as well as her knowledge of developments in psychology and neurology through the 1870's, suggests that Eliot's portrayal of neurosis in *Daniel Deronda* (1876) was directly informed by the matrix of medical and spiritual issues I have outlined.[19] In particular, Eliot's work with Lewes on *Problems of Life and Mind*, her research into medical history for *Middlemarch*, and her friendship with Herbert Spencer and other intellectuals working in the fields of biology, sociology, and psychology made her aware of the current issues in these and related fields. Lewes's influence here is paramount. Writing at a critical moment in medical history before the disciplinary separation between neurology and psychology, Lewes's theoretical shifts between psychological and physiological explanations for human behavior mark his attempt, like Eliot's own, to explore the tenuous middle ground between body and mind. As Karen Chase has noted, Lewes moved from an early belief in psychology as a separate science of mind to a later position that asserted the physiological basis of psychology.[20] Eliot's portrayals of psychological processes through the physiological framework of nervous disease in *Daniel Deronda* are thus consistent with Lewes's emphasis on the biological basis of behavior in the later period of his career.

By thus appropriating, in part, the authorized discourse of science and medicine, as well as the popular interest in spiritualism and mesmerism, Brontë and Eliot were able to codify concerns about self and society through their figurations of nervous disease. However, Brontë and Eliot drew on literary as well as medical history in their portrayals of neurosis. Working in essentially realistic genres, they employed stereotypes of nervous sensibility in order to codify a perceived disjunction between imaginative and material realms of experience. Before the publication of *Villette*, representations of nervous sensibility were generally confined to gothic or sentimental fiction. Late-eighteenth-century gothic tales such as Ann Radcliffe's *Mysteries of Udolpho* and *The Italian*, and Matthew G. Lewis's *Monk*, were designed to evoke sensational nervous reactions in both heroines and readers. Closely allied to romanticism and popular concepts of sensibility, these tales helped to establish stereotypes of nervous sensitivity that Jane Austen parodied in early novels such as *Northanger Abbey* and *Sense and Sensibility*. These stereotypes also found expression in the period's sentimental fiction; and in her study of eighteenth- and nineteenth-century magazine literature, *Heroines in Love*, Mirabel Cecil claims that "by the end of the eighteenth century sentiment, under the guise of sensibility, had arrived in magazine stories in such a big way that it threatened to swamp them. Heroines became frail and pale, priding themselves on being able to swoon at length and weep at will" (45). The fictive connection between illness and sensibility was thus well established by the time Brontë began writing *Villette*; indeed, it was a familiar literary trope that had descended to the level of parody and cliché. Brontë's expansion of the genre constituted a significant departure from traditional depictions of the nerves, linking nervous sensibility to an emerging psychological realism and making illness a condition of narrative authority rather than an expression of sentimental distress.

Eliot's portrayal of neurosis, like Brontë's, drew upon established literary stereotypes. But by the time Eliot wrote *Daniel Deronda*, nervous sensibility had been revived and transformed into another form of popular fiction—the sensation novel. Popularized around the 1860's by such writers as Wilkie Collins and Mary Braddon, sensation novels, like their gothic predecessors, relied on nervous sensibility for sensational or somatic effects.[21] But Collins, Braddon, and other writers like them focused less on the supernatural than Radcliffe or Lewis did. Their plots emphasized criminal behavior, nervous sensitivity, and incipient madness, and they refigured the haunted mansion of gothic fiction as the Victorian asylum. Eliot's use of sensation fiction paradigms to portray the workings of nervous disease is made clear in the barely disguised violence and murderous fantasies of her nervous heroine. But Eliot, like Brontë, transformed the genre she drew upon to explore the physical, psychological, and narrative implications of nervous illness. Thus, while fictions of the nerves were not solely a Victorian phenomenon, their literary and cultural significance underwent important developments during the nineteenth century that corresponded, in part, to the medical developments I have outlined.

Despite the common stereotypes they employ to represent nervous sensibility, *Villette* and *Daniel Deronda* portray strikingly different kinds of nervous heroines. Whereas Lucy is plain and retiring, Gwendolen is flamboyant and aggressive; while Lucy is a vicarious spectator of life's drama, Gwendolen seeks center stage. Yet Lucy and Gwendolen experience nervous sensibility as part of the structure of consciousness; it tempers their perceptions of and reactions to the outside world. Lucy's vision of a ghostly nun and Gwendolen's vision of a dead man's face precipitate nervous attacks that implicate them in a long literary tradition of female nervousness and hysteria. But unlike those of many of their gothic predecessors, Lucy's and Gwendolen's confrontations with the supernatural are assigned neurological causation. Lucy claims that her "nerves are getting overstretched" and describes her ailment variously as "a strange fever of the nerves and blood" (231), "a deadlier paralysis" (229), and a "long accumulating, long pent-up pain" (234). Although her malady is more persistently physical in its symptoms than Gwendolen's, both suggest forms of hysteria, a condition so loosely defined in the popular nineteenth-century imagination that it could range from heightened excitability to madness. Eliot stresses Gwendolen's "peculiar sensitiveness" (53) and her "unusual sensibility" (89). Gwendolen's mother worries about the "fits of timidity or terror" (95) that come over her eldest child and cause Gwendolen to experience moments of "hysterical violence" (407). Both heroines are thus set apart by the quality of their nerves; their maladies occur in the uncharted spaces between physical reality and psychological interpretations of that reality.

Perhaps the most striking similarity between Brontë's and Eliot's novels lies in the figurative vocabulary they employ to portray the experience of nervous illness. In both novels disorders of the nerves reveal disturbing fissures in the concept of self, challenging the assumed wholeness and continuity of identity. They portray the heroines' neuroses as a series of visionary experiences and violent self-divisions that compel Lucy and Gwendolen to experience their own physicality as potentially alien and radically unstable. Their fluctuating bodies, precariously balanced between pain and imagination, provide immediate points of reference for psychic events. Yet at other moments Lucy and Gwendolen experience a terrifying detachment from their bodies; their neuroses create a state of personal disorder that threatens to overwhelm any immediate sense of identity. In this way, the troublesome dialectic of body and mind that we saw in both Alice James's diary and contemporary medical studies of neurosis is refigured in Lucy's and Gwendolen's responses to nervous illness.

Lucy and Gwendolen experience neurosis as a literal dis-order of the self, and each attempts to reimpose order on the chaos of her nerves. These attempts take the form of spatial metaphors, symbolic locales that provide substitutes for an increasingly vague and disordered sense of reality. Unlike Alice James, who lamented "over my poverty in the way of receptacles for my overflow" (105), Lucy and Gwendolen find numerous receptacles for the overflow of their nervous sensibilities. Both heroines are obsessed with privacy, persistently seeking structures to contain emotional and pathological secrets. As I go on to suggest, these physical spaces parallel Lucy's and Gwendolen's narrative domains; in each case the heroine's response to neurosis is to reshape her threatened reality into more concrete and durable forms.

As Karen Chase has noted, Brontë is preoccupied with symbolic spatial relationships in her novels.[22] Just as Alice James uses the metaphor of "bottled lightning" to describe her nervous condition (60), Lucy seeks containers—boxes, bottles, drawers, desks—to express her conflicting sense of restriction and release. Embodying systematic acts of sexual, emotional, and physical repression, Lucy's spaces allow her to organize and corporealize her psyche when it is threatened by nervous disorder. Thus each contact Lucy has with Dr. John is systematically hidden and restructured in her system of emotional organization. The bottle of Dr. John's letters that Lucy buries in the school's garden is the most prominent example of this process, but Lucy's battles with Mme. Beck over control of her dresser drawers and with M. Paul over her desk fit into this general pattern of emotional and spatial displacement. Lucy's search for symbolic locales and her subsequent acts of containment constitute reconstructions of her relationship to a threatened material and personal reality.

Like Lucy, Gwendolen finds that the psychological process of securing her hysterical fears necessitates corresponding acts of physical enclosure. She too is preoccupied with containers, though her focus is on the keys that will keep them locked. Gwendolen becomes so obsessed by a secret painted panel in her mother's house that she keeps it locked and hides the key in her bedroom. When her younger sister steals the key to view the panel more closely, Gwendolen snaps at her, "How dare you open things which were meant to be shut up?" (56). Gwendolen's sense that there are things "meant to be shut up" in her own psyche worries her throughout the text. Whereas Deronda's journey through the novel is toward receiving the key to open his grandfather's trunk and thereby claim his spiritual and familial inheritance, Gwendolen's keys are meant only to lock, never to open. Although Deronda attempts to open up Gwendolen's psyche, believing he has "found a key now by which to interpret her" (488), Gwendolen's neurosis remains stubbornly impenetrable to both Deronda's hermeneutic powers and her own. Furthermore, like the progressive violence of her neurosis, Gwendolen's locked spaces contain progressively more dangerous objects and ideas. While traveling with Grandcourt, Gwendolen acquires a dagger and then locks it in her dressing case. Later she tells Deronda, "I dared not unlock the drawer: it had a key all to itself; and not long ago, when we were in the yacht, I dropped the key into the deep water. It was my wish to drop it and deliver myself. After that I began to think how I could open the drawer without the key" (756). For Eliot, the spaces of Gwendolen's neurosis codify anxieties about the very nature of physical and mental experience and the precarious balance between them.

If enclosed spaces figure the body for these two heroines, tempests and horizons figure their states of mental and emotional release. In *Villette* thunderstorms and ocean tempests both express and provoke the violence of Lucy's illness. Lucy describes her symptoms of hysteria in metaphors of the ocean, claiming, "To this hour, when I have the nightmare, it repeats the rush and saltiness of briny waves in my throat, and their icy pressure on my lungs" (94). In this passage Lucy's imaginative and physical realities merge; she projects the watery figuration of her neurosis into her corporeal experience. The "salty waves" with their "icy pressure" on Lucy's throat and lungs correspond to the choking symptoms or "globus hystericus" that constituted one of the few consistent symptoms of hysteria in medical definitions from Hippocrates to Freud. Water metaphors carried a similarly pathologic significance for Alice James. When she recalled the worst outburst of her illness it was as "that hideous summer of '78, when I went down to the deep sea, its dark waters closed over me and I knew neither hope nor peace" (230). The drownings envisioned by Brontë and James, like the "deep waters" of Gwendolen's psyche, indicate the turbulent inner life associated with victims of nervous disorders. Both Alice James's real body and Lucy's and Gwendolen's figurative ones are projected into the natural world through a rhetoric that links personal fragility with tempestuous external events.

Like Lucy's reaction to storms, Gwendolen's reaction to open spaces is characterized by passionate fear and dread. Indeed, Gwendolen is as frightened by wide horizons as she is obsessed with locked boxes, for while locked spaces set tangible boundaries, expansive vistas threaten to disperse her immediate sense of self:

Solitude in any wide scene impressed her with an undefined feeling of immeasurable existence aloof from her, in the midst of which she was helplessly incapable of asserting herself. The little astronomy taught her at school used sometimes to set her imagination at work in a way that made her tremble: but always when some one joined her she recovered her indifference to the vastness in which she seemed an exile. (*Daniel Deronda*, 94–95)

Gwendolen's dread of the sublime in nature—her essentially antiromantic intellectual and emotional stance—places her in contrast with Daniel's idealistic quest for cultural heritage and spiritual identity in

the East. Gwendolen's hysteria thus works against the broader movement of the text, which reveals increasingly wider intellectual and
geographic horizons. More than any other of Eliot's novels, *Daniel
Deronda* extends beyond either provincial or national terrain. Gwendolen's need to participate in a small world that circulates around
her individual existence is challenged by her successive confrontations with people who move in a world far larger than hers. Thus
when Herr Klesmer criticizes the artistry of Gwendolen's hitherto
admired singing voice she experiences "a sinking of heart at the sud-
den width of horizon opened round her small musical performance"
(79). Later, after her marriage to Grandcourt, Gwendolen suffers
from a sense of solitude in a world that is vast and indifferent. Indeed, Gwendolen's fear of horizons becomes most acute, and most
directly linked to violence and neurosis, during the yachting vaca-
tion that precipitates Grandcourt's death, for the voyage forces
Gwendolen to contemplate a wide, uninterrupted horizon that preys
on her worst nervous fears. These symptoms of Gwendolen's illness,
her moments of immobility in open spaces, can be compared to the
exaggerated postures of Charcot's hysterics, for as Gillian Brown
has noted in her study of agoraphobia, "The preeminent figure of
immobility for the nineteenth century is the hysteric, whose strange
postures freeze normal bodily motion and activity" (135).

Lucy's and Gwendolen's use of spatial metaphors to express the
terms of their neuroses is replicated in their use of narrative spaces.
Like their locked boxes, Lucy's and Gwendolen's narratives serve as
projections of their hysteria, symbolic transformations of the "formless vague" into the narrative concrete. Yet their neuroses serve different functions in the novels' narrative structures. As both narrator
and heroine, Lucy controls the terms of her own signification; she is
the self-actuating subject of her narrative. Conversely, Gwendolen
is one step removed from narrative control; her experience of neurosis is mediated through the discourse of Eliot's narrator, and both
her body and its expressions of hysteria are constructed as the object of the narrative gaze. Whereas *Villette* compels us to ask how
central Lucy's nervous system is to her narrative role and whether
neurosis enhances or competes with her ability to tell a story, *Daniel
Deronda* raises questions about the cultural and textual conse-

quences of the heroine's neurosis as it is mediated through the authorized narrative voice.

The status of the body in *Villette* corresponds to the dual nature of nervous disease. It is both a truth and a lie. This contradiction is implicit in Lucy's nervous condition and shapes her view of her interpretive and narrative roles. Conflating the boundaries between subject and object, viewer and viewed, Lucy's narrative reflects the ambivalent status of her nervous body and challenges simple correlations between language and physicality. This dynamic relationship between Lucy's nervous sensibility and her narrative role is played out most explicitly in the "Concert" chapter of *Villette*. While attending a performance with Dr. John and his mother, Lucy feels a vague but irresistible impulse draw her gaze away from the public performance to a private drama taking place in the royal box of Labassecour. As the king enters, Lucy sees beyond the regal persona to the "silent sufferer" within. She reads "the strong hieroglyphics graven as with iron stylet on his brow" as a mirror of her own nervous sensibility, and she attributes the workings of "Hypochondria" to a nature that they both share (290). By transforming the king's body into a signifier, reading symbolic meaning into the "peculiar and painful fold" on the king's furrowed brow, Lucy enacts her own corporeal dilemma. On the one hand her body, like the king's, is a detached object for public interpretation. A figuration that signifies disease, it is always already a sign. On the other hand, Lucy's body is a vehicle of absolute truth, an irreducible instance of material, sensory reality. It precedes and circumvents language. The king's illness thus provides Lucy with external evidence of her inward conviction that the body is both a psyche, or imaginative construct, and a soma, or physical entity. Extrapolating from her own psychosomatic experience, Lucy reads the world as the soma of her psyche. By projecting her own sensibility into others and reading their neuroses as her own, Lucy blurs the boundaries between her body and her narrative. In this way, the king appears as both an independent sufferer of immediate pain and a symbolic extension of Lucy over which she wields hermeneutic control. Lucy's neurosis thus leads her to perceive herself as both an inviolable text and a creative interpreter.

At the same time that Lucy finds herself poised between two

views of the body, she seeks to legitimize her acts of interpretation through the testimony of her nerves. Lucy interprets through sensibility rather than reason; her authority is of the body rather than the mind. While watching the king she claims, "If I did not *know*, at least I *felt*, the meaning of those characters written without hand" (290). Brontë suggests that Lucy is able to read the subtle symptoms of human emotion precisely *because* her nerves are sensitized, because she too is a silent sufferer. Thus the permeability between Lucy and her surroundings is at once a proof of her interpretive prowess and a symptom of her illness. Lucy's hermeneutic sensitivity, enhanced by nervous disease, allows her to interpret the world through what Eliot termed "the subtler possibilities of feeling" and thereby to grasp its invisible and subjective truths (*Daniel Deronda*, 72).

The correlation between narration and neurosis in *Villette* is integral to Brontë's view of her narrator-heroine. She explicitly links the symptoms of Lucy's illness to her narrative role. In a striking moment of self-recognition, Lucy laments, "Ginevra gradually became with me a sort of heroine. One day, perceiving this growing illusion, I said, 'I really believe my nerves are getting overstretched: my mind has suffered somewhat too much; a malady is growing upon it—what shall I do? How shall I keep well?' Indeed there was no way to keep well under the circumstances" (231). What Brontë indicates here is that far from being an aberration of character, Lucy's nervous disease constitutes the fabric of her narrative consciousness. In making Ginevra into a heroine, Lucy both fulfills a narrative function and uses fictional categories to express her own emotional needs. Indeed, nervous disease becomes Lucy's vocation; she is called to it as ecstatically as a nun (the figure of her neurosis) is called to religious orders: "I concluded it to be a part of his great plan that some must deeply suffer while they live, and I thrilled in the certainty that of this number, I was one" (229). Lucy's sense of being chosen for suffering is empirically confirmed in the concert scene when, after watching the king suffer throughout the performance, Lucy realizes how unique her sensibility is: "Full mournful and significant was that spectacle! Not the less so because, both for the aristocracy and the honest bourgeoisie of Labassecour, its peculiarity seemed to be wholly invisible: I could not discover that one soul present was either struck or touched" (291). Much like the correlation between illness and language that I outlined in Chapter 1, here nervous sensibility translates into narrative perspicacity. Throughout *Villette*, the fixity of Lucy's narrative gaze marks unique moments of spiritual sympathy that set her apart from those with ordinary sensibilities and project her into their lives with an uncanny power to interpret the drama within. Brontë reveals that to read bodies as texts and to transform one's own neurosis into narrative are not mutually exclusive paradigms. Rather, Lucy's nervousness enhances her narrative authority at the same time that it necessitates acts of narrative containment. Like Alice James, who often described her aesthetic and neurasthenic sensibilities in the same terms and rejoiced at the "bliss of finding that I too was a 'sensitive' " (47), Lucy finds that the subtlety of her perceptions is inseparable from the condition of her nerves.

If Lucy's gaze anticipates medical correlations between neurosis and hypnosis, her visions of the nun and her impetuous visit to a priest reveal the direct relationship between neurosis and spirituality. Both events suggest that Lucy's hysteria is, in part, a form of spiritual expression and repression. Lucy is not oblivious to this interpretation of events. She blames her confession on the influence of her "nervous system" and views the confessional as another form of receptacle like her boxes and bottles (258). She claims "the mere pouring out of some portion of long accumulating, long pent-up pain into a vessel whence it could not be again diffused—had done me good" (234). The inviolable relationship between confessor and priest prevents the "diffusion" that Lucy cannot otherwise contain. Just as boxes function as metaphors for her body, Lucy's confession functions as a physical expression of her disease. And like Alice James, who described her diary as "an outlet to that geyser of emotions, sensations, speculations and reflections which ferments perpetually within my poor old carcass" (25), Lucy uses the act of confession as a narrative outlet for the overflow of sensation. Lucy compares her confession to a heart attack or stroke, describing "a feeling that would make its way, rush out, or kill me—like . . . the current which passes through the heart, and which, if aneurism or any other morbid cause obstructs its natural channels, seeks abnormal outlet"

(258). The apparent conflation of verbal and physical modes becomes evident in Lucy's metaphor. Lucy bestows a physical body on the verbal act of confession. But what appears to be a contradiction is actually a function of her neurosis. Because Lucy's disease encompasses both psyche and soma, her rhetoric insistently links imaginative and physical domains.

If confession constitutes an expression (literally a pressing out) of Lucy's disease, her vision of the nun, as Goldfarb has observed, functions as a symbol of repression (152–54). Yet the spiritual ecstasies historically associated with nuns and saints indicate that Lucy's nun is a more complex symbol of neurosis than has hitherto been noted.[23] In the way a nun channels sexual desire into spiritual devotion, Lucy channels both sexual and spiritual desire into disease. The nun thus becomes a metaphor for all acts of displacement in *Villette*, a liminal figure that reveals the dual structure underlying Lucy's malady. Brontë's emphasis on the spiritual aspect of Lucy's neurosis further suggests that personal expressions of faith (both Lucy's and perhaps Brontë's own) were being encoded in the public rhetoric of Victorian medicine. Thus Dr. John Bretton legitimizes Lucy's first vision of the ghostly nun by diagnosing it as "a case of spectral illusion . . . following on and resulting from long-continued mental conflict" (330). Although later in the novel the nun is revealed as a man in disguise, the diagnosis of Lucy's sensibility remains intact; indeed, much like Brontë's description of her own nervousness as a "horrid phantom," the nun becomes the continuing trope for Lucy's disease, a synonym for nervous excitability (Gaskell, *Life*, 377). Studying Lucy's face, Dr. John exclaims, " 'Ho! the nun again?' . . . 'She has been, as sure as I live,' said he; 'her figure crossing your eyes leaves on them a peculiar gleam and expression not to be mistaken' " (338). In Dr. John's diagnosis the nun functions as both the object of Lucy's neurosis and its sign. The ghostly figure/figuration simultaneously bestows a body upon Lucy's elusive malady and erases the body in the spiritualized robes of sisterhood. And if the nun bears a metonymic relationship to Lucy's neurosis, Lucy's gleaming eyes function as synecdoches of her sensitized body. Indeed, Lucy's body is all eyes; her disease is that of the visionary. The nun signals her visitations through ocular symptoms, as if wielding a hypnotic as well as pathological effect. In this peculiar grafting of gothic metaphor, spiritual expression, and medical diagnosis we can see how competing discourses could share the same rhetorical and imaginative spaces and how nervous sensitivity could signal both spirituality and sexuality, both imagination and disease.

Visionary Sensibility: *Daniel Deronda*

If Lucy's sensibility takes the form of narrative spectatorship, Gwendolen's constitutes a form of spectacle. She is never the audience—that role belongs to Eliot's narrator—for Gwendolen's neurosis is always on narrative display. But Gwendolen's hysteria is not fully explained in or contained by the text's dominant narrative structure. Her struggle for control over an increasingly fragmented inner reality takes shape in her visions, which form a kind of "heterodiegesis," or counternarrative. Gwendolen's visions and hallucinations, like those of Bernadette of Lourdes or Louise Lateau, constitute a form of spiritual (though not religious) narrative in conflict with secular paradigms. While her budding conscience, nurtured by Deronda's influence, conforms to the text's moral and cultural proscriptions, Gwendolen's hysterical visions constitute a challenge to the privileged spiritual discourse of Mordecai, Mirah, and Deronda and threaten to undercut the novel's dominant narrative voice.

Eliot makes Gwendolen's potential to challenge narrative authority explicit in the opening lines of *Daniel Deronda*. The first chapter begins in contemplation of Gwendolen's visual power and an assessment of its effects:

Was she beautiful or not beautiful? and what was the secret of form or expression which gave the dynamic quality to her glance? Was the good or the evil genius dominant in those beams? Probably the evil; else why was the effect that of unrest rather than of undisturbed charm? Why was the wish to look again felt as coercion and not as a longing in which the whole being consents? (35)

In this series of questions Gwendolen is made the object of both Daniel Deronda's and the narrator's gaze while her own is systematically dissected and revealed as the "coercive" glance of the mes-

merist. Entering into the mind of the hero as he watches Gwendolen
from across the room, Eliot's narrator suggests that the "evil" in
Gwendolen's nature lies in her ability to appropriate and disrupt authorized forms of vision. Unlike Lucy, who controls the focus of her
own narrative, Gwendolen's ability to cross the boundaries between
subject and object signals a transgression of power relationships, a
dangerous reversal of proper specular roles. Like the invisible magnetic fluid that was once believed to run between the mesmerist and
his subject, Gwendolen's gaze threatens to enter the implicitly male
viewer and to drain him of independent volition.[24]

Like Brontë, Eliot associates private neuroses with public performances. Throughout *Daniel Deronda* Gwendolen vacillates between watching and wanting to be watched by others; so when her
family's finances are threatened, the only careers Gwendolen can envision for herself are those of actress and singer or wife. But each
option eventually precipitates the symptoms of Gwendolen's disease,
for each involves increasing the discrepancy between Gwendolen's
public role and private sensibilities. In her first and only dramatic
performance—a tableau of the living statue Hermione in *The Winter's Tale*—Gwendolen perfects a role she has already perfected in
life: that of object and spectacle for an implicitly male viewer. But
her portrayal of Hermione's stasis belies the inner turmoil Gwendolen experiences. During the performance Gwendolen both becomes the statue she plays and transforms that statue into an image
of her own private hysteria. She freezes "with a change of expression that was terrifying in its terror. She looked like a statue into
which a soul of Fear had entered: her pallid lips were parted; her
eyes, usually narrowed under their long lashes, were dilated and
fixed" (91). Gwendolen's private drama is thus exposed to the public eye while her own gaze is "fixed" like one in a trance. And although the audience attempts to ignore the revelations of Gwendolen's performance, Gwendolen finds these "occasional experiences,
which seemed like a brief remembered madness, an unexplained exception from her normal life" (94) increasingly difficult to ignore.
They intrude upon the "normal" narrative flow of events, hinting at
visions that are for Gwendolen's eyes alone.

However, such specular moments constitute expressions rather than origins of Gwendolen's hysteria. Even as a child, Gwendolen perceives her nervous sensitivity as different from the sensibilities of those with whom she lives. Both a source of pride and a revelation of self-division, Gwendolen's neurosis is actively violent in expression:

There was a disagreeable silent remembrance of her having strangled her sister's canary-bird in a final fit of exasperation at its shrill singing which had again and again jarringly interrupted her own. She had taken pains to buy a white mouse for her sister in retribution, and though inwardly excusing herself on the ground of a peculiar sensitiveness which was a mark of her general superiority, the thought of that infelonious murder had always made her wince. (53)

Like both Alice James and Lucy Snowe, Gwendolen feels that her peculiar sensitiveness sets her apart from others and marks her superiority to their duller sensibilities. Her somewhat gullible and lovestruck cousin Rex feels that Gwendolen's "excitability" should make her "able to love better than other girls" (95). But her childhood violence and nervous sensitivity grow into more threatening adult forms, deadening her capacity for love and channeling her emotional life into disturbing moments of spiritual horror. Unlike Lucy, whose nervous disease renders her virtually powerless in all but feeling, Gwendolen's illness, with its potential outbreaks of "infelonious murder," constitutes an active danger to those around her. Her diminished power of self-control reveals fissures in the smooth functioning of social and narrative relations, challenging civility and civilization with unpredictable outbursts of the nerves.

The implicit threat of Gwendolen's nerves becomes explicit after her marriage to the ghoulish aristocrat Henleigh Grandcourt, for marriage, like the stage, reveals the division in Gwendolen's public and private narratives. The correlation that the text makes between theater and marriage is codified in Gwendolen's hysterical response to her wedding night. In an unstaged scene that mirrors her performance of Hermione, Gwendolen experiences an outburst of hysteria as her husband watches in uncomprehending silence. She "screamed again and again with hysterical violence. . . . He saw her pallid, shrieking as it seemed with terror, the jewels scattered around her on the floor. Was it a fit of madness? In some form or other the Furies had crossed his threshold" (407). Because Eliot constructs the scene through Grandcourt's eyes, we see how the eruption of Gwendolen's nervous sensibility temporarily displaces Grandcourt's mastery and defies narrative explanation or control. Gwendolen's private "furies" invade the patriarchal threshold, threatening to usurp Grandcourt's power to command. Her outburst of hysteria thus highlights the fissure between acceptably public, properly specular femininity and the uncontrolled aggression of the private self.

Like Lucy, who in a fit of nervous agitation seeks out a priest, Gwendolen seeks confession for the violence of her sensibility. She warns Deronda, "I am frightened at everything. I am frightened at myself. When my blood is fired I can do daring things—take any leap" (508). Deronda, impotent in the face of Gwendolen's private struggles, nevertheless recognizes the spiritual power of her neurosis. He advises Gwendolen, "Try to take hold of your sensibility, and use it as if it were a faculty, like vision" (509). Deronda's advice proves ironic, for visions are the very manifestations that Gwendolen most dreads. Like Lucy, Gwendolen is plagued by hallucinations, but the visual symptoms of Gwendolen's disease are far more threatening than Lucy's silent nun. They foreshadow her own potential for violence, her ability to disrupt the status quo with psychic and psychotic power, and they constitute a form of "inward vision" (757) that competes with Gwendolen's public life. This hallucinatory energy of Gwendolen's neurosis corresponds to what Terry Castle has identified as the role of the phantasmagoria in nineteenth-century fiction and psychology. Castle describes how the phantasmagoria "was a favorite metaphor for heightened sensitivity and . . . neurasthenic excitement" ("Phantasmagoria," 48). She claims, "The mind itself now seemed a kind of supernatural space, filled with intrusive spectral presences—incursions from past or future, ready to terrify, pursue, or disable the harried subject" (59).

As her neurosis progresses, Gwendolen's spectral presences take increasingly narrative forms; that is, they seem to tell a story that follows a connected pattern of cause and effect.[25] The icon of Gwendolen's neurosis is a painting portraying a fleeing figure and a dead man's face. This visual narrative is transmuted again and again in Gwendolen's moments of nervous dread. It embodies her need to commit "some fiercely impulsive deed" (737), and it foreshadows her trial of conscience when that event—Grandcourt's death—comes about. Gwendolen's visions are insistently mobile; she sees punishing furies and figures in flight. They imply a logical progression from desire to action to punishment, and they tell a story of Gwendolen's life that is different from either the one she lives in public or the one she reveals to Deronda in private. Eliot describes Gwendolen's life of nervous fears as "a long Satanic masquerade, which she had entered on with an intoxicated belief in its disguises, and had seen the end of in shrieking fear lest she herself had become one of the evil spirits who were dropping their human mummery and hissing around her with serpent tongues" (831).

The periodic intrusions of this Satanic masquerade in the larger narrative, as well as Gwendolen's (rather than the narrator's) power to "see the end" of her visions—to anticipate their frightening possibilities for narrative closure—highlights both the diegetic form and prophetic function of Gwendolen's neurosis. Unlike Lucy's encounters with the nun, which are eventually given a rational explanation, Gwendolen's hysterical visions reveal the tenuous boundaries between her private life and the world outside. The scene of Grandcourt's drowning punctuates this rift between public veneer and private violence. As Gwendolen and Grandcourt leave on the boat, "both of them proud, pale and calm," they create a "scene [that] was as good as a theatrical representation for all beholders. . . . It was a thing to go out and see, a thing to paint" (745). Eliot highlights the specular nature of the scene by placing it in a dramatic frame. As they walk to the boat our vision is divided between Gwendolen's placid exterior and the tempestuous drama within. "She was not afraid of any outward dangers—she was afraid of her own wishes, which were taking shapes possible and impossible, like a cloud of demon-faces. . . . Quick, quick came images, plans of evil that would come again and seize her in the night, like furies preparing the deed that they would straightway avenge" (745–46). The iconographic echoes between Gwendolen's imaginative "seizures" and the painting in her mother's house foreshadow Grandcourt's transformation into the dead face from which Gwendolen flees. When the boat returns, even Gwendolen cannot fully explain the circumstances of Grandcourt's death. After seeing him fall into the water she stands, frozen like Hermione, unable to throw him a rope. Filled with murderous triumph, Gwendolen delays her rescue attempt until it is too late. Although Deronda assures Gwendolen of her innocence, Gwendolen insists, "I did kill him in my thoughts. . . . I only know that I saw my wish outside me" (760–61). Because Gwendolen realizes the tenuous boundaries between her fantasies and actions, she assumes full moral responsibility for the crime. The violence of Gwendolen's sensibility puts to test the assertion of Eliot's narrator that "Macbeth's rhetoric about the impossibility of being many opposite things in the same moment, referred to the clumsy necessities of action and not to the subtler possibilities of feeling. . . . A moment is room wide enough for the loyal and mean desire, for the outlash of a murderous thought and the sharp backward stroke of repentance" (72). Because Gwendolen's life is continually poised between murderous thoughts and moral repentance, she is unable to make clear distinctions between her internal and external narrative domains. Instead, the circumstances of Grandcourt's death raise the complex ethical questions surrounding *inaction* and challenge the proverbial innocence of the bystander or spectator. Gwendolen finds that her "subtler possibilities of feeling" have tangible (and homicidal) effects on external reality. The two become fused because, for Gwendolen, neurotic fantasies impinge on and are inseparable from rational actions. Here, Eliot seems to be putting to fictional practice Lewes's theory that "to imagine an act is to rehearse it mentally. . . . Hence it is that a long-meditated crime becomes at last an irresistible criminal impulse" (459). Gwendolen's visions thus function as dramatic rehearsals for later events. But it is not only Gwendolen's imagination that seems to condemn her. The very act of spectatorship implicitly becomes the scene of violence in *Daniel Deronda*, for to wield narrative power is to accept responsibility for the events one observes and depicts. Through the terms of Gwendolen's narrative fantasies, Eliot demonstrates how specular authority is always implicated in a violent exchange between subject and object. However, Eliot distances herself from the implications of this principle by displacing the text's explicit narrative violence into the hysterical visions of her heroine. Ultimately, Gwendolen is held responsible for the violence of narrative authority, just as in the opening scene she is blamed for its disruption.

Although Eliot continues throughout the novel to valorize Gwendolen and Deronda's bond of conscience and to grant Mordecai the official role of prophet, the form of Gwendolen's hysteria finally challenges and mimics the dominant narrative structure.[26] Gwendolen's power to make her "inner visions" come true, to see her wishes take shape outside her body, constitutes a spiritual and prophetic dimension to her character that is in conflict with the novel's authorized spiritual voice. Ultimately, Deronda's loyalties are divided between the task of morally reclaiming Gwendolen and bringing her back to a sense of cultural community, or pursuing his own, separate cultural and spiritual heritage through his grandfather's legacy and Mordecai's guidance. Eliot implies that Deronda must choose between prophets precisely because his "was not one of those quiveringly-poised natures that lend themselves to second sight" (527). But the status of prophetic truth is jeopardized in *Daniel Deronda* by the rhetoric of spirituality, for the language Eliot uses to describe Mordecai's religious visions is too close to her descriptions of Gwendolen's violent sensibility. Both the Jewish mystic and the murderous hysteric exhibit natures "quiveringly-poised" on the verge of "second sight." On the one hand, Mordecai initially expresses his spirituality to Deronda in the form (so familiar to Gwendolen's experience) of a "possessing spirit which had leaped into the eyes and gestures" (437). But the overlapping rhetorics of the visionary and the hysteric move in two directions. The prophetic fulfillment of Gwendolen's visions is signaled in apocalyptic echoes of biblical rhetoric. As Gwendolen steps from the boat that has carried Grandcourt to his death she cries, "It is come, it is come!" (750). These parallels between Mordecai's religious inspiration and Gwendolen's hysterical violence are, in part, reflections of Eliot's interest in all aspects of human spirituality, for despite their moral incompatibility, Gwendolen and Mordecai share a common psychic experience. But Gwendolen's spectral experiences also carry a potential challenge to Mordecai's prophetic authority because, like medical correlations between saints and hysterics, Eliot's rhetoric encodes the possibility that all visionary powers are a function of nervous disease.

Incurable Narratives

Answers to the questions raised in *Villette* and *Daniel Deronda* about narrative authority and nervous disease are postponed until the moment of narrative (and perhaps therapeutic) closure. The endings of *Villette* and *Daniel Deronda* have raised a number of critical questions, not the least of which is whether Lucy and Gwendolen are eventually cured of their neuroses. Although there has been a fairly broad critical consensus that Lucy overcomes her malady and Gwendolen attempts to bring hers under rational control, the means to and effects of such cures have been subjects of debate. Most critics of *Villette* have agreed on the fact of Lucy's cure, but not on its causes. Goldfarb claims that Lucy works through her neurosis symbolically by means of the sexual iconography of her buried bottle of letters, and thus successfully transfers her repressed sexual desire for Dr. John into her "asexual" marriage to M. Paul (153–54). Similarly, John Maynard argues that Lucy has rescued herself "from the verge of psychological disaster . . . by acknowledging her feelings and accepting a life of emotions and desire" (210). A number of feminist readings have attributed Lucy's cure to her achievement of independence. They point to Lucy's successful school and claims of happiness while M. Paul is away as proof of her newfound emotional and physical health.[27]

With similar diagnostic confidence, some critics of *Daniel Deronda* have asserted Gwendolen's moral growth and achievement of psychic health, while nevertheless noting varying degrees of irony in Eliot's ending. Gwendolen's release of Deronda from his unofficial role as confessor and therapist and her final vow to become "one of the best of women, who make others glad that they were born" (882) is cited as proof of her progression from selfish neurotic to selfless idealist. Roger Whitlock, for example, sees Eliot valorizing the rational over the emotive sides of the text and claims that "Deronda is triumphant; the verbal and rational mode is triumphant; the daylight world is finally the only world recognized" (23). But Whitlock admits that "such a conversion makes little sense" (23) in the world that Gwendolen is left with at the end of the text, and most critics recognize, like Deirdre David, that "the burden of Eliot's fictions of resolution seems to fall more heavily on Gwendolen than it does on Deronda. . . . It is difficult for us to imagine what she will do with the understanding that she has so painfully achieved" (204).

If we accept these readings of *Villette* and *Daniel Deronda* it would seem that many of the disruptive cultural and intellectual implications of Lucy's and Gwendolen's nervous maladies are undercut by the need for narrative closure. One must, it appears, cure the heroine in order to end the text. As in a medical case history, the state of wellness collapses the need for narrative. Yet most readings of *Villette* and *Daniel Deronda* fail to account for lingering evidence of neurosis and fail to recognize that Lucy's and Gwendolen's attempts to achieve self-control continue to receive authorial skepticism amidst formal gestures of closure. In fact, both texts resist closure by leaving their heroines' fates uncharted and their lives in emotional turmoil. In *Villette* the reader is left to speculate whether M. Paul dies at sea, and in *Daniel Deronda* Gwendolen is left without a husband, a fortune, a career, or a confidante. While this narrative irresolution is by no means unique to texts about neurosis (indeed, almost any text can be seen as in some way open-ended), the issue of narrative closure is highlighted in Brontë's and Eliot's novels by their emphasis on neurosis as a form of narrative production. We can find proof of the discomfiting reaction the ending of *Daniel Deronda* produced in contemporary audiences in the anonymous American sequel that appeared soon after its publication. Entitled *Gwendolen*, the sequel united Gwendolen and Daniel after Mirah's death in the East and thus provided a sense of thematic closure absent in Eliot's novel.

Most important for this study, the endings of *Villette* and *Daniel Deronda* raise questions about the validity of their heroines' newfound health. Despite Lucy Snowe's independence, hard work, and happiness, *Villette* ends with a storm. The violence of weather that affects Lucy's nerves throughout the text is no less disruptive in its conclusion. Once again Lucy's rhetoric erupts into hysterical violence as the storm rages out of control:

I know some signs of the sky; I have noted them ever since childhood. . . . The wind shifts to the west. Peace, peace, Banshee—"keening" at every window! It will rise—it will swell—it shrieks out long: wander as I may through the house this night, I cannot lull the blast. The advancing hours make it strong: by midnight, all sleepless watchers hear and fear a wild south-west storm.

That storm roared frenzied for seven days. It did not cease till the Atlantic was strewn with wrecks: it did not lull till the deeps had gorged their full sustenance. (595–96)

Recalling her childhood sensitivity to storms, Lucy links her current reaction to earlier outbursts of hysteria. Once again, the "shrieks" and "keening" of the wind provide analogs of Lucy's neurosis. The violence of the tempest is transformed into narrative expression, challenging Lucy's placid claims of health and happiness. Brontë leaves us in the midst of this emotional and meteorological outburst, thereby extending her portrayal of neurosis beyond the boundaries of the text and refusing either narrative or interpretive closure.[28]

Eliot's text is similarly indeterminate. By the end Deronda recognizes the precarious position in which he must leave Gwendolen, and he admits failure in the responsibility he had assumed. Faced with her confusion and despair he claims, "I am cruel too, I am cruel" (877). And though Gwendolen promises Deronda that she will try to overcome her fears, she reacts to his absence with a final fit of hysteria:

When he was quite gone, her mother came in and found her sitting motionless.

"Gwendolen, dearest, you look very ill," she said, bending over her and touching her cold hands.

"Yes, mamma. But don't be afraid. I am going to live," said Gwendolen, bursting out hysterically.

Her mother persuaded her to go to bed, and watched by her. Through the day and half the night she fell continually into fits of shrieking, but cried in the midst of them to her mother, "Don't be afraid. I shall live. I mean to live." (879)

Gwendolen's motionless and cold body recalls her many other moments of frozen horror in the novel, and her rational will to live is belied by the testimony of her "shrieking" hysterical outburst. The only evidence of a cure at the end lies not in Gwendolen's behavior but in her assurances of good intent. The narrator moves on to more traditional narrative conclusions—Daniel and Mirah's wedding and Mordecai's beatific death—leaving Gwendolen to recover in her mother's arms. But Gwendolen's close relationship with her mother, unlike Caroline Helstone's, bears only slight promise of renewal. Throughout *Daniel Deronda*, Gwendolen's nervous disorder proves impervious to her mother's aid. The end of Eliot's novel thus remains radically unresolved, for Gwendolen has embraced Deronda's moral vision without eradicating her own nervous symptoms. In essence, Deronda's narrative closes while Gwendolen's is abandoned. The two competing narratives—the one that erupts in Gwendolen's mind and the one that tells her story for her—are never allowed, as Alice James's were, to merge into one.

Ultimately, the effect of narrative indeterminacy and curative failure in *Villette* and *Daniel Deronda* extends the disruptive energy of nervous illness beyond the space of the text. Here fictional form accurately mirrors medical function, for despite their fascination with the psychological and spiritual implications of nervous disease, Victorian doctors were rarely more successful than Brontë and Eliot in envisioning effective remedies for nervous suffering. The causes of and cures for nervous illnesses remained open questions throughout the nineteenth century, yet this failure to categorize and control psychosomatic energies led to the proliferation of a cultural discourse in which they assumed spiritual and religious significance. For Brontë and Eliot, as for many of their medical contemporaries, neurosis was an imaginative category as well as a painful reality, and both medical and fictional "narratives" sought, in some respects, to explain and contain the visionary capacity of neurosis through linguistic structures. Together they participated in a rhetoric of the nervous body that constructed it as a cultural symbol, an icon of disorder and doubt. They found that neurosis provided a vocabulary for spiritual expression that was not limited to the province of saints. By using nervous disease (both fictional and real) as a frame through which to view Victorian culture, we can see how the neurotic became both a privileged interpreter of that culture and a reflection of its values.[29] In exploring the wider psychological and spiritual implications of neurosis, Brontë and Eliot participate in an emerging cultural narrative about the metaphysics of mind and body in which the ambiguity of the nervous system came to symbolize the contested nature of consciousness and to posit a material basis for spiritual experience. At the same time, their fictions give independent voices to the necessarily marginalized victims of nervous disease, exploring the ontological crises produced by "subjective sensations." In depicting the nervous sufferer's attempts to reconstruct a coherent sense of physical reality, to merge public and private versions of the self, Brontë and Eliot reinterpret the assumptions of Alice James's complacent "medical men." *Villette* and *Daniel Deronda* thereby pay tribute to the individual experience of suffering while also recognizing that private bodies are always in some ways determined by and representative of the larger culture in which they move.

CHAPTER 3

Neuromimesis and the Medical Gaze

⚕

During an 1881 performance of *La dame aux camélias* in Moscow, an interchange occurred between Sarah Bernhardt and her audience that became the focus of medical debate. According to a Russian alienist who attended the performance and later described it to the French sociologist Gabriel Tarde:

In the fifth act, at the most dramatic moment, when the entire audience was so silent that you could have heard a pin drop, Marguerite Gautier, dying of consumption, coughed. Immediately an epidemic of coughing filled the auditorium, and during several minutes, no one was able to hear the words of the great actress. ("Foules et sectes," 367)[1]

In Bernhardt's performance there were two acts of mimesis—Bernhardt's imitation of disease and the audience's imitation of Bernhardt. The experience at the Moscow theater served, in part, as a sign of Bernhardt's dramatic triumph: her portrayal of Marguerite Gautier was convincing and dynamic enough both to mimic real disease and to affect the audience physically. Bernhardt's coughing demonstrated a successful mirroring of life, or in this case death, in art. Although the layers of fictional distance between the Moscow audience and any real experience of disease would seem enough to dispel any worries about the dangers of such a performance, a few contemporary physicians and sociologists saw the event as a sign of the audience's (and, by implication, modern civilization's) incipient nervous decay. According to this argument, successful dramatic mimesis posed a medical threat—the duplication of fictional events on real bodies through the weakness of the nerves and the instability of human identity. At a time when modern plays, novels, operas, and newspapers frequently were "blamed for the spread of nervousness" (Drinka, 154; see also Foucault, *Madness and Civilization*, 157), and were thought to heighten emotional and physical suggestibility (Aubry, 11; Tarde, *Imitation*, 84; Nordau, 26), the behavior of the Moscow audience at Bernhardt's performance seemed a compelling example of the dangers inherent in the act of spectatorship. By demonstrating the potential for interaction between real bodies and fictional ones, the Bernhardt incident suggested that audiences could be deeply affected by dramatic events in ways that were not always healthy or cathartic. Like Lucy Snowe's emotionally charged response to Vashti's performance, Bernhardt's Moscow audience experienced a sympathetic, and involuntary, physical reaction to the deathbed drama. Crossing the boundaries between fiction and reality, spectator and spectacle, the audience projected themselves into the sickroom and onto the stage. They thereby raised questions about the innocence (and immunity) of the bystander, implicating the act of watching, or by extension reading, in the visual or textual scene.

The terms of debate in which the Bernhardt incident was framed are familiar and not by any means limited to medical, fictional, or theatrical events of the late nineteenth century. More recent arguments about the social effects of pornography, televised violence, and suicide clusters (to name a few) have raised similar questions about suggestibility and incorporation. To what extent do people duplicate the behavior they view? How are events in the outside world assimilated into the self? What is the relationship of the viewing act to the object of vision? Who, if anyone, controls the gaze, and who is controlled by it?[2] My interest here is not in formulating a definitive answer to these questions, were that even possible, but rather in studying the ramifications of asking them in relation to literary and medical texts of the nineteenth century. By focusing on the various medical, fictional, and readerly audiences to illness, and by demonstrating the tensions that accompany their moments of identification with the body of the sufferer, this chapter explores the interplay of roles—particularly gender roles—involved in acts of spectatorship.[3] It demonstrates how both fictional and real audiences—that is, characters on the novelistic stage and potentially suggestible readers—are invited to participate vicariously in the drama of disease, negotiating the territory between sympathy and detachment.

Imitation, Contagion, and the Crowd

The theatrical setting of the Bernhardt incident made literal the implicitly dramatic structure of a phenomenon Sir James Paget identified in 1875 as "nervous mimicry" or "neuromimesis" (172–73).[4] A form of involuntary behavior associated with hysteria, neuromimesis could refer to any mimicking of organic disease. More specifically, however, he used the term to designate a state of suggestibility in which viewing, hearing, or reading about a disease aroused corresponding symptoms. The emphasis on mimesis in this form of neurosis seemed to ally it with other modes of representation in drama, fiction, and art. It constituted a pathological instance of the human faculty for imitation. But neuromimesis, though in many senses a disease of the imagination, was not dismissed as merely a curious psychic phenomenon or nervous chimera. Its ability to shift into the realm of the "real"—to produce palpable effects on the body—qualified it for medical attention. The underlying idea was not a new one; concerns about excessive emotional engagement, novel reading, and questions of sensibility and sympathy in general had received considerable medical attention in the eighteenth century (Mullan, 217, 220–24). In addition, some theories of insanity posited the potentially contagious power of mental derangement or what was later called "*folie à deux.*"[5] But Paget's codification of these beliefs into a single theory of nervous suggestibility marked a new interest in systematizing the relationship between body and mind. Although neuromimesis did not receive the sustained interest that diseases such as hysteria and neurasthenia provoked (appearing in late-nineteenth-century medical encyclopedias sometimes under its own heading and sometimes under hysteria or malingering), it gained increasing attention in the 1880's, fed by some of the same concerns about suggestibility that appeared in medical and legal debates about insanity, hypnosis, and newly emerging theories of crowd psychology.[6]

The widespread currency of suggestion and imitation as explanatory principles of human behavior indicates, as I have argued, the embattled status of subjectivity in the nineteenth century. Incidents like the Bernhardt performance seemed to reveal a fundamental permeability not only between body and mind but also between self and other. This dissolution of ontological boundaries suggested the possibility of a kind of mental or neurological contagion comparable to epidemics of organic disease (Ray, 180). Described as a kind of mass hypnosis, or free-floating transmission of emotions, nervous contagion could sap the moral strength and force of will, allowing people to be influenced by or to identify themselves with the actions or directions of others. Combining medical concerns about weak nerves with sociological interests in intermental psychology, speculations about nervous contagion developed in conjunction with late-nineteenth-century crowd theory, which in turn grew out of the various nineteenth-century reactions to and reassessments of the French Revolution.[7] Drawing on bacteriology as a model, Gustave Le Bon claimed that "ideas, sentiments, emotions, and beliefs possess in crowds a contagious power as intense as that of microbes" (126). Like Le Bon, who was responsible for popularizing the subject of crowd psychology, most crowd theorists agreed that the motivating force was some form of "moral contagion," "suggestion," "imitation," or "hypnosis" (terms that were not used interchangeably, though they referred to related behavioral processes), that would move through groups of people, transforming individual identities into the phenomenon of "the crowd."[8]

Like the more general fear of contagious diseases that spurred nineteenth-century drives for sanitary reform, the concept of a moral epidemic became a means through which both the scientific community and the population at large expressed concerns about physical and mental proximity of different peoples. Peter Stallybrass and Allon White have argued that " 'contagion' and 'contamination' became the tropes through which city life was apprehended" precisely because of bourgeois fears about promiscuous physical contact with the lower classes (135). Theories such as Le Bon's (which was actually drawn from a number of different writers) revealed that "contact" and "contagion" could be more than physical; the very morals, emotions, or intelligence of one person could be temporarily transferred to another as part of the homogenization of humanity that took place in the midst of a crowd.

Although the development of crowd theory and the related concept of nervous contagion were most prevalent in continental writings (in addition to Le Bon and Tarde, they were treated at length in Paul Aubry's 1888 *Contagion du meurtre*, which footnotes the Bernhardt incident, and in Vigouroux and Juquelier's 1905 *Contagion mentale*), the subject of suggestibility, in one form or another, was addressed in a variety of developing fields—psychology, sociology, criminology—and received considerable exposure in England and America.[9] Long before Le Bon had popularized crowd theory, however, Alexander Bain had taken up the problem of emotional transference in his chapter "Sympathy and Imitation" in *The Emotions and the Will* (1859). Bain warned that actors had a special power to express and transfer emotions to others—even false emotions. Great actors could, according to Bain, "[manifest] emotion . . . so as to render it infectious to all beholders" (213). Among audiences, Bain claimed, there was "a susceptibility greater in some men than in others to the outspoken feelings of their fellows, by which they yield more promptly to sympathetic influences" (213).[10] The infectious nature of these sympathetic influences indicated to some members of the medical community a general (and possibly hereditary) weakness of character that could make people susceptible to the influence of any popular demagogue.

Aubry's study is perhaps the most sensational in assessing the threat of neuromimesis to the general population, predicting murder, suicide, and political anarchy as the consequences of nervous disease. He was not alone, however, in seeing troublesome implications in this form of suggestibility. In 1863 Isaac Ray warned that "intimate association with persons affected with nervous infirmities, such as chorea, hysteria, epilepsy, insanity, should be avoided by all who are endowed with a peculiarly susceptible nervous organization, whether strongly predisposed to nervous diseases, or only

vividly impressed by the sight of suffering and agitation." Furthermore, he said, "No one can safely consider himself as exempt from
the operation of the principle in question. They who are most confident of their power of resistance, often furnish the most striking illustrations of its irresistible influence" (174). Nine years later, Daniel
Hack Tuke recounted numerous cases of nervous mimicry in his
study *Illustrations of the Influence of the Mind upon the Body in
Health and Disease*. In his attempt to prove that "witnessing an af-
fecting occurrence produces bodily effects" of a serious nature, Tuke
cited cases in which suggestibility led to premature death, where
"imagination had the same effect as . . . reality" (84, 78). In particular, he recounts a case of "involuntary Attention" in which "a gentleman who had constantly witnessed the sufferings of a friend afflicted with stricture of the oesophagus, had so great an impression
made on his nervous system, that after some time he experienced a
similar difficulty of swallowing, and ultimately died of the spasmodic
impediment produced by merely thinking of another's pain" (87).
In this and other examples, Tuke assesses the serious consequences of
nervous mimicry, emphasizing the powerful hold that pain and suffering—even someone else's pain—could claim over one's thoughts,
feelings, and actions. For Tuke, to view suffering was potentially to
collapse the rational boundaries between imagination and reality
and to relinquish the power of self-control.[11]

Similarly disturbing was the indiscriminate nature of nervous susceptibility, its refusal to distinguish between the strong and the weak.
The American crowd psychologist Boris Sidis observed that "the
spirit of suggestibility lies hidden even in the best of men; like the
evil jinnee of the Arabian tales is corked up in the innocent-looking
bottle. . . . Not sociality, not rationality, but . . . suggestibility is what
characterizes the average specimen of humanity, for *man is a suggestible animal*" (17). Paget noted that although hysterics were the
most prone to neuromimesis, even ordinary nervous systems could
be influenced by the power of imagination and the natural urge to
imitate or participate in what we see: "Many persons, even such as
have good nervous systems, must be conscious that it requires effort—that is, a full exercise of will—to avoid these imitations, and
to disbelieve or disregard sensations imitative of those endured by

others" (*Clinical Lectures*, 182). For Paget the central question was one of willpower. One needed a strong will to preserve the boundaries of identity, allowing one to face the spectacle of disease and remain uninfluenced. "Hence," he claimed, "among these patients [suffering from nervous mimicry] are the most numerous subjects of mesmerism, spiritualism, and the other supposed forces of which the chief evidence is the power of a strong will over a weak one" (ibid., 181).

The American neurologist Silas Weir Mitchell, who included a chapter on nervous mimicry in his 1885 *Lectures on Diseases of the Nervous System, Especially in Women*, took Paget's argument even further. According to Mitchell, a battle of wills lay at the heart of the doctor-patient relationship in all cases of nervous disease. Mitchell argued that the power of suggestion, which was central to mimetic diseases, should be appropriated by the physician in the pursuit of a cure: "If you cause such hysteric women as these to believe that you can cure them, you enlist on your side their own troops, for as you can create symptoms, so can you also create absence of symptoms. There is in all this something like the so-called magnetizing of which we used to hear and see so much" (66). A kind of medical Svengali, Mitchell advocated the physician's ability to manipulate patients out of their neuroses through sheer force of personality. This emphasis on the physician's medical mystique, his capacity to exert mental control over the curative process, corresponds to myths of medical authority in the literature of the period. In one striking example, Sarah Grand's definition of medical success, as her heroine describes it in *The Heavenly Twins* (1893), seems to echo Mitchell's ideal:

"You have some mysterious power over my mind. All great doctors have the power I mean; I wonder what it is. Your very presence restores me in an extraordinary way. You dispel the worry in my head without a word, by just being here, however bad it is. . . . But I want to discover the secret of a great doctor's success," she pursued. "What is your charm? There is something mesmeric about you, I think, something inimical to disease at all events. There is healing in your touch, and your very manners make an impression which cures." (635)

Grand's description, with its focus on the impressionistic mental qualities of great doctors, is articulated by a character who has already been diagnosed as hysteric. Although the feminist Grand elsewhere challenges the often rigidly gendered constructions of nervous susceptibility, her nervous heroines nevertheless participate in the very paradigms of suggestibility that doctors like Mitchell proposed. Although many of Mitchell's case histories involved men, Mitchell singled out nervous women and children as the most vulnerable to sympathetic, neuromimetic symptoms; he urged "the need for care in discussing symptoms before [them]" (*Lectures*, 74). According to Mitchell, information about disease constituted a dangerous form of knowledge to be kept from the weak and impressionable. Such privileged knowledge was the province of the physician—and more specifically the strong physician—since, according to Mitchell, Paget, and Tuke, doctors were not immune to mimetic tendencies in the sickroom.

Mitchell stresses the specular nature of the sickroom using rhetoric that persistently invokes theater and audience as a model for doctor-patient interaction. His lengthy chronicle of case histories, which ranges from a physician who unconsciously mimics the facial contortions of a patient suffering from "unilateral grimace" (ibid., 62) to men who experience sympathetic morning sickness at their wives' pregnancies, to an entire infirmary of schoolgirls who involuntarily adopt each other's symptoms until separated and sent to different hospitals, is laced with theatrical terminology. Although Mitchell insists that their pain is real and their behavior, in most cases, is inherent and involuntary, he describes these patients as "actors" in a "pathological drama" (ibid., 86), and claims "the actor receiv[es] . . . from a too sympathetic audience, hints which enable him the better to sustain his part" (ibid., 71). Sympathy here is thus doubly dangerous—it initiates the patient's symptoms through the act of watching and it perpetuates them through the act of being watched.

Although Mitchell's medical attitude toward healing is consistently aggressive, preaching the need for a strong personality in the sickroom, anxieties about maintaining this role emerge occasionally in his fiction. In his semi-autobiographical novel *Characteristics*, published in 1891, Mitchell recounts his hero Owen North's observations on human nature during his practice as a physician and his recovery from paralysis after the Civil War. We can see North's anxiety about the physician's viewing relationship to his patients when he recounts a morphine-induced dream that enacts the drama of neuromimesis on the doctor's body and reveals the implicit threat to medical and masculine authority that this neurosis conveyed. The dream proceeds along the following lines: An obese patient enters North's office seeking treatment for an unnamed affliction, simultaneously warning the doctor of a curious phenomenon—every time he describes his symptoms to a physician, the physician immediately begins to suffer from the same symptoms. Mitchell's hero accepts the challenge and agrees to treat the patient, confident of his own clinical detachment and strength of will. As the patient begins to describe symptoms such as severe back pain and blindness in one eye, North immediately begins to experience the same symptoms. The patient subsequently tells North:

As I came up the street I left eleven symptoms with different doctors. One was difficult to satisfy; he got an enlarged liver, emphysema of the left lung, and varicose veins. I have seen but one reasonable doctor, and it, or she (for the doctor was a woman), said she always carried away some of her patients' symptoms, and would have nothing to do with me. (16–17)

Mitchell's fictional dream highlights the psychic danger he felt that doctors faced if their wills were weak, and the distinct gender roles assigned to different constructions of the medical gaze. Although she is described as the only reasonable doctor, the female physician in this dream is only reasonable in admitting the limitations of her sex. She refuses to see the patient precisely because her gaze is already, by definition, neuromimetic. Lacking the masculine strength of will necessary for medical practice, she overidentifies with patients and takes on their maladies through the power of suggestion. Consequently, the hero's authority is challenged by his association with female forms of looking and his submission to disease. "To be ill," he claims, "is a feminine verb, and agrees best with that gender" (ibid., 91). The dream reveals that neuromimesis, because it is allied with femininity and passivity, poses a threat to the medical profession by depriving the physician of his visual predominance and clinical detachment.[12]

Lest there be any doubt about the consequences of excessive sympathy, Mitchell further instructs us of its dangers in an anecdote Owen North tells later in the novel. Describing the case of a colleague, North reads from a document in which the man describes the causes of his failure as a physician:

If a case were painful, I suffered too. If it ended ill, I was tormented by self-reproaches. In a word, I was too sensitive to be of use. Weak or hysterical women liked me and my too ready show of sympathy. It was, in fact, real, and quite too real for my good or my comfort. Moreover, I hated to be told that I had so much sympathy. It is a quality to use with wisdom. I could not control it. (Ibid., 215)

The intrusion of the "too real" experience of emotional trauma upon the doctor's body produces a state of excess (he is "too sensitive," "too ready," "too real") in which the categories of somatic and psychic experience become indistinguishable, and self and other temporarily collapse into a unified experience of suffering. Consequently, upon consulting a colleague, the doctor is told to leave the profession because, without hardening his sympathy, "it and you are useless" (ibid., 216).

In both cases Mitchell's cautionary stories function as parables for defining the effective (rather than affective) physician, identifying qualities that he believed every doctor needed to confront and control. Although Mitchell's medical identity crises are highly dramatized, his concerns were not unique. Sir William Osler's advice to medical students about the value of a judicious "callousness" over "keen sensibility" made essentially the same point. Osler stressed that "the first essential is to have your nerves well in hand," since the physician or surgeon "who shows in his face the slightest alteration, expressive of anxiety or fear . . . is liable to disaster at any moment" (95–96).[13] The problem, as both Mitchell and Osler present it, is that although doctors need some form of sympathy in order to understand and treat their patients, that same sympathy can undermine their effectiveness (*Characteristics*, 8, 233; *Counsels and Ideals*, 95). It is the struggle to channel a potentially "feminizing," boundary-collapsing sympathy into a more appropriately "masculine," carefully delineated medical role that constitutes, for Osler, Mitchell, and the fictional Dr. North, the challenge of the medical profession.[14]

Sympathy, Gender, and Medical Vision

As one might expect from Mitchell's fictional examples, the association between the clinical eye and such qualities as strength, self-control, detachment, critical distance, and dispassionate judgment could function as a covert and "natural" means of excluding women from the medical profession.[15] This occurred, in part, because visual authority played a crucial role in the transition from traditional to modern medicine. With a new emphasis on close observations of symptoms, doctors were instructed in medical theaters that placed considerable importance on specular elements of diagnosis and the display of the body in medical training.[16] Like Bentham's architectural Panopticon, which perfected the act of observation and transformed it, as Foucault argues, into an organized form of discipline, medical practice was frequently structured around the control and extension of the visual field.[17] For example, the microscope, which had become a common medical tool by the 1860's, was a crucial instrument in enhancing the doctor's real and mythic powers of sight; it functioned as an extension of his clinical eye and a symbol of his scientific authority. One popular American handbook for physicians published in 1882 advised them to display their microscopes prominently along with their diplomas (Shorter, *Bedside Manners*, 82, 85). Thus vision, which had come to define (at least in part) the doctor's claim to medical and scientific legitimacy, also became a symbol of masculine authority within some aspects of the medical profession. In 1870 the physician Augustus Kinsley Gardner, describing the New York Medical College for Women, noted that "the study of medicine is not unmingled pleasure, and the dissecting room is no bed of roses. More especially is medicine disgusting to women, accustomed to softnesses and the downy sides of life. They are sedulously screened from the observation of the horrors and disgusts of life" (71). Gardner's emphasis on visual taboos—the screens used to protect women from the danger and disgust (as well as the power) of observation—suggest that the doctor's vision was a crucial symbolic territory. Even in the rare instances when women were admitted to traditionally male medical colleges, they attended separate anatomy lectures in order to preserve and protect female modesty. This practice emphasized the widely accepted correlation between specular and sexual difference and highlighted the transgressive scopic positioning of the aspiring female physician.

The medical profession also constructed arguments against female doctors based on issues such as their greater emotional response to scenes of pain and suffering and their sympathetic, and thus inherently weak, sensibilities. The American surgeon Edmund Andrews claimed in 1861 that "the primary requisite for a good surgeon, is *to be a man,*— a man of courage. . . . A surgeon should be calm. His sympathy should not boil over into a hysterical excitement; it *must not disorder the lightest motion of his hand*" (588, 595).[18] Another doctor noted that women should be disqualified from practicing medicine because of their excitability: "Man with his coarser brain, and less impressible nervous system, can witness scenes with perfect coolness that would blanch the cheeks and make the hearts of most women stand still. No woman can control her nervous system. . . . Hysteria is second nature to them" (Weatherly, 75). Indeed, in this period of "medical imperialism," when discoveries in the scientific community were frequently compared to imperialist expansion, the metaphors for medical observation invoked masculine adventure as the model for visual authority.[19] One example can be seen in the accounts of Dr. Marion Sims (who invented the prototype for the modern gynecological speculum). In a striking parallel to the language of African exploration, Sims describes his first clear view of the vagina and cervix: "I saw everything, as no man had ever seen before. . . . I was on the eve of one of the greatest discoveries of the day" (234–35).[20] Women's bodies—and especially black women's bodies, since Sims began his research on slaves—were the natural territory that Sims was seeking to colonize in the name of modern medicine. At a time when women's diseases were an important focus of medical attention, the profession tended to perceive women as appropriate objects of medical vision rather than as potential viewers or explorers themselves.[21]

It is thus as a testament to the New Woman's capacity for clear sight and rational thought that Sarah Grand chooses medical texts as the symbol of forbidden masculine knowledge that her strong-minded heroine appropriates and explores. In *The Heavenly Twins*,

Evadne's reading habits are set in contrast with those of male medical students in a striking feminist reversal of Mitchell's neuromimetic fantasies:

After studying anatomy and physiology, she took up pathology as a matter of course, and naturally went on from thence to prophylactics and therapeutics, but was quite unharmed, because she made no personal application of her knowledge as the coarser mind masculine of the ordinary medical student is apt to do. She read of all the diseases to which the heart is subject, and thought of them familiarly as "cardiac affections," without fancying she had one of them; and she obtained an extraordinary knowledge of the digestive processes and their ailments without realizing that her own might ever be affected. She possessed, in fact, a mind of exceptional purity as well as of exceptional strength, one to be enlightened by knowledge, not corrupted. (23)

We can take Grand's representation of resisted neuromimesis as one strategy by which women entered the medical profession, proving themselves capable of mastering the same ideals of scientific objectivity and emotional detachment that their male colleagues supposedly came by so naturally. This was not, however, as Regina Morantz-Sanchez has pointed out, the only strategy available. At the same time that arguments against women doctors focused on their lack of visual authority and excesses of emotion, changes in medical knowledge and practice provided women with new rationales for legitimate entry into the medical profession. In *Sympathy and Science*, Morantz-Sanchez notes that the development of anesthesia in the middle of the nineteenth century softened the traditional image of the doctor from one who must necessarily inflict pain in order to produce a cure to one who could alleviate pain. This transformation helped to undermine arguments against women becoming doctors by "rendering harsher images of the doctor obsolete" and calling into question the efficacy of "heroic" models of medical treatment (53, 30). Martin Pernick has further argued that increasing support for noninterventionist therapies fostered new arguments for a more feminine model of the physician (110–17). The emergence of moral and environmental therapies within the medical establishment—that is, therapies that relied on changing the patient's moral and physical environment as the basis for cure—ultimately provided women with a more viable role in the medical profession.[22] A number of early women physicians such as Elizabeth Blackwell and Harriot Hunt used the domestic ideology that defined women as inherently more moral, sympathetic, and sensitive than men to argue that these unique qualities made women ideally suited to certain branches of medicine. Many of their female patients agreed. After experiencing Mitchell's famous "rest cure" and describing its failings in her story "The Yellow Wallpaper," Charlotte Perkins Gilman praised the bedside manner of the American physician Mary Putnam Jacobi in terms that echo both Mitchell's professional functions and his fears: Dr. Jacobi, Gilman claimed, "seemed to enter into the mind of the sufferer and know what was going on there" ("Addresses," 66).[23]

A further strategy that aspiring women physicians used to forge a place for themselves within the profession was to invoke the doctor's vision against their male colleagues, exposing the masculine clinical eye as erotic and thus morally inappropriate for female patients. Both Hunt and Blackwell, as well as vocal feminist patients such as Catherine Esther Beecher, equated the examined woman with the fallen woman and advised female independence from male practitioners (Wood, 14–15).[24] In an interesting parallel to this interpretation of medical authority, recent feminist critics such as Jacqueline Rose and Coral Lansbury have pointed out the alliance between Victorian pornography and medical theaters and dissecting rooms. Rose discusses the pornographer Henry Ashbee, who in his 1877 *Index Librorum Prohibitorum* "compares his own activity as a collector of the literary taboo with the forms of investigation legitimated by the new science" (Rose, 112). Ashbee claims that his pornographic extracts will both distance and "disgust" his readers, thereby preventing them from reading the originals for any but scholarly purposes: "As little, it is my belief, will my book excite the passions of my readers, as would the naked body of a woman, extended on the dissecting table, produce concupiscence in the minds of the students assembled to witness an operation performed upon her" (lxx). Although Ashbee intended to sanitize his collection of erotica through this comparison, associating his *Index* with other taxonomic classifications and transforming the study of pornography into a new science of sexuality, in effect he associated medicine with pornography by revealing their specular similarities.[25] It is these similarities that inspired Harriot Hunt to call for women's presence in medical theaters and dissecting rooms, admonishing her male colleagues: "Think, young men, how irreverently, how irreligiously you handle the body of a sister in the dissecting room—would it not impart respect and sanctity to the occasion if women witnessed these dissections? Talk of impropriety!" (271). Similarly, Elizabeth Blackwell described the examination of a poor woman by a male colleague as "a horrible exposure; indecent for any poor woman to be subjected to such a torture; she seemed to feel it, poor and ignorant as she was" (72). Paget's descriptions of the type of conversations that occurred in medical theaters confirm some of Hunt's and Blackwell's claims. Paget recalls in his *Memoirs and Letters* that "it was not, then, generally thought amiss that one of my teachers told many stories, some of which were obscene, some very nasty" (50).[26] It seems significant, then, that Hunt entitled her 1855 autobiography *Glances and Glimpses*. For Hunt, to transfer the power of clinical vision to female physicians was to purge medicine of its patriarchal authority over women's bodies and to disrupt traditional associations between femininity and passive, limited, or obstructed forms of viewing. In *Glances and Glimpses* Hunt asserts that women's eyes become stronger the more they are allowed to see:

Many would be afraid to make a movement, or stir a step, if they saw the blood circulating, the tendons pulling, the lungs inhaling, the innumerable nerves, arteries, veins, etc., which sustain our existence; but let knowledge illuminate such an one, and a reverent awe is induced, and fear dispelled. So with social life—particularly with woman. When learning ceases to be uncommon with them, you will cease your remarks about "blue stockings," "masculine women," "anti-woman movement," etc. etc. The artificial hedges which have grown up around us, are withering and dying, and it will take some desperate mind ever to think of planting them again. Sunlight has penetrated through naked branches, and the eye has become strong enough for more. (326)

Hunt's rhetoric is calculated to shock with its discussion of the nakedness of the body exposed to the doctor's gaze; in this passage, the eye becomes a scalpel revealing the body's (and society's) underlying structures. In order to prove her command of forbidden anatomical knowledge and her corresponding strength of vision, Hunt lists the contents of the inner body part by part. This recital stands as her testimony to the potential strength of women's eyes and the determination of women doctors to appropriate the power of vision. The "nerves, arteries, veins" that branch through the body in Hunt's description form the "naked branches" through which women will finally be allowed to see themselves and the world around them with newfound clarity. Thus for Hunt, the simple act of viewing human anatomy inspires her with visionary energy.

Suggestible Readers

While the debate over gender and visual authority was taking place in nineteenth-century medical schools, journals, and newspapers, Victorian fiction addressed many of the same anxieties about sympathy, spectatorship, and disease. The evocation of sympathy was an expected goal of fictional production, and Victorian critics assumed audience involvement to be a normal part of the reading experience. As I suggested in Chapter 1, however, there was cause for censure if that involvement threatened to provoke a disruptive emotional state in the reader. Walter M. Kendrick has noted that a belief in the "life" or "reality" of fictional characters and their accompanying power to evoke sympathy was "a pervasive demand of mid-Victorian criticism" (24). At the same time, critics argued that "the novelist's principal duty [is] . . . to direct and limit sympathy, not merely to induce it" (ibid., 25). Like Mitchell's anxiety over the control of medical sympathy, critics demanded that authors regulate readerly emotion in such a way that it respected proper ethical and artistic boundaries. They focused on the reader's potential suggestibility and the ways in which emotional excess could be encouraged by specific kinds of narratives. As one might expect, debates arose over the effects of sensation fiction and whether they exceeded such boundaries. Melodrama, romance, and the sentimental novel came under similar critical scrutiny. In addition to this influence on individual readers, the sheer popularity of sensational and sentimental genres could be seen as a form of audience participation. Gabriel Tarde recognized this when he compared the effects of reading to crowd psychology, arguing for reading as a controlled form of mass behavior. Tarde claimed that women's reading of popular romantic novels, poetry, and women's magazines constituted a form of collective experience and might provide a harmless substitute for the ferocity of the female mob (*L'opinion et la foule*, 29–30). Although Tarde argued against the dangers of such fiction, he based his argument on the same assumptions about readerly, and especially female, suggestibility as those who saw possibilities for emotional contagion in popular fiction. This common framework of belief about the effects of reading marked many of the debates throughout the century as Victorians struggled to understand the relationship between agency and imagination. Kendrick has described the history of these debates, which go back to Samuel Johnson's cautions against the danger of fictional examples: if the power of example is so great as "to take possession of the memory by a kind of violence, and produce effects almost without the intervention of the will, care ought to be taken that . . . the best examples only should be exhibited; and that which is likely to operate so strongly, should not be mischievous or uncertain in its effects" (Johnson, 22).[27] Although Victorian critics and journalists generally dismissed arguments about the sensation novel's power to promote real acts of violence, its popularity was thought to be "indicative of a certain morbid condition in the public mind," with such novels as Mary Elizabeth Braddon's *Lady Audley's Secret* possessing "power of an uncomfortable kind" ("Novels and Novelists of the Day"; 188, 189).[28] In effect, popular nineteenth-century theories of reading implied a transmissibility of emotions from text to reader that paralleled medical and psychological discussions of suggestibility. As Alice James complained, "I can't read anything suggestive, that survives or links itself to experience for it sets my silly stomach fluttering and my flimsy head spinning so that I have to stop" (50).

By examining the conditions under which nineteenth-century authors sought to evoke sympathy or detachment, proximity or distance in their collective readerly audiences, and by identifying how particular specular roles interact with narrative structures, we can see how a text's presentation of a visual scene attempts to shape, and gender, the viewing or reading experience. One way to dissect these specular strategies and examine their constituent parts is to look at how texts establish alliances between the projected reader and the fictional spectators and narrators.[29] In this process, the act of reading is guided by gender assumptions that inform the viewing relationships portrayed in the text, regardless of the reader's actual gender. I do not mean to suggest by this that the gender of the reader is not an important part of the reading experience, or that studies based on that assumption are misdirected.[30] My argument assumes that a reader's response to a given text is determined by many factors, including gender. The purpose here is to show how gender configurations that are located in the rhetoric of spectatorship complicate the reading experience by offering conflicting roles and sites of identification. In this formulation, neuromimesis becomes a model for any affective, sympathetic, collective, and implicitly "feminized" process of reading or viewing, whereas the medical gaze corresponds to an implicitly masculine form of visual empowerment and its various hermeneutic manifestations—irony, critical distance, objectivity.

Mary Ann Doane, discussing the relationship between spectatorship, sympathy, and femininity in *The Desire to Desire*, affirms the centrality of the medical model in constructions of the female gaze:

Female spectatorship is generally understood in its alignment with other qualities culturally ascribed to the woman—in particular, an excess of emotion, sentiment, affect, empathy. . . . From this perspective, the female gaze exhibits, in contrast to male distance, a proximity to the image which is the mark of overidentification and hence a heightened sympathy. But the concept of sympathy is a physiological/medical one as well, of particular interest to the female subject. The meaning of "sympathy" in physiology and pathology is, the *Oxford English Dictionary* tells us, "a relation between two bodily organs or parts (or between two persons) such that disorder, or any condition, of the one induces a corresponding condition in the other." Sympathy connotes a process of contagion within the body, or between bodies, an instantaneous communication and affinity. (67)

Sympathy and contagion are, according to Doane, aligned with female spectatorship as an essential part of the cultural model of femininity. Indeed, this correlation between overidentification and femininity has a lengthy tradition in Western culture, going back at least as far as Plato, who gives as one reason for banishing poetry from the Republic the fact that to "delight in giving way to sympathy" and to be "in raptures at the excellence of the poet who stirs our feelings most" is "deemed to be the part of a woman" (300).[31] By transforming the act of reading into an act of gendering, Plato helped shape the values of western literary criticism along lines that privilege critical detachment and devalue affective responses to literary texts.

In particular, affective responses to representations of pain, disease, or death in nineteenth-century fiction need to be scrutinized in order to determine to what extent they participate in the same cultural assumptions as medical discussions of neuromimesis. We have already seen in *Villette* how Lucy Snowe's identification with the emotional and physical pain of those she views—the King of Labassecour, Ginevra, Paulina, the actress Vashti—links neurosis to narrative, providing a model of the sensitive narrator-reader who is physically attuned to scenes of suffering. Brontë's and Eliot's emphases on the specular relationship between those suffering from nervous disease and those who watch or are watched by them is one example of the larger correlation between audience and contagion. But representations of neurosis are not the only instances in which viewing and suffering interact. Regardless of the specific pathology invoked, scenes of illness carry the potential for drama and invite the reader, like Bernhardt's audience, to participate vicariously in fictional events. In the second half of this chapter I focus on one of the most emotionally powerful (and potentially manipulative) narrative maneuvers in Victorian fiction: the deathbed scene. Because of their common dramatic structure (in most cases, one finds an invalid, a bed, a doctor, and/or an audience of friends and family in the room watching the passage from life to death), deathbed scenes invoke highly systematic, often densely layered viewing relationships that are frequently, though not always, as I will show, based on the cultural correlations between gender and spectatorship.

Affective Hermeneutics: *Uncle Tom's Cabin*

Like the link between saints and hysterics I outlined in the preceding chapter, the symptoms or attributes associated with neuromimesis have a long cultural tradition in the values and myths of Christianity. By taking on the sins of the world and by suffering in response to the suffering of others, Christ is allied with the same qualities as the female spectator—sympathy, passivity, emotion, overidentification. We can see this correlation at work in one of the most celebrated deathbed dramas of the nineteenth century—that of Eva in Harriet Beecher Stowe's *Uncle Tom's Cabin* (1852).[32] Eva enacts a Christian model of suffering, dying for the sins of slavery and taking into her own body the pain she sees in the slaves around her. Stowe stages Eva's illness so as to leave the reader in no doubt about its symbolic value. In one of her many moments of spiritual illumination, Eva explains the motive of her illness to Uncle Tom:

> "I can understand why Jesus *wanted* to die for us."
> "Why, Miss Eva?"
> "Because I've felt so, too. . . . I've felt that I would be glad to die, if my dying could stop all this misery. I *would* die for them, Tom, if I could," said the child, earnestly, laying her little thin hand in his. (400)

Eva's death thus becomes a proof of her Christian faith and an imitation of Christ's own neuromimetic sacrifice. Eva's "instinctive sympathy" (380) makes her, according to her father, "too sensitive" (403) to the brutalities of slavery. As Eva complains to him:

> You want me to live so happy, and never to have any pain,—never suffer anything,—not even hear a sad story, when other poor creatures have nothing but pain and sorrow, all their lives;—it seems selfish. I ought to know such things, I ought to feel about them! Such things always sunk into my heart; they went down deep; I've thought and thought about them. (403)

In this passage, Eva enacts not only the Christian and feminine model of selflessness but also the struggle over the proper signification of literature—the appropriate response to "a sad story." Eva asserts that there is a moral imperative to feel pain when confronted with pain and a hermeneutic imperative to suffer in reaction to stories of suffering.[33] Like Harriot Hunt's penetrating eye, Eva's sympathy cuts "down deep" into her body, sinking into her heart. Here Stowe seems to be proposing a neuromimetic theory of art in which the body becomes the measure of a work's social value and artistic success. The deeper the reader's or viewer's physical response, the better the audience and the better the text. By these criteria, Eva becomes the ideal Christian interpreter and *Uncle Tom's Cabin* the pinnacle of artistic success, for the text (and its numerous dramatizations that toured through America) was arguably the most emotionally and historically influential of its day.

John Kucich has discussed the function of sentimentality for the Victorian reader in terms that are useful for an examination of Eva's deathbed scene. Kucich claims that sentimentality is, on the one hand, restrained, enclosed, conservative, and thus safe for the reader because it controls emotion by positing a shared community of feeling in which that emotion is expressed. On the other hand, sentimentality is excessive in its demand for the reader to participate in the text's overflow of emotion (*Excess and Restraint*, 43–57). It is this latter force that interests me here, for in Eva's deathbed scene we are invited (indeed rhetorically coerced) to view her with the same emotions that the slaves for whom she dies do. Eva's Christian neuromimesis thus becomes the model for the reader's textual stance, a stance that is inevitably feminized by the rhetoric of overidentification that forms the basis of sentimental fiction.

Eva's sensitivity is more traditionally feminine and self-consciously Christian in expression than the tempestuous sensibilities and spiritual expressions of either Lucy Snowe or Gwendolen Harleth, perhaps because Stowe is less interested in exploring the psychological ramifications of sensibility than in evoking the sentimental force of Christian self-sacrifice. In the sickroom, Eva's sensitivity to the pain of her father's slaves is mirrored in their reciprocal sensitivity to Eva's spiritualized death. The sight of her "spiritual face, the long locks of hair cut off and lying by her . . . struck at once upon the feelings of a sensitive and impressible race," and as Eva bursts into tears over their inability to read the Bible for themselves, they respond with "many a smothered sob" (Stowe, 418, 419).[34] When read in the context of Stowe's hermeneutics, we can see that despite their illiteracy, the slaves are, in fact, better readers of Eva's death than the white spectators. And while Stowe's assertion that the slaves are members of "a sensitive and impressible race" reaffirms stereotypes of the childlike Negro, it is also part of Stowe's valorization of affective spectatorship. Thus the unabashed sentimentality of this exchange is internally consistent with Stowe's artistic (and humanistic) criteria, allowing the reader, as Philip Fisher has argued, to participate in the "moral purposes [of sentimental fiction] by accepting analogies between his own experiences of suffering and those of the characters within the novel." In this way, the sentimental novel "depends upon experimental, even dangerous, extensions of the self of the reader" (109, 98). Fisher's assessment of danger differs from that defined by Victorian critics, emphasizing the role of sentimentalism as a "radical methodology" that seeks to claim humanity for and extend compassion to figures from whom complete humanity "has been socially withheld" (99)—slaves, prisoners, children, the aged, the insane, and even animals; but his emphasis on the transgressive emotional power of sentimental fiction, its ability to extend the boundaries of the self, suggests that political danger may have been one of the historical subtexts in arguments against sentimental and sensation fiction.[35]

Hypnotic Spectatorship: *Trilby*

Of course, not all deathbed scenes have as many historical repercussions as Eva's, nor do many Victorian invalids die from sympathy for others' pain. Nevertheless, the cultural assumptions that neuromimesis embodies inform the reading and viewing structure of other fictional deathbeds. In another popular novel that had widespread success when staged—George du Maurier's *Trilby* (1894)—the overlapping rhetorics of science and sexuality reveal a densely layered viewing structure that anatomizes the effects of medical vision.

Set in Paris, the plot of *Trilby* reflects the late-nineteenth-century fascination with suggestibility, which, in addition to its central role in theories of hysteria and crowd behavior, had gained increasing popular attention during the 1890 trial of Gabrielle Bompard, who claimed to have committed murder while under the hypnotic influence of her lover.[36] Although the parallel between Bompard's defense and Trilby's narrative is not an exact one, the common emphasis on suggestibility as a form of specifically sexual danger is striking. Like Bompard's, Trilby's emergence into the public eye is a result of her seducer's hypnotic powers; her brilliant singing career takes place under the direction of Svengali's gaze. As Ruth Harris has pointed out, Bompard's trial sparked a volatile medical debate over the potential susceptibility of the average person to hypnotic influence and the consequent breakdown of moral restraints. Both the trial, which was covered extensively in French and foreign presses, and the novel, which sparked fan clubs, benefits and marketing promotionals across America, transmitted the emerging scientific discourses of hypnosis, hysteria, and crowd psychology to the popular imagination, demonstrating to nineteenth-century audiences the vulnerability of the human psyche. In turn, Bompard's trial and du Maurier's novel created their own forms of audience participation, thus exemplifying the very theories of suggestibility and crowd behavior in which their audiences were being instructed. According to Harris, the trial apparently drew so much public attention that some 20,000 spectators visited the Paris morgue to see the trunk in which the body had been disposed ("Murder Under Hypnosis," 197). Jonathan Freedman has noted the mimetic (and pedagogical) relationship between the wildly enthusiastic response of the fictional audiences to Trilby's performances and the similarly demonstrative historical audiences that viewed the dramatized version of *Trilby* in America.[37]

Apart from the historical reception of and response to du Maurier's novel, and its position within the discourses of suggestibility in the 1890's, we can see how the text of *Trilby* raises issues of visual hegemony in ways that help to shape the implied reader's hermeneutic alliances. The coercive relationship between Svengali and Trilby is central to du Maurier's positioning of the readerly audience because of the way it constructs a rigidly gendered set of viewing options. The choice, as du Maurier presents it, is either to become a voyeur who participates in Svengali's scopic manipulations of Trilby by watching her performance from a stance of aesthetic distance and sexual desire, or to overidentify with the heroine and become feminized, indeed hypnotized, by her performance into a state of emotional collapse.

One of the tropes that du Maurier uses to emphasize the sexual dynamics between Svengali and Trilby is the medical gaze. Their relationship constructs an erotics of clinical vision, and Trilby believes that her death would provide Svengali with the desired specular access to her body. Paralyzed by this thought, she claims "Svengali used to be always talking about the Morgue, and my going there some day. He used to say he'd come and look at me there, and the idea made me so sick I couldn't [even kill myself]" (215). In this grim parody of post-mortem examination, Trilby becomes a cadaver for Svengali's visual experimentation and appropriation. The act of looking translates into the act of dissection, revealing an imaginative link between sexuality, spectatorship, and death that takes the medical theater as its point of reference. Trilby's fear of becoming part of what Bram Dijkstra has called the "cult of the woman as corpse" (46) is particularly significant since she is also a member of the social class most often used in nineteenth-century medical demonstrations—as either cadaver or patient.

Although Svengali's necrophilic viewing fantasy is never overtly fulfilled in *Trilby*, it remains an important factor in his visual authority.[38] Indeed, Svengali fulfills his threat in other ways, despite the fact that his own death precedes Trilby's. Thus the scene at Trilby's deathbed emerges out of a rhetoric of spectatorship that is already well established by the end of the narrative. On her deathbed, Trilby is still subject to Svengali's influence, for upon seeing his photograph with eyes "full of stern command," she goes into a final trance, her "eyes dilated, and quite a strange light in them" (239).[39] Much like Poe's imaginative experiment in "The Strange Case of M. Valdemar," du Maurier's exploration of how hypnosis can suspend the boundaries between life and death challenges the integrity of the subject through the agency of science. But du Maurier further engages the reader in the scene through an explicitly gendered process of visual identification. As Svengali's photographic presence looms over Trilby's bedside, replacing the gaze of the (in this case absent) physician, she performs a final concert in her "ineffably seductive" (240) voice for the tearful visitors. Du Maurier shapes the scene so that we, along with the other spectators, are encouraged to respond to her deathbed performance with both fascination and horror. Ultimately, the power of Svengali's vision to transcend the grave and claim Trilby as his "instrument" during her moment of transition from life to death creates an imaginative link between aesthetic appreciation, medical experimentation, and necrophilia. By revealing the uncanny source of our aesthetic pleasure, du Maurier questions how we view what we view, identifying both our own susceptibility (like Trilby's and her various audiences') to readerly suggestion and our compromised innocence in viewing the scene before us. Through this means, du Maurier simultaneously encourages and disempowers the sympathetic audience, emphasizing Svengali's (and our own) role in a coercive economy of vision that is never challenged in the text.[40]

Visual Transgression: *Middlemarch*

If *Uncle Tom's Cabin* encourages a neuromimetic reader and *Trilby* attempts to eroticize the reading experience by associating it with the medical gaze, both of these texts nevertheless construct relatively stable, binary models of gendered viewing. That is, Stowe seeks a traditionally "feminine" hermeneutics while du Maurier presents, if not a strictly "masculine" one, at least a pair of intratextual options that limit the reader to either the loss of self through hypnotic suggestion or the assertion of self through voyeuristic perversion. At this point I turn to two novels—Eliot's *Middlemarch* and James's *Wings of the Dove*—that attempt to complicate these interpretive paradigms, establishing multiple axes of viewing in relation to their central scenes of illness.

The various representations of medical subjects in *Middlemarch* (1871–72) demonstrate the tension between different formulations of visual authority as they are acted out in the "pathological drama." As a result of his progressive views, Lydgate functions as a representative of the "new science" and the authority it claimed. But despite her apparent sympathy with Lydgate, and his vision of medical reform, Eliot reveals through him the structures of medical voyeurism, following the trajectory of his gaze through the theater to the sickroom. As Jacqueline Rose has pointed out, Lydgate's preoccupation with Madame Laure, his need to "go and look at this woman" on the stage, takes place during his Parisian medical education and as a diversion from his study of galvanism (109). But Lydgate's shift from the viewing authority of the medical world to passive spectatorship at the theater has the effect of propelling him (like

Bernhardt's audience) into the events on stage. As the melodramatic murder becomes real and the actress's fictional swoon ceases to be a fiction, Lydgate jumps onto the stage and demonstrates his medical expertise. But Lydgate finds that this incident has more levels of fiction and reality than he had at first assumed, and he eventually realizes that his flirtations with dramatic tragedy and emotional excess have gotten out of control. Once he has extricated himself from the melodrama on and off stage, Lydgate resolves to maintain his authority in the future by taking "a strictly scientific view of woman" (183). This resolution demonstrates, according to Rose, "how the question of female sexuality and the question of science are implicated in each other" (110). Indeed, what most disturbs Lydgate about this Parisian interlude are the implications of his own sympathy. During his infatuation with Madame Laure, Lydgate loses the will to control his emotions. He experiences (like Mitchell's fictional doctor) a passive, uncritical, and uncontrolled participation in the visual scene. When he discovers that, in fact, he is neither protecting nor "treating" Madame Laure, but that she has all along been in control of the drama, Lydgate's masculine authority and medical expertise are threatened. He has not correctly diagnosed the situation. Lydgate's resolution to stick to scientific modes of vision thus becomes an affirmation of the "proper" critical stance of the physician; it attests to the threat of feminization posed by affective modes of viewing.

The complicity of Lydgate's "scientific view of woman" with cultural assumptions about normative femininity is again made evident in his bedside manner. Eliot emphasizes Lydgate's clinical mode of vision by comparing it to Dorothea's overidentification with scenes of suffering and to Rosamond's narcissistic femininity in the sickroom. At the examination of Edward Casaubon and the bedside of Peter Featherstone, Lydgate views the invalids through the lens of their female attendants, a detour in which he is frequently accompanied by Eliot's narrator. Upon being called to Lowick to attend Casaubon, Lydgate finds that Dorothea "was usually by her husband's side, and the unaffected signs of intense anxiety in her face and voice about whatever touched his mind or health, made a drama which Lydgate was inclined to watch" (321). Like Mitchell, Lydgate views the sickroom as an occasion for drama (a drama, in this case, that he can control), and he studies these scenes with the detached gaze of the medical spectator. In this instance, Dorothea becomes the instrument through which we view the sickroom scene. It is the anxiety on Dorothea's face that invests Casaubon's medical condition with dramatic interest; her selfless devotion to him in sickness, despite her intellectual reservations about his scholarship, becomes the focus of our attention and sympathy.

In a similar instance upon a visit to Featherstone, Lydgate's "dull expectation of the usual disagreeable routine with an aged patient" is brought into dramatic focus by Rosamond's presence; Featherstone's illness makes an "effective background to this vision of Rosamond" (143–44). Of course, unlike Dorothea, Rosamond is acutely aware that she is the object of Lydgate's gaze. "Every nerve and muscle in Rosamond was adjusted to the consciousness that she was being looked at. She was by nature an actress of parts that entered into her *physique*" (144). Rosamond's nerves and muscles thus compete with Featherstone's for the physician's attention, and Featherstone's routine physical ailments are visually abandoned in favor of Rosamond's dramatic and more immediately compelling "physique." Although this is meant to indicate the first wavering of Lydgate's resolution to take a strictly scientific view of woman, in fact, Lydgate's initial sexual attraction to Rosamond is rhetorically implicated in his scientific seeing.

Though both in very different ways demonstrate the gender alliances deployed in the sickroom, Dorothea's model sympathy and Rosamond's performative femininity are not the only examples of gendered viewing in Eliot's text. Mary Garth, whose nursing Lydgate barely notices until she is pointed out as Rosamond's cousin, presents a challenge to traditional constructions of femininity and spectatorship. Eliot invests Mary with crucial moments of specular and narrative authority that temporarily disrupt (like Harriot Hunt's anatomy lesson) the dominance of medical vision.

Eliot portrays Mary's sickroom gaze as neither passive nor sympathetic but rather aggressively independent. Paid for her services, Mary invests little emotional energy in her care of Peter Featherstone. She performs her duties and shrinks from becoming the ob-

ject of anyone's gaze, thereby distancing herself from the false emotions of the sickroom and Featherstone's petty tyrannizing. Ultimately, Featherstone's final attempt to burn his will and thus manipulate events after his death is thwarted by Mary's rebellion. This
rebellion is specifically constructed as an appropriation of vision, for
Mary's resolution is fueled by watching Featherstone struggle to
maintain control. Her vision grows proportionally stronger as his
grows weaker. Thus while the scene begins with Featherstone
"look[ing] straight at her with eyes that seemed to have recovered
all their sharpness" (350), her refusal to burn the will reduces his
eyes to a "blank stare" (351). With a detachment worthy of Mitchell's model physician, Mary begins to study the invalid, framing the
scene with all the trappings of a tragedy: "Mary, standing by the fire,
saw its red light falling on the old man, propped up on his pillows
and bed-rest, with his bony hand holding out the key, and the money
lying on the quilt before him. She never forgot that vision of a man
wanting to do as he liked at the last" (352).

Mary's vision is dramatically complete—a miniature allegory of
death: Featherstone is propped up in center stage with appropriately
purgatorial lighting and surrounded by all the futile symbols of
earthly authority (the useless key, the rejected money). His bony
hand is even held out in a gesture that points to the skeleton he will
become. By framing her vision of Featherstone's impending death in
the trappings of allegory and melodrama, Mary simultaneously detaches herself from and constructs the scene before her. Instead of
being consumed by sympathy for Featherstone's mortal impotence
or experiencing a tragic catharsis, Mary is urged "to speak with
harder resolution than ever" (353). Her last vision of him alive is his
final attempt to stare Mary down and break her will, but Featherstone's vision has by this point deteriorated to the point where "he
looked at her like an aged hyena, the muscles of his face getting dis-
torted with the effort of his hand" (353).

The transference of visual power from Featherstone to his nurse
is accompanied by a transference of economic authority, for as Mary
soon realizes, her bedside rebellion has shaped the fortunes of many
other people. During the reading of the will after Featherstone's fu-

neral, the narrator views the "little drama" Featherstone had so carefully planned from Mary's perspective (358). She feels a "throbbing excitement . . . in the consciousness that it was she who had virtually determined the production of this second will, which might have momentous effects on the lot of some persons present" (369). This sense of power both heightens Mary's interest in the scene and detaches her from it by virtue of her superior knowledge. Here again Mary asserts her authority through the act of looking:

All eyes avoided meeting other eyes, and were chiefly fixed either on the spots in the table-cloth or on Mr. Standish's bald head; excepting Mary Garth's. When all the rest were trying to look nowhere in particular, it was safe for her to look at them. And at the sound of the first 'give and bequeath' she could see all complexions changing subtly, as if some faint vibration were passing through them. . . . Fred blushed, and Mr. Vincy found it impossible to do without his snuff-box in his hand, though he kept it closed. (370)

Just as Lucy Snowe watches with fascination the King of Labassecour, Mary silently observes the changes taking place on others' bodies. But unlike Lucy, Mary distances herself from these blushes and vibrations, refusing to participate in the scene before her except as a critical onlooker. Essentially, Mary reads this scene using the same strategies that Lydgate used to read Casaubon's illness; only here Eliot reverses traditional gender affiliations, delineating the subtle physical changes in the primarily male audience while Mary looks on with almost clinical interest in the result of her experiment.

Of course, to reverse the specular power structure is not to displace it, and Mary's authority is a fleeting one. What this scene suggests, however, is that despite the cultural correlation between gender and certain kinds of spectatorship, specular cross-dressing nevertheless could, and did, take place. While Dorothea is turned into the object of vision—most obviously, perhaps, by the painter Naumann, but also by Lydgate, Ladislaw, Casaubon, and Chettam—and while Rosamond participates in the trope of female narcissism, able only to view herself and be viewed, Mary asserts her authority and defines herself as subject through a transgressive act of looking. In these brief moments of specular reversal—from Lydgate's brush with emotional excess to Mary's flirtation with clinical distance—Eliot presents the reader with a sometimes conflicting array of scopic positionings.

This conflict within specular roles extends to the narrative voice and structure of *Middlemarch*, which many critics have discussed in terms of Eliot's scientific metaphors and in terms of the narrator's evocation of sympathy as the highest test of moral value. What has not been discussed is the intricate relationship between these narrative patterns and the gendered positions and identifications they invoke.[41] Lydgate's model of scientific perception, which is so often echoed in the narrator's "optic" metaphors, is legitimized as the dominant critical stance for realism.[42] Eliot's narrative is equally invested, however, in the sympathetic viewing patterns that Dorothea emblematizes. Eliot frequently asks her readers for acts of imaginative generosity toward even her most unsympathetic characters, encouraging our compassion for Casaubon in his petty egotisms and for Bulstrode in his confrontation with a venal past. Of course, neither scientific objectivity nor sympathetic communion is fully achieved (or achievable) in the novel. And even as an ideal, Eliot's vision of self-immersion in the currents of sympathy is not immediately resolvable with her valuation of scientific objectivity, creating the doubleness of voice in *Middlemarch* that has long concerned Eliot criticism. In asking her readers to trace a path between seemingly opposing critical positions and narrative stances—stances that were, as I have argued, distinctly gendered—Eliot posits not only the capacity of a single consciousness to hold multiple ways of seeing and feeling, but also its capacity to fluctuate in gender affiliations. The narrative voice does not so much transcend gender, as Gilbert and Gubar have argued (*Madwoman*, 523), as emphasize its instabilities. Like Marian Evans's own pseudonymous cross-dressing as George Eliot, or Mary Garth's moments of clinical detachment, we are asked to negotiate alternative identifications by following the competing models of gendered viewing within *Middlemarch*. By emphasizing both the differences between individual characters' fields of vision and the differences within them, Eliot seems to recognize a potential fluidity in specular roles that applies as much to authors, narrators, and readers as to the fictions they create.

Interpretive Androgyny: *Wings of the Dove*

In the deathbed scenes I have so far discussed, the dramatic structure has been based on the presence of the invalid within the focus of vision. In my final example I examine the consequences of the invalid's visual absence in one of the most sustained fictions of illness, Henry James's *Wings of the Dove* (1902). In the 1909 preface, James claims that his interest lies as much (if not more) with those who come into contact with the afflicted and are changed by it, as with the invalid herself. "Their participation," he claims, "becomes their drama too." As he goes on to explain, they are "drawn in as by some pool of a Lorelei . . . terrified and tempted and charmed; bribed away, it may even be, from more prescribed and natural orbits, inheriting from their connection with her strange difficulties and still stranger opportunities, confronted with rare questions and called upon for new discriminations" ("Preface," 5).

Placed in the position of Bernhardt's audience, James's characters are "drawn in" to the deathbed drama and moved to participate in its outcome. They do not mimic her symptoms, for Milly's illness has few, if any, visible signs, but they are nevertheless changed by having observed and entered into the spectacle of her decline. However, James makes it clear that his interest is not in disease or death per se but in the "rare questions" and subtle "discriminations" involved in viewing illness. He thereby transforms medical questions into aesthetic ones. As a consequence of these priorities, James's strategy in *The Wings of the Dove* is to view Milly Theale's illness obliquely, investing meaning in her absence of symptoms and in the reflection of her disease on the lives of others. As Kate Croy marvels, Milly, even in the act of dying, "won't smell, as it were, of drugs. She won't taste, as it were, of medicine" (215). Defined by negations, Milly's illness actually facilitates her status as an object of aesthetic pleasure, and we are asked as readers to consume Milly's body as delicately as her disease has, appreciating the subtleties of feeling and "good taste" that Milly's invisible and unspeakable malady embodies.[43]

On the face of it, James's interest in the "drama" experienced by those who come into contact with Milly would seem to contradict his emphasis on silence and absence in the text, for drama is pre-eminently a medium of presence; it involves events that take place immediately before the eye. The dramatic interest of the deathbed was powerful enough to make Alice James lament that her own death "will probably be in my sleep so that I shall not be one of the audience, dreadful fraud! a creature who has been denied all dramatic episodes might be allowed, I think, to assist at her extinction" (135). Alice's desire to witness the spectacle of her own deathbed as both audience and actress has an uncanny correspondence to the ambiguity and doubling of roles in her brother's most famous deathbed drama. In *The Wings of the Dove*, James is interested in the play of presence and absence, participation and detachment, as it takes place within the text or, by extension, within the reader. James asserts in his preface that Milly's illness, and the fight for life it engenders, represents "the soul of drama . . . which is the portrayal, as we know, of a catastrophe determined in spite of oppositions. My young woman would *herself* be the opposition—to the catastrophe announced by the associated Fates" ("Preface," 4). Milly's body thus becomes the stage upon which the drama of her resistance is played out. But for James, drama also necessitates an audience able to appreciate and interact with the heroine, to transform her drama (willingly or unwillingly) into its own. Thus when Kate Croy explains to Merton Densher how she has distanced herself from Milly's illness by "only watching" the drama from afar, he argues that she is already implicated, "since here you are, in spite of all you say, in the midst of it" (216). It is Kate's belief that she can remain an innocent bystander, untouched by the deceptions and omissions that constitute her relationship to Milly, that ultimately determines Kate's own tragedy. She discovers, in the final line of the novel, that as a result of Densher's and her interactions with Milly, "we shall never be again as we were" (403). Thus, even though Kate is more directly involved than any other character in influencing the outcome of the story, she is finally not capable of observing it from the critical distance that her directorial role has implied.

The reader's role as audience to this drama is mediated because, as many critics have observed, James's indirect style complicates the act of interpretation by making us rely on other characters' impressions as guides to our own. We are poised between competing viewing strategies. Although there are as many perspectives on the drama as there are characters in the text, these perspectives encompass the extremes of affective involvement and clinical detachment. On the one hand, we are called upon to participate in the text as neuromimetics, to sympathize with Milly by experiencing the delicate fluctuations of her sensibilities (much as Henry James tried to do with Alice). The intratextual model for this viewpoint is Susan Stringham, whose relationship with Milly is predicated upon their unspoken reciprocity of emotion. Not only does Susan sympathize with Milly's illness, assuring her friend at one point, "I'd die *for* you" (127), but Milly, in turn, sympathizes with Susan's sympathy. Milly determines that "the basis, the inevitable basis, was that she was going to be sorry for Susie, who, to all appearance, had been condemned in so much more uncomfortable a manner to be sorry for *her*" (240).

This convoluted framework of feelings is maintained throughout the text, and Susan's nerves are perpetually attuned to the scene before her. Upon first meeting Susan, Densher describes how her nerves "quivered, clearly, they hummed and drummed, they leaped and bounded in Mrs. Stringham's typical organism—this lady striking him as before all things excited, as, in the native phrase, keyed-up, to a perception of more elements in the occasion than he was able to count. She was accessible to sides of it, he imagined, that were as yet obscure to him" (206). Densher identifies Susan's "American nerves" (206) as the source of her heightened powers of perception. She is, according to Densher, a more subtle reader of the scene than he. Susan takes a similar view of her hermeneutic superiority. She feels that no one else understands or appreciates Milly as well as she can, and she sets herself up as the proper interpreter of Milly's life and Milly's disease. When Densher seems to challenge this authority by asserting a prior knowledge of Milly in New York, Susan jealously snaps at him, "You know nothing sir—but not the least little bit—about my friend" (207). As readers, we are lured into identifying with Susan's essentially neuromimetic stance because we share her interpretive project. By asking us to make subtle aesthetic, social, and moral discriminations about Milly and the consequences of her illness—that is, to "key-up" our perceptions to the level of Susan's—James invites us to join in Susan's affective response to disease.

However, our identification is hindered by the fact that Susan is not always successful in her interpretive ventures. Like Milly, she misreads the complex motives of and relationships between Mrs. Lowder, Merton Densher, and Kate Croy and thus unknowingly participates in their deceptions. As Kate points out, it is Susan who is responsible for introducing Milly into this particularly predatory circle of people (171). While never questioning Susan's devotion, James seems at times to question her judgment, and even Milly is inclined to take Susan's authority lightly as a consequence of Susan's perpetual self-negation. Milly recognizes, as does her companion, that Susan "had now no life to lead; and she honestly believed that she was thus supremely equipped for leading Milly's own" (81). Susan's self-effacement—her adoption of another life to replace her own—is the product of her neuromimetic stance taken to its logical extreme: to sympathize absolutely is to erase the boundaries of individuality. As Gordon Hutner has pointed out, Milly is confronted with a surfeit of sympathy that threatens to overwhelm her; she "has to meet the 'face of sympathy,' to struggle against the 'machinations of sympathy,' to tolerate 'sighing sympathy' and 'amiable sympathy' " (210). Indeed, although Susan Stringham is redeemed by her sympathetic devotion to Milly, her appropriation of her friend's life is finally no less systematic than other characters' attempts to appropriate Milly's money. Each makes Milly the means to his or her own particular end. Thus while Susan's affective response to Milly's drama establishes an important, and partially validated, reading strategy, it is by no means presented as an untainted or unproblematic one.

The most clearly opposing alternative is Sir Luke Strett's objective, clinical vision of Milly, which corresponds, as a reading strategy, to the narrator's own ironic distance. By remaining detached from emotional involvement in the drama, Sir Luke's perspective provides the reader with a corrective against what James presents as the dangers of Mrs. Stringham's overidentification.[44] Although Sir Luke plays a relatively small part in the narrative events, throughout most of the text his medical vision looms over Milly. If Milly's

illness forms the text's dramatic center, around which other characters circulate, the physician's function is to direct the action while
watching the drama unfold. Susan Stringham explains that all she
knows about Sir Luke's diagnosis is that "he's watching" Milly
(246). When Sir Luke visits Mrs. Stringham to discuss Milly's case,
his prescription for the invalid consists of a set of casting and stage
directions. According to Mrs. Stringham, he tells her Milly must be
made happy: "He gave it to me, that is, as *my* part. The rest's his
own" (246). Milly is instructed to live and fall in love "by the doctor's direction" (247). Sir Luke becomes her "smooth strong director" (253), and she accepts his authority over her life without reser-
vation.

If Susan "knows" Milly through their silent sympathy, Sir Luke
Strett's knowledge is based on detached observation and medical authority. Milly realizes, "She hadn't gone to him to be liked, she had
gone to him to be judged; and he was quite a great enough man to be
in the habit, as a rule, of observing the difference" (155). Like
Mitchell's ideal physician, Strett exhibits a specular strength powerful enough to direct Milly through her illness, though not to cure
her.[45] Sir Luke advises her, in Milly's words, "that I'm not to worry
about anything in the world, and that if I'll be a good girl and do
exactly what he tells me he'll take care of me for ever and ever"
(143). Even when his detachment seems to falter and he exhibits an
interest in Milly's life story apart from her illness, she perceives this
sympathy in terms of his medical gaze: "In his appreciation of these
redundancies he dressed out for her the compassion he so signally
permitted himself to waste; but its operation for herself was as directly divesting, denuding, exposing. It reduced her to her ultimate
state, which was that of a poor girl—with her rent to pay for example" (155). Sir Luke's interest in the details of his patient's life is
envisioned by Milly as a physical examination. Milly experiences his
compassion not as she does Susan's—with reciprocal sympathy—
but rather as an operation in which she is exposed by his gaze. As if
cutting into her naked body, the doctor's questions probe and reduce
Milly to her spiritual and anatomical essence. Milly feels that he has
illuminated the elusive truth of her disease. And although James ultimately pulls back from the crude corporeality of his metaphor, re-

placing the nakedness of Milly's body with the nakedness of her imagined poverty, the examination remains the dominant image of the scene.

By glorifying the doctor's understanding of her and taking his silent diagnosis of her case far more seriously than Susan's sympathy, Milly authorizes Sir Luke's interpretation of her story. " 'He knows all about me, and I like it,' " Milly tells Kate. " 'He asked me scarcely anything—he doesn't need to do anything so stupid. . . . He can tell. He knows' " (143). Milly compares Susan's and Sir Luke's approaches to her illness, investing the physician's with legitimacy by contrasting it with Susan's ineffective, if noble, neuromimesis: "Susie positively wanted to suffer for her; Susie had a noble idea that she might somehow so do her good. Such, however, was not the way in which the greatest of London doctors was to be expected to wish to do it. He wouldn't have time even should he wish" (253). Milly's expectations about the emotional detachment proper to a great doctor correspond, as we have seen, to nineteenth-century medical ideals, explicitly distancing Sir Luke from Susan's affective response to suffering. His gaze commands Milly because it is seemingly objective; unlike Susan, who observes Milly from a stance of perpetual intimacy, Sir Luke's authority is determined by his status as an important London doctor with other calls upon his time. His vision takes in these wider horizons, assessing Milly's proper place within them.

The power of Sir Luke's gaze is not limited, however, to its effects on Milly. His worldly authority is perhaps most evident in Merton Densher's dread of being seen and judged by the doctor. While Densher is in Venice, uncomfortably fulfilling his agreement with Kate to "make up to a sick girl" (216), he reflects on the indignity of his situation: "He was glad there was no male witness; it was a circle of petticoats; he shouldn't have liked a man to see him. He only had for a moment a sharp thought of Sir Luke Strett, the great master of the knife. . . . He had a vision of great London surgeons . . . as incisive all round; so that he should perhaps after all not wholly escape the ironic attention of his own sex" (299). A contrast between masculine and feminine values is explicit in Densher's comments. Unmanned by the "circle of petticoats" into which he has allowed himself to be drawn, Densher dreads being subjected to male scrutiny. He finds himself placed in a feminine specular position, while retaining his own consciousness of a "proper" masculine authority and code of honor to which he has not adhered. Here the gaze of the doctor (or more specifically the surgeon) becomes a paradigm of objective authority because it is inherently "incisive," cutting through and seeing into social complications like Densher's with a lacerating irony. Although the threat of the doctor's gaze proves (like all things in this text) to be more vivid in imagination than in reality, Densher's anxieties confirm the gender distinctions we have already seen in nineteenth-century medical literature and suggest their crucial importance to the viewing structure of James's text.

Sir Luke Strett's authority, objectivity, and detachment would thus seem to ally him with James, or James's narrative voice, as an authorial cipher within the text. The "irony" of Strett's perspective, his role as "director" of the drama, combined with his "incisive" view of textual events, place him in a specular position similar to that of the writer/narrator. Yet James retreats from investing any single character with interpretive authority, instead revealing layers of interpretive possibility that never allow the reader to uncover a final transcendent truth. Thus Sir Luke's incisiveness, when looked at from another textual angle, becomes an optical illusion, merely a prop for Milly to use in staging her own decline.[46] It is potentially misleading to take Milly's rhetoric about Sir Luke's worldly authority as proof of his controlling position in the drama, because his directorial role is also part of a fiction that Milly herself has constructed. Milly shifts responsibility for her role onto Sir Luke in order to perpetuate the beautiful fiction of her passivity. By setting up the doctor as the authorizing figure of her illness, Milly is able to shape others' perceptions of and participation in her death, thereby asserting herself as subject through an act of self-deflection. Marcia Ian has noted this tendency in James to view the achievement of selfhood as a process of visual manipulation and concealment: "For James, permitting the self to be known by another makes selfhood impossible. . . . To know is to reduce and limit; to be known is to be annihilated or at least violated and imperiled" (112). If we accept this as an interpretation of Milly's motives, it becomes clear why she is better able to accept and capitalize on Sir Luke's clinical view of her than on Susan's neuromimetic one. The very distance of the doctor's exposing gaze, paradoxically, allows Milly to control her own self-representation, to shape the visual field in which she moves, whereas Susan's sympathy threatens to invade and annihilate the boundaries that protect Milly's sense of self.

Ultimately, James asks us not to view textual events exclusively from either the doctor's perspective or Susan Stringham's, but rather to engage, simultaneously, competing interpretive strategies. James implies that neither Sir Luke's detachment nor Susan's sympathy is sufficient alone. He forces us to evaluate the consequences of each specular position (along with the many others in the text that fall somewhere between) and to determine how far our own view of Milly corresponds to those presented and critiqued within the text. This intermingling of critical perspectives proposed in *The Wings of the Dove* is consistent with James's view of the critic's role expressed in his other writings. In his *Notebooks*, for example, James describes the ideal reader as "admiring, inquisitive, sympathetic, mystified, skeptical" (220–21). Hutner has discussed this conflicted stance of the Jamesian critic as one in which "critical readers are . . . always torn between two opposing yet complementary impulses" (200). By maintaining a balance of sympathy with what James describes as an "uncompromising swarm of authors, the clamorous children of history," the Jamesian critic "deals with the experience of others, which he resolves into his own" ("Science of Criticism," 99). Thus the critic, for James, "is immensely vicarious . . . for he deals with life at second-hand as well as at first" (ibid.), participating in a tension between self and other that parallels both the controlled sympathy of Mitchell's ideal physician and the temporary loss of individuality that occurs in the midst of Tarde's and Le Bon's similarly "uncompromising swarm"—the crowd. The parallel between crowd and critic is not, of course, an exact one, for James's ideal critic consciously and voluntarily enacts the transference of sympathy. Nevertheless, James's participation in the discourse of suggestibility is clear. It is only in "being indefatigably supple," in allowing the self the kind of permeability that James's characters resist, that James's critic participates in a controlled version of the experience of Bernhardt's coughing audience ("Science of Criticism," 99).

James's emphasis on what we might call interpretive androg-yny—a mingling of traditionally gendered critical stances—is en-hanced in *The Wings of the Dove* by a strategic lack of information. We are forced to attend to (and potentially adopt) the ways in which various characters view Milly precisely because so much of her de-cline and eventual death take place off the textual stage. Milly's deathbed scene is perhaps the most crucial absence in James's text, for like the burned letter that Densher never opens, it allows the imagination free reign. In his study *Silence in Henry James*, John Auchard claims that in *The Wings of the Dove* "a rarified silence de-velops as the dominant atmosphere of a novel where, when the hero-ine disappears, she transforms into a more vital figure" (86). Milly's vitality in the act of dying is enhanced precisely because we are forced to imagine it. Although Susan and Sir Luke are present at Milly's deathbed, we experience the scene indirectly through Den-sher's imagination after he has retreated to London. We are thereby allied with his developing awareness of guilt and sympathy and forced to evaluate the sincerity of his emotional response.

Densher's geographic distance from Milly's bedside is replaced by an imaginative proximity that is, ultimately, a mark of his grow-ing identification with the woman he has deceived. He feels com-pelled to communicate his emotional experience and to envision heroic narratives that will provide substitutes for the scene he has not been allowed to witness. Unable to talk about his ostensible lover with his real one, he finds in Mrs. Lowder a willing audience to his imaginative reconstruction of Milly's death. He describes how "Milly had held with passion to her dream of a future, and she was sepa-rated from it, not shrieking indeed, but grimly, awfully silent, as one might imagine some noble young victim of the scaffold, in the French Revolution, separated at the prison-door from some object clutched for resistance. Densher, in a cold moment, so pictured the case for Mrs Lowder" (369).

Faced with Milly's specular absence, which prefigures the more lasting absence of her death, Densher feels an obsessive need to en-vision scenarios that make the invalid present in his imagination and endow her death with mythic grandeur. He replaces the real Milly's death with fictional refigurations that serve to enhance his sense of participating in a tragedy. Furthermore, Densher forces Mrs. Lowder not only to listen to his laments but also to participate in his catharsis. Significantly, James depicts Densher's grief as a sentimental deathbed drama played in front of a responsive female audience: "It was almost as if she herself enjoyed the perfection of the pathos; she sat there before the scene, as he couldn't help giving it out to her, very much as a stout citizen's wife might have sat, during a play that made people cry, in the pit or the family-circle. What most deeply stirred her was the way the poor girl must have wanted to live" (368). Although James is clearly poking fun at Mrs. Lowder's bourgeois sentimentality and recognizing the danger of similar overtones in his own work, his portrayal of Densher's emotional confusion in this scene is poised between sincerity and skepticism. As in Lucy Snowe's and Gwendolen Harleth's acts of confession, Densher pours out the excess of his emotion into Mrs. Lowder's sturdy (even stout) container. But unlike those two heroines, Densher also feels the need to provoke parallel excesses in his audience. He accentuates the pathos in his description of Milly in order to trigger the anticipated emotional response in Mrs. Lowder. We view this exchange with irony, but James complicates the scene by emphasizing the involuntary nature of Densher's response. According to James, Densher "couldn't help giving it out" in such a way. Even in the midst of sincere confusion about his own emotions, Densher is unable to resist manipulating and aggrandizing the presentation of his grief. His sympathy for Milly is inseparable from his continued role-playing, and we can neither embrace nor dismiss the reality of his response.

Densher's consciousness of his own moral failings and divisions of motivation, though not necessarily redeeming his character for the reader, is nevertheless a mark of his developing powers of self-interpretation. It brings him closer to the complex perspective we have been invited to adopt. In imagining his own relation to Milly's death, Densher describes his sense of distance from the event:

He himself for that matter took in the scene again at moments as from the page of a book. He saw a young man far off and in a relation inconceivable, saw him hushed, passive, staying his breath, but half understanding, yet dimly conscious of something immense and holding himself painfully together not to lose it. The young man at these moments so seen was too distant and too strange for the right identity; and yet, outside, afterwards, it was his own face Densher had known. (369)

Densher's divided perspective in this description represents a fusion of visual modes, for he is at once neuromimetically inside the scene in an "inconceivable relation" to the invalid experiencing "something immense," and outside watching himself ironically from a distance and as a stranger. We can read Densher's divided gaze as an improvement upon his earlier insensitivity because it is an affirmation of James's hermeneutics. Densher's vision recognizes, simultaneously, both presence and absence, participation and detachment, moral responsibility and aesthetic voyeurism. And although Densher never articulates an understanding of his own specular balancing act, it is through his divided perspective that we gain our understanding of (and access to) Milly's death.

Ultimately, James impugns the innocence of both the neuromimetic and the clinical gazes, implicating all forms of spectatorship in the manipulation and appropriation of the specular object. Unlike Stowe, who reverses the hierarchy of interpretive values by valorizing sentimentality and sympathy over critical distance, and unlike Eliot, who examines ways in which scopic authority can be produced and transgressed, James neither challenges the correlation between gender and spectatorship nor embraces either specular position. While recognizing that excesses of sympathy like Susan Stringham's involve a loss of self and a corresponding appropriation of the other, James also recognizes that critical distance like Sir Luke Strett's is not, by itself, a viable position because it lures us into a false sense of superiority to textual events. With a kind of meta-irony, James critiques the very ironic perspective he so often adopts. He emphasizes that no one in *The Wings of the Dove* is able to remain morally untouched by his or her connection with Milly, and no one (including Milly herself) can be fully absolved of responsibility for her death. James invites us to confront the consequences of this revelation as it relates to our own interpretation of the text and to recognize how aesthetic voyeurism both shapes and undercuts the "part" we have been assigned—that of audience *in absentia* to Milly's deathbed drama.

It becomes clear from reading Victorian deathbed scenes that fictions of illness reproduced correlations between gender and specta-

torship codified in nineteenth-century medical rhetoric. Although
the medical literature articulates the gender values ascribed to acts
of looking more explicitly, both in theories of nervous mimicry and
in arguments over the validity of women doctors, concerns about
suggestibility and detachment appear in both medical and fictional
representations of disease. Together they form part of an emerging
cultural narrative about contagion that incorporated and gendered
the concept of audience. Recognizing the interdependence of hermeneutic relationships between doctor and patient, we can see how
the clinical gaze became a contested symbolic maneuver through
which the Victorian medical profession attempted to define, and
sometimes mystify, the basis of its authority. At the heart of this
strategy lay a fear of psychic and somatic permeability, of unstable
social and ontological boundaries, that was embodied, variously, in
the neuromimetic, the woman doctor, and the crowd. By designat-
ing fixed boundaries and codes of medical vision, Victorian doctors
could defuse the threat of their own emotional excess—the threat of
feminization.

   In the literature of disease, we find writers as ideologically and
artistically diverse as Stowe, du Maurier, Eliot, and James simultaneously affirming, criticizing, and occasionally reshaping traditional
constructions of visual authority in their attempts to come to terms
with Victorian concepts of gender. Their concerns about viewing relationships, and their skepticism about the innocence of spectatorship—whether erotically exploited as in *Trilby* or demystified as in
Middlemarch—may be taken as examples of wider cultural anxieties
about the transgressive power of vision. Just as theories of neurosis
attempted to contain the disruptive spiritual energy of saints and
hysterics, theories of suggestibility and spectatorship attempted to
come to terms with the permeable boundaries of identity. By examining the specular structure of illness and how it could threaten the
stability of gender roles, we can see how Victorian writers both acted
out Mitchell's "pathological drama" and transformed the terms of
his script. By implicating the reader in the consequences of spectatorship—either incorporating us, so to speak, in the midst of Bernhardt's audience or distancing us like the viewing doctor—they confronted a potentially fluid gendering of visual positions in the act of

interpretation. Ultimately, these narratives of contagion—both medical and literary—posited an unstable relationship between individuality and collectivity, detachment and sympathy, self and others. They identified gender identity as the most precarious category of visual identification, perpetually subject to the threat of nervous collapse.

CHAPTER 4

The National Health

Defining and Defending Bodily Boundaries

In 1903, upon discovering that a dramatic decrease in the height of soldiers in the British army since 1845 had necessitated reducing the minimum height requirement to 5 feet during the Boer War, Lord Rosebury complained, "It is no use having an Empire without an Imperial Race" (quoted in Shee, 797). Emphasizing physical development as a foundation for a dominant political body, Rosebury articulated a widespread concern about the relationship between health and racial survival that grew increasingly prominent in the latter decades of the nineteenth century.[1] For many Victorians, the pursuit of health constituted an act of patriotism, and the status of the body became a matter for political debate. Sir Duncan Gibb of the London Anthropological Society argued that "the vital energies of a people had a great deal to do with the state of the body, and that the capacity of the chest should count for something very considerable as an indication of national power" (quoted in Hoffman, 172). A synecdoche of Anglo-Saxon strength, Gibb's ideal of the capacious chest that could expand to fit the expanses of Britain's empire matched his vision of a country that flexed its physical and political muscles in unison. In this vision, the lungs become quite literally a measure of nationalist inspiration, helping to construct the somatic fiction by which fitness and empire were conceptually and ideologically linked.

Rosebury's and Gibb's idealizations of the racially superior body

as an implicitly masculine national symbol can be seen as a structural counterpart to the gendered female body of the invalid and hysteric. If the sickroom manipulated vision and sympathy in order to
reinforce the relationship between illness and gender, Victorian attitudes toward health expressed a similar desire to convert the physical into the ideological. This chapter turns, therefore, to the intersecting categories of gender, class, and race as they were deployed in
those carefully choreographed spectacles of national health—the
playing fields and the imperial frontiers. By moving my emphasis
here from sickness to health, I seek to demonstrate not a simple opposition between these concepts, or between the gender categories
they invoke, but rather their dynamic and often contradictory relations. As the health of the individual body came to be closely allied
with the health of the social body, anxieties about the one were projected onto the other: issues of military strength, world competition,
national growth, and the defense of national borders translated into
anxieties about physical strength, athletic prowess, evolutionary
progress, and the defense of biological boundaries against disease.

If, as I have argued, contagion and suggestion were the dominant
metaphors through which Victorians expressed fears about the
breakdown of individual and social boundaries, definitions of health
provided a means of restabilizing them. Like the crowd, the healthy
body functioned as a fantasy about collectivity. It emphasized the
possibility for group definition by creating a racial or national ideal.
However, unlike the crowd, which demonstrated the personal and
political dangers of commingling, the healthy body transformed collectivity into a measure of national identity. Through the comparative statistical measurement of groups—whether of cranial or chest
capacity, nutritional intake, reproductive success, or rate of mortality—nineteenth-century scientists sought to define social and evolutionary progress through a hermeneutics of bodily detail.[2] Ultimately,
this process equated the pursuit of health with the pursuit of empire,
establishing a somatically based territorial imperative.

In effect, the desire to construct and maintain an "imperial race"
that would constitute an adequate reflection of the British Empire
(or its American and European counterparts) both enabled the process of expansion by grounding imperialist ideology in physiology
and in many ways paralleled and even substituted for empire build-

ing itself. In other words, racial fantasies like Lord Rosebury's that proposed a collective bodily ideal served some of the same ideological functions as imperial expansion and domination. As the acquisition of new territories became more competitive in the late Victorian period, particularly in the scramble for Africa, the substitution of a national or racial body for a territorial one became an increasingly important symbolic gesture. By examining how an idealized healthy physique became a figure of national identity and, under the influence of social Darwinism, came to represent one of the central fictions of imperialist ideology, we can see how the comparative statistical measurement of groups marked an attempt by nineteenth-century science to define social and evolutionary progress through a hermeneutics of bodily detail. Medical classifications of body types—attempts to define sexual and racial characteristics and their relationship to pain, mortality, and disease—thereby constructed what we might call an anatomy of imperialism.

In identifying the ideological function of bodily ideals, this chapter necessarily examines larger mappings of social identities. It charts how culturally, sexually, and racially "other" bodies (against which such ideals usually were defined) appeared through the filters of scientific theory and exotic adventure narrative. Here again, visual metaphors predominate—we find the scientist and the imperialist, the writer and the reader, allied in acts of physiological and geographical tourism. When Dr. Aziz claims, in *A Passage to India*, that "this pose of 'seeing India' which had seduced him to Miss Quested at Chandrapore was only a form of ruling India; no sympathy lay behind it" (Forster, 306), he identifies tourism as an empowered mode of seeing. It functions as a counterpart to and extension of imperialist conquest, defined (like the effective physician) by the absence of sympathy in its scopic positioning.[3] My analysis of the symbolic value of health thus continues and complicates the gendering of visual positions outlined in Chapter 3 by suggesting their entanglement in racial and class politics. It addresses not merely the means through which perceptions of cultural difference shaped nineteenth-century views of the body, but how different angles of vision overlap or are displaced in the process of classification, conflating and redefining categories of race, ethnicity, class, or gender in often contradictory attempts to organize and contain the anxieties produced by imperialism and its decline.

The Ideology of Exercise

Concern about physical deterioration and the laws of health and hygiene grew steadily during the second half of the nineteenth century, producing a variety of popular health advice books, patent medicines, water cures, and journals devoted to "physical culture." According to Bruce Haley, "No topic more occupied the Victorian mind than Health—not religion, or politics, or Improvement, or Darwinism. . . . Literary critics thought of Health when they read a new book of poems; social theorists thought of Health when they envisioned an ideal society" (3). Although the promotion of health drew some of its energy from sanitation reformers and revelations about the physiological effects of slum conditions in London and other large cities, advice manuals generally targeted a middle-class audience and often stressed the importance of physical fitness in combating racial degeneration and improving the national health.[4] Predictably, definitions of health and advice about exercise took different forms for men and women. These differences corresponded to a conceptual division of labor in the process of empire building. Female health was most often measured in terms of reproductive capacity and nervous energy, focusing on the constitutional demands of motherhood to ensure the future of the next generation.[5] In contrast, male fitness was measured through characteristics such as height, musculature, lung capacity, and athletic prowess, characteristics that, if present in sufficient quantity, ensured the strength and stamina of soldiers. The ideology of exercise was merely one component in a trajectory of cultural fears about "race suicide," which extended from arguments for immigration restriction and eugenics to those against higher education for women and birth control (Smith-Rosenberg and Rosenberg, 26–28). One popular health manual complained of the "present race of pigmies" in England and provided advice about behavior, exercise, and diet intended to remedy this degenerative trend (Chavasse, 327). An American advice book claimed that the modern world "demands *unusual* bodies . . . *for the welfare of the race,*" arguing for the promotion of athletic competitions that would show "the *best* men, and methods of development of men." These men would, in turn, enable the nation to "*hew down whole forests till you have cleared a continent*" (Blaikie, 272–73). The equation of physical health and strength with racial destiny and territorial expansion suggests the extent to which individual fitness came to be perceived as a question of collective behavior and goals.

In his study of women's athleticism in the nineteenth century, Paul Atkinson has described what may stand as the most striking icons of the collective ideal in physical culture—a set of male and female statues that were displayed at the 1893 Chicago World's Fair, constructed from the averaged measurements of Harvard and Harvard Annex students. An anthropometrical study accompanying the exhibit provided a statistical comparison between these modern statues and the proportions of classical Greek statuary in order to assess the condition of the modern body and the physiological effects of higher education.[6] Although the sculptor deemed the male statue to be further from the Greek ideal than the female figure, greater interpretive energy was focused on the latter because of the greater controversy over women's higher education. In comparing the statues to their Greek counterparts at least one observer was comforted to find the female figure "fairly healthful, fairly attractive, and, above all, thoroughly womanly" (quoted in Burstall, 150). In this attempt to register the effects of a changing culture and educational system on a collective physique, we can see the prevailing interest in reducing bodies to their constituent details and reassembling them in symbolic forms, as a search for transcendent cultural meaning. In its trajectory from flesh to marble, the statuary exhibit provides a striking reversal (and multiplication) of the Pygmalion myth. A group of women require transformation into a statue in order to affirm their essential womanliness. But womanliness here is not merely an issue of "vital statistics"—indeed, the categories of measurement would perplex a modern reader of *Playboy*, including, as they did in many such projects, everything from head length and arm span to rib cage breadth and lung capacity (Atkinson, 40–41). At stake in the definition of healthy femininity are the external signs of internal fitness. Growing out of the medical attacks on women's higher education by Clarke and Maudsley, and participating in a widespread anxiety about declining birth rates among upper- and middle-class women, the medical profession increasingly defined female fitness in reproductive terms. By giving three-dimensional form to these issues and placing them on display, the World's Fair exhibit served to legitimize cultural anxieties about gender identity, reproductive capacity, and collective physical fitness. At the same time, its results promoted the cause of Victorian feminism by establishing the *stability* of the feminine physique. Ultimately, the statues provided visible proof that higher education was not, in fact, detrimental to the health and anatomical development of American women (Atkinson, 38–39).

The cultural resonance of these statues extends well beyond the Victorian debate about higher education. The investment of moral and cultural, as well as biological and evolutionary, meaning in minutely detailed body measurements was a prominent scientific strategy in research ranging from the criminological studies of Cesare Lombroso to the skull measurements made by Paul Broca (see the discussion in the third section of this chapter). What is perhaps most striking about the exhibit, however, is its attempt to recover the originary and normative form of human anatomy through the agency of classical art. As Atkinson has noted, the legitimizing function of the Greek ideal achieved widespread acceptance in fields as varied as Victorian anthropometry, education, and health reform (38–40). In particular, a perceived change in female anatomy as a result of tight corseting made the comparison of individual and collective bodies to classical statuary an effective strategy for both feminist dress reformers and physicians concerned with female reproductivity. For the novelist Sarah Grand, the anticorseting argument marked a feminist commitment to women's freedom and equality. In *The Heavenly Twins*, her rebellious child heroine employs the Greek ideal to parody the conventions of Victorian femininity, interrogating a tightly laced visitor:

"Why are you tied so tight in the middle?" Angelica asked at last in a voice that silenced everybody else in the room. "Doesn't it hurt? I mean to have a *good* figure when I grow up, like the Venus de Medici, you know. I can show you a picture of her, if you like. She hasn't a stitch on her."

"She looks awfully nice, though," said Diavolo, "and Angelica thinks she'd be able to eat more with that kind of figure." (132)

Angelica's personal justification for a "good figure" through the legitimizing agency of classicism employs the same paradigm as Victorian physicians who sought to protect women's powers of reproduction from the dangers of high fashion. If higher education was, in Clarke's argument, a potential drain of energy from body—or more specifically uterus—to brain, the corset was a potential deformation of the reproductive organs.[7] In seeking to quantify the deterioration of the modern female body, the physician Andrew Combe claimed, like Angelica, that one could measure its deviation from the "natural shape" by placing "a cast of the Venus de Medicis beside any young woman" in stays (181). Here again, the peculiar overlap between past and present versions of anatomy sets forth an equation in which classical art is invested with the authority of natural history. In Grand's and Combe's arguments, as in the statuary exhibit, art does not simply reflect nature; it is also the criterion of the "natural," providing unique access to a historical trajectory of body forms.

Physical exercise was the logical answer to the problem of female health for feminists and physicians alike. Women's colleges—especially in America—responded to the challenges of Clarke and Maudsley by developing campus gymnasiums and conducting anthropometrical studies that sought to regulate the balance between mental and physical development. Faced with widespread concern about women's illnesses and their potential link to declining middle-class birth statistics, many advice manuals argued that exercise was a patriotic duty to ensure women's strength and reproductive fitness as mothers of the next generation: "In our Christian lands, we find, if history be correct, that the great men have almost invariably had remarkable mothers. . . . The Sandwich Island proverb, 'If strong be the frame of the *mother*, her sons will make laws for the people,' suggests truths that will hold good in many other places besides the Sandwich Islands" (Blaikie, 50). In particular, physicians and health reformers saw exercise as an antidote to female nervousness, religious enthusiasm, and sentimentality, which, as we have already seen, formed a triad of temperamental dangers that could inhibit reproductive health: "The genuine child of Nature is not a morbidly emotional child. The girl who lives in the open air, who knows every bird and flower and brook in the neighborhood, has neither time nor inclination to spend in reading the sentimental histories of departed child-saints, and takes small delight in morbid conversation" (Bissell, 509).[8] In striking contrast to traditional correlations between nature and emotion in romantic poetry, Bissell sees a vigorous communion with nature as the antidote to emotional indulgence and a preventative against nervous illness. She argues, in effect, that what Lucy Snowe or Caroline Helstone may have needed was a good long walk.

The underlying agendas and moral justifications used to define fitness and to encourage appropriate forms of exercise could differ widely, however. A perceived contradiction between competition and "womanliness," in addition to fears that women's reproductive capabilities would be injured or overtaxed by excessive physical activity, made women's participation in vigorous or competitive sports a controversial social and medical subject. Women received conflicting signals about the value and propriety of exercise in promoting their health. Although throughout the century health advice books had encouraged women to exercise moderately, prescribing activities such as walking, croquet, archery, and light horseback riding, many also argued that too much athleticism, like too much intellectual activity, could interfere both with gender roles and with reproductive capacities. Literature frequently encouraged these stereotypes. In Anthony Trollope's *Orley Farm* (1862), for example, the aggressively horsey Tristram sisters become the object of narrative ridicule when their expertise in riding with the hounds and competing with the best horsemen in the county make them unfit for marital consideration. Despite such cautionary tales, however, increasing numbers of women participated in sports, and as they grew more vigorous and competitive, women pushed beyond the advice of the medical profession and established their own claims to fitness as a right separate from the issue of reproduction. Feminist reformers thus participated in the steadily increasing public interest in physical culture, appropriating the rhetoric of national fitness while contesting, or at least complicating, its ideological agenda.[9]

If definitions of female health were both implicitly and explicitly framed in terms of reproductive competition and species survival, male health was even more directly linked to the rhetoric of fitness. J. A. Mangan has made a persuasive argument for the connection between the development of public school games as a British institution and the physical training of British youth to promote imperialist expansion. In his book *The Games Ethic and Imperialism*, Mangan claims that the concept of "manliness" changed during the nineteenth century from connotations of "seriousness, self-denial and rectitude" to those of "robustness, perseverance and stoicism" (18), the latter qualities being of greater use for imperialist enterprises. The Reverend J. E. C. Welldon, headmaster of Harrow from 1881 to 1895, claimed that "if there is in the British race, as I think there is, a special aptitude for 'taking up the white man's burden' . . . it may be ascribed, above all other causes, to the spirit of organized games" (quoted in Mangan, 45). This idea was elaborated, Mangan notes, in the writings of another influential headmaster, Hely Hutchison Almond, who claimed that the promotion of health and hygiene was more important to the nation than democracy, and whose educational ideal was to make his boys "wholesome and manly, carrying the banner of the cross to distant lands, and with strong arm, iron will and earnest purpose winning Christian victories among ignorant natives and coarse traders, protecting rough colonies from effeminacy and vice, and spreading 'the contagion of their vigour' " (ibid., 25). Although Almond usually framed his views of health in the approved Victorian rhetoric of "muscular Christianity," we can see the influence of social Darwinism and the concept of natural selection in his description of the physiological benefits of sportsmanship.[10] Singling out the traits most useful for sheer physical survival, Almond suggested that Britain needed sportsmen more than students in order to succeed in imperialist ventures. He asked:

Which of the two—the student or the sportsman—is the more likely to be sensitive to and to interpret correctly faint and momentary impressions on eye and ear; to know what is indicated by the fall of a pebble, or the distant shimmer of steel, or to discern other visible or audible indications of the neighbourhood of a foe; or to march through a donga without finding out what there is about its sides. . . . Which of the two is the more likely to throw off the germs of disease, to recover soon from wounds, or to endure exposure and fatigue? (663–64)

Almond's correlation between sensory awareness, physical fitness, and military superiority emphasizes not only the healthy body's strength but also its hermeneutic sensitivity. As we have seen, the nervous sufferer often figured as an acute interpreter of subtle psychic, somatic, and social signals. However, Almond's healthy body (here exclusively male) proves similarly acute in interpreting the rough natural terrain of the battlefield. Furthermore, Almond's rhetoric envisions health as a form of internal combat—not just the absence of sickness, but the ability to conquer disease, to wrestle with it biologically and throw it to the ground. This internal combat, in turn, could be externalized and extended into the social body: the development of "such thews and sinews," wrote J. G. Cotton Minchin in 1901, "must give the hegemony of the world to the country that can produce these athletes" (52).

The idea that the essence of national identity was reflected in the body (and particularly the male athlete's body), and that if the bodies of its citizens could be shaped and strengthened by hard exercise or careful breeding, the social body would be correspondingly strengthened and made more fit, became one of the guiding precepts of Victorian educational theory.[11] Educators adopted these views in conjunction with contemporary scientific and medical theories, which saw in the details of the individual body the collective history and potential future of the race. The most obvious application of these ideals can be seen in the Rhodes Scholarships, which promoted physical fitness as a crucial component of the educational system: the scholar/sportsmen who received them were to be "the best men for the world's fight" (Green, 287). Having overcome his own childhood frailty gun-running on the South African frontier, Cecil Rhodes saw health and imperialism as inseparable goals for England, and he identified the educational system as the most important place to develop a strong national identity.[12]

Domestic Fitness: *The Egoist*

Connections between physical fitness, intellectual superiority, and biological destiny appear as frequently in nineteenth-century litera-

ture as they do in the sciences and the educational system. The somatic fictions through which the individual body became a measure
of national identity and imperialist power were, at least in part, produced by literature that emphasized ideals of health, fitness, and empire, both at home and abroad. As I suggest in the final section of
this chapter, the values that Rhodes and Almond promoted coin-
cided with the often aggressively masculine genre of imperialist fantasy and adventure fiction. Foreign lands provided idealized locales
for the demonstration of sociobiological fitness. Nevertheless, it is
in the sphere of domestic politics that we find the clearest articulation of health as a cultural imperative. When, in Meredith's *Egoist*,
the "pattern" aristocrat Sir Willoughby Patterne demands that his
wife must have "health above everything" (74) in order to provide a
"promise of superior offspring" (72), he acts as an eloquent
spokesman for those Victorians who were eager to prove and maintain the comparative fitness of the Anglo-Saxon race over other races
and cultures. In Meredith's novels, the related discourses of evolutionary theory, reproductive fitness, athleticism, and imperialism become part of a figurative vocabulary that codifies and genders acts
of self- and social definition.

Bruce Haley has described Meredith's portrayal of masculine values in both *The Ordeal of Richard Feverel* (1859) and *The Egoist*
(1879) as subscribing to the idea of "the Athlete as Barbarian"—
that is, promoting a view of athleticism that allies it with acts of
primitive physical conquest (Haley, 227).[13] Although, as Haley points
out, Meredith was himself a fitness enthusiast, a prodigious walker,
and a man whose conversation frequently turned to the subject of
"the maintenance of the British physique" (228), his narrative irony
was, nevertheless, frequently turned against characters who exhibited similar preoccupations with health and fitness.[14] Both Sir Austin
Feverel's educational "system" in *The Ordeal* and Sir Willoughby
Patterne's scientific pursuits in *The Egoist* involve principles of health
as they relate to the proper development and perpetuation of the
British aristocracy. But for Meredith they serve as examples of how
health can be transformed into a cultural obsession. As if parodying
the many and varied exercise plans, nutritional guidelines, and general systems of fitness promoted by nineteenth-century health man-

uals, Meredith's texts dissect the very process of systematization, identifying egoism as the driving force behind larger "systems" of Victorian science, culture, and belief.

For Meredith's patriarchs, health is a form of property, maintained as assiduously as a hereditary estate. Preserving one's health, or the health of one's offspring, against disease and degeneration constitutes as much of a baronial responsibility as preserving one's timber or game. Each necessitates a system of surveillance and each represents a form of patriotism. In *The Ordeal*, Sir Austin's health inspections of his son Richard constitute a kind of familial police state, a paternal panopticon that ensures the reproductive integrity and value of future generations. In discussing his "system" with the family physician, Sir Austin plots a rigid trajectory for his son's life that includes "manly sports and exercises" (36), ignorance of women (37), regular "medical examinations" (38), and an arranged marriage at the age of thirty (40): " 'On my System he must marry,' said the Baronet, and again dissected the frame of man, and entered into scientific particulars" (40). In Sir Austin's system, domestic harmony is subordinated to domestic science. Because he envisions the family as a structural counterpart of the state, Sir Austin's pet project seeks to shape the physique of the British race and thereby ensure the future of British aristocracy.

Though Sir Austin's system focuses primarily on developing manhood, women's health is scrutinized for reproductive fitness once Richard reaches the age to marry. Sir Austin's careful inspection and verbal anatomization of a number of marriageable young women, his minute inquiries into their health and habits, anticipate the detailed scrutiny of bodily and behavioral norms that preoccupied nineteenth-century science. Developing his own catalogue of aristocratic offspring and seeking out potential abnormalities, Sir Austin leaves no detail unexplored; in particular, he refuses to be taken in by blooming complexions that hide structural degeneration. Searching for a young woman who is neither the inferior product of aristocratic "wild oats" nor a member of the robust, but coarse, peasantry, Sir Austin attempts to systematize, and thus maintain control over the object of his son's desire and the terms of his reproduction. A focus of satire in Meredith's text, Sir Austin's "wild oats" theory articulates contemporary ideas about male sexual excess espoused by both scientists and health reformers, who argued that too frequent use of the reproductive organs, whether through conjugal intercourse, adultery, or masturbation, caused a deterioration in health and a degeneration of offspring.[15]

The Egoist, which many critics view as a sequel to *The Ordeal*, continues Meredith's unmasking of the cultural and ideological structures that support the "systems" of men like Sir Austin and Sir Willoughby. Although *The Egoist* can hardly be considered a text about imperialism in the way Haggard's or Conrad's fiction can, it would be a mistake to dismiss the importance of imperialist ideology either to Willoughby's interest in fitness or to Meredith's critique of egoism.[16] Meredith persistently links Willoughby's ideas about manliness and fitness to his admiration of and attempts to associate himself with England's military forces. Like the connection Almond draws between public school gamesmanship and imperialism, Meredith shows how Willoughby's "admirable passion to excel," which "was chiefly directed in his youth upon sport" (*The Egoist*, 46) is sustained in his adult ideals of military superiority. In the opening scene of the text we are introduced to Sir Willoughby in the act of reading and admiring the account of his distant relative Lieutenant Crossjay Patterne's bravery in "the storming of some eastern riverain stronghold." Meredith's narrator notes that "the humour of gentlemen at home is always highly excited by such cool feats. We are a small island, but you see what we do." As a result of this armchair nationalism, Willoughby develops "a taste for a soldier's life" and a habit of talking about his " 'military namesake and distant cousin, young Patterne—the Marine' " (39). Imagining his cousin as a strong young soldier and thus an appropriate reflection of himself and his country, Willoughby invites him to visit the Patterne estate only to discover that the lieutenant is a somewhat coarse looking, stocky, middle-aged marine—unfit to represent Sir Willoughby's ideal of British manhood. The Baronet is able to retain his "enthusiastic patriotism" (60) only through reasserting the centrality of class hierarchy to British society; that is, by socially "cutting" his relative and thereby preventing the real from encroaching upon the ideal. He later attempts to repair this failure of the common soldier to reflect the glory of British manhood by bringing the lieutenant's son, Cross-jay, to the estate in order to shape his character and physique into a more aristocratic masculine ideal. Willoughby thereby seeks to redeem the Patterne name (however distantly) and, by extension, the British empire, from the taint of the lieutenant's coarseness.

By choosing this scene to open his novel and introduce his protagonist, Meredith asserts the primacy of military and imperialist ideals to the concept of national identity and their constitutive part in Sir Willoughby's egoism. The imaginative link Meredith makes between the Patterne estate and the British empire is repeatedly asserted in Sir Willoughby's military deportment, his claims of sporting prowess, and his need to dominate and claim admiration from family, tenants, and neighbors alike. His fiancée Clara Middleton's first impression of Willoughby's "noble conquering look, splendid as a general's plume at the gallop" (90) is a characteristic one. Meredith thus parodies the way in which military and imperialist ideals feed the national ego and foster an attitude of complacent superiority.

If the first chapter of *The Egoist* is devoted to military egoism, the second chapter explores the scientific variety, for Willoughby's ideals of health and masculinity are just as much a product of nineteenth-century scientific thought as they are an expression of British nationalism. Carolyn Williams has noted Meredith's preoccupation with evolutionary theory in *The Egoist*, distinguishing between the ironic misinterpretation of Darwin in Willoughby's "science" and Meredith's own validation of natural selection in the development of the novel. This double valence of the evolutionary narrative allows Meredith to critique potential appropriations of evolutionary theory in the social realm, while nevertheless proposing a Darwinian (or more specifically Spencerian) agenda of his own. As such, Meredith enters the debate over what constitutes fitness, negotiating the territory between physical and intellectual trajectories of evolutionary progress.

Although Williams deftly unpacks the layers of irony in Meredith's account of natural selection, her argument ignores its persistent link with nationalist and imperialist ideologies. Throughout the novel, the rhetorics of military conquest and species survival overlap. Thus, when Willoughby states his allegiance to modern science, it sounds suspiciously like his patriotic fervor:

A deeper student of Science than his rivals, he appreciated Nature's compliment in the fair one's choice of you. We now scientifically know that in this department of the universal struggle, success is awarded to the bettermost. You spread a handsomer tail than your fellows, you dress a finer top-knot, you pipe a newer note, have a longer stride; she reviews you in competition, and selects you. The superlative is magnetic to her. . . . She cannot help herself; it is her nature, and her nature is the guarantee for the noblest races of men to come of her. In complimenting you, she is a promise of superior offspring. Science thus—or it is better to say—an acquaintance with science facilitates the cultivation of aristocracy. Consequently a successful pursuit and a wresting of her from a body of competitors, tells you that you are the best man. What is more, it tells the world so. (71–72)

Conflating his own courtship narrative with what Gillian Beer has called "Darwin's plots," Willoughby transforms an obsessive concern with the survival of the Patternes into a natural, "universal" law. Having already inserted himself into the account of his cousin's military prowess, Willoughby now goes on to insert himself into Darwin's account of natural selection. Willoughby's metaphoric "general's plume" becomes a bird's "finer top knot"; his military bearing is expressed by the superior animal's "longer stride"; the lieutenant's "storming" of the "stronghold" is transformed into a mating ritual—the "wresting of her from a body of competitors." Meredith suggests that both forms of "competition"—the imperialist ventures of British military forces and the evolutionary principles that determine a species' survival—are being used by the Egoist for the sole purpose of proving both to himself and to the world that he is indisputably "the best man."

As in *The Ordeal*, female health plays a significant (and predictably reproductive) role in the rhetoric of national fitness, validating homosocial bonds and rivalries. Throughout the text Willoughby merges romantic and evolutionary narratives, assuming that one's marital prospects demonstrate one's evolutionary success and are thus part of a natural world order. The stress he places on the word "nature" in his description of the courtship ritual ("She cannot help herself; it is her nature, and her nature is the guarantee

for the noblest races of men to come of her") emphasizes the correlation between women and nature and suggests Willoughby's need
to validate more than just his pedigree. Willoughby seeks to confirm
his sense of social identity by subjecting it to scientific principles and
inviolable biological laws. These, in turn, allow him to maintain a
stable set of assumptions about class and gender. However, what
Willoughby's courtship actually demonstrates is the very lack of anything natural or inevitable in his attempt to coerce Clara into hon-
oring their engagement and fulfilling the marriage contract. Thus,
at the same time that the pursuit of science feeds Willoughby's sense
of social and biological complacency, it also places a tremendous
burden on his courtship, for he relies upon nature—that is,
woman—to provide unassailable proof of his fitness to perpetuate
the species. Clara's increased dissatisfaction with and ultimate re-
jection of the baronet is perceived by Willoughby as a betrayal by
nature because it has the power to undermine his masculinity and
thus his entire system of self-worth. Meredith stresses that "all the
health of her nature" (141) makes Clara recoil against marrying a
man she does not love. Early in the novel we have been presented
with a Darwinian narrative that seems to lead to an inevitable conclusion—Sir Willoughby "looked the fittest; he justified the dictum of
Science" (73); "Clara was young, healthy, handsome; she was therefore fitted to be his wife, the mother of his children, his companion
picture" (76); and finally, "Thus did Miss Middleton acquiesce in
the principle of selection" (73). By the end of the story these premises
are, in effect, exploded. Clara defies the coercive authority of Darwin's plot (as it is enacted in Willoughby's imagination) when she
chooses the shy Vernon for her mate and leaves Willoughby with the
fading and sickly Laetitia.

Contrary to both Williams's and Haley's emphases on the rhetoric of male fitness, in Willoughby's interpretation of Darwin female
health becomes the determining gauge of evolutionary success. Only
the healthy female body is able to validate the male, for Willoughby
depends on the fitness of his mate both to prove his own superiority and to ensure that of their offspring. Thus throughout the text
the discourse of natural selection is manifested through the rhetoric
of female health. In describing Clara's fitness as a mate Willoughby

claims, "I would . . . have bargained for health above everything, but she has everything besides" (74), and later he insists, "My bride must have her health if all the doctors in the kingdom die for it!" (97). Clara's "splendid healthiness" (286) is set against Laetitia's "hollowed cheeks" (61), and Willoughby strains to retain his hold on Clara as a result of this comparison:

> The fact that she was a healthy young woman returned to the surface of his thoughts like the murdered body pitched into the river. . . . His grand hereditary desire to transmit his estates, wealth and name to a solid posterity, while it prompted him in his loathing and contempt of a nature mean and ephemeral compared with his, attached him desperately to her splendid healthiness. The council of elders, whose descendant he was, pointed to this young woman for his mate. He had wooed her with the idea that they consented. O she was healthy! . . . She was the first who taught him what it was to have sensations of his mortality. (286)

Meredith demonstrates the essentially moribund and unnatural quality of Willoughby's desire for Clara through his metaphor of a "murdered body." Her health haunts him because he has invested it with the significance of scientific law. The traditional courtship ritual is thereby inverted, for despite the scrupulous care with which Willoughby chooses his fiancées, they ultimately end up choosing (or more frequently not choosing) him. Clara's attempts to secede from their union transform her body into a symbol of Willoughby's failure; his subsequent fantasies involve violent erasures of the health he cannot possess: "Ten thousand Furies thickened about him at the thought of her lying by the road-side without his having crushed all the bloom and odour out of her . . . to lie there untouched, universally declined by the sniffling, sagacious dog-fiend, [man]" (278). Even his request for a last kiss is "intended to swallow every vestige of dwindling attractiveness out of her" (279). Willoughby thus justifies Clara's earlier discovery that "egoists have *good* women for their victims; women on whose devoted constancy they feed; they drink it like blood" (206). A vampiric prototype, Willoughby's thirst for female health to sustain his unnatural ego constitutes an attempt to colonize the female body and thereby control the narrative of natural selection, subsuming both into his own systems of meaning.

Ultimately, Willoughby's need for a healthy female body to validate his social and biological superiority is figured as a form of pathology—a moral disease that is capable of depleting the health of others. His sexual desire is articulated through metaphors of toxicity and infection. Thus, after a stroll with her fiancé, Clara feels as if "poison of some sort must be operating in her. She had not come to him to-day with this feeling of sullen antagonism; she had caught it here" (96). Eventually Clara puts a name to Willoughby's disease—egoism—and finds that this malady both afflicts and constitutes Willoughby's identity: "This word was her medical herb, her illuminating lamp, the key of him" (137). Subsequently, Laetitia perceives "Miss Middleton's fever of distaste. [Laetitia] shrunk from it in a kind of dread lest it might be contagious" (202–3). Once the "disease" of clear thinking has spread from Constantia to Clara to Laetitia, Willoughby is forced to appropriate the role of physician, promising: "I will cure you, my Laetitia. Look to me, I am the tonic" (476). But this declaration, by identifying Willoughby's ego as not only the instrument of contagion but also the source of cure, signals Meredith's continued skepticism about Willoughby's power to overcome his own pathologies, much less to cure others.

Although Meredith clearly satirizes what he sees as a cultural preoccupation with fitness, taking his patriarchs to task for masking (and magnifying) egoism in the guise of science and medicine, he undercuts this criticism and declares his own allegiance to the narrative of natural selection through his championing of intellectual fitness and idealizations of the "natural" body. The characters most preoccupied with fitness—Sir Austin and Sir Willoughby—are not necessarily the most fit. While their elaborate systems and scientific dictums inevitably fail, Meredith's physically healthiest characters inevitably triumph. Richard Feverel eventually finds a woman who lives up to his father's ideal—but he finds her instinctively (they meet accidentally in an outdoor setting) rather than systematically, allowing Meredith to separate the romantic from the scientific narrative. Similarly, in *The Egoist*, the fitness of Clara's marriage to Vernon is signaled in their plans for a honeymoon of vigorous alpine walking. Meredith thereby reveals the contradictions of corporeal metaphor; by collapsing the relative values of health and disease, he attempts to challenge scientific and imperialistic appropriations of

health as a symbol of national "fitness," while nevertheless maintaining faith in both the narrative of evolution and the primacy of
romantic desire.

The Egoist, then, reveals some of the ideological underpinnings
that linked evolutionary fitness, reproductive health, athleticism, and
militarism in a collective fantasy about the national physique. But
Meredith's emphasis on female health as the register of evolutionary progress reveals the tension in his argument between critiquing
evolutionary imperatives and affirming them. Meredith never makes
it entirely clear whether the triumphant romantic narratives that end
these novels challenge systems such as Sir Willoughby's and Sir
Austin's or reconstruct them. By calling on the reader to define what
"real" health consists of—in effect, to substitute what the text defines as unhealthy (because obsessive) systems of health with new,
apparently nonobsessive, more "genuinely" healthy principles—
Meredith reinscribes health as the determining category of value.
The novels enact the very systematizations of health that they criticize, constructing new standards of measurement for the reproductive project. Meredith's robust romances thus constitute the domestic version of what I will go on to identify as fantasies of national
health through imperialist adventure. It is through these collective,
and sometimes competing, narratives of fitness—produced by literary texts as well as advice manuals, anthropometric studies, public
school athletics, and the physical culture movement—that we can
see the ideological centrality of the healthy body to nineteenth-century conceptions of national identity.

The Anatomy of Empire

We have already noted the attention paid to bodily measurement
as an index of physical fitness, and the educational projects that
linked sports and fitness programs to the maintenance of an empire.
What has so far been only implicit in this equation is the correlation
between defining health and defining difference that preoccupied the
late-nineteenth-century human sciences. Debates in fields such as
medicine and anthropology suggest that health and fitness, far from
being clear and accepted categories, were important areas of ideo-

logical contest. While classical statuary might provide a temporal yardstick for measuring the relationship between ancient and modern bodies, it offered little information about comparative health and physical development between groups of people in the modern world. One means of determining the relationship between fitness and difference lay in anthropometrical studies of contemporary populations. Combining eighteenth-century scientific techniques with post-Darwinian concerns about comparative development, these studies located racial, sexual, and class differences in the measurement and description of body types, systematizing and grouping random individual variations into meaningful collective ones. Statistical measurements of comparative brain weights, body structures, and staminas, promoted by early eugenicists such as Francis Galton and the French craniometrist Paul Broca, formulated a basis for group definition and classification. Indeed, the comparative measurement of civilized and savage peoples seemed to offer both a diachronic and a synchronic scale. Insofar as the bodies and behaviors of savages provided living access to primitive human ancestry, as many Victorians assumed, they could be used to measure the comparative evolutionary development of civilized nations. Insofar as those differences could be correlated with differences of class, race, and, in some cases, gender, as in Cesare Lombroso's catalogue of criminal atavism, they seemed to provide a comprehensive system for measuring differential relations both between and within cultures.

In effect, statistics that measured and compared features such as height, muscular development, facial shape, and sensory awareness, as well as rates of mortality and reproduction, served to alleviate Victorian concerns about evolutionary progress by refashioning individual bodies into collective cultural symbols. A kind of statistical Frankenstein's monster, these abstractions gave the dominant culture an image of itself that could be used to determine the future of the race in relation to other races and cultures. This collective envisioning of the social body corresponded to another collective phenomenon—the imaginative engagement with questions of physical and racial vulnerability in late Victorian popular fiction. If, as I argued in Chapter 2, narratives could provide a means of reshaping a threatened physical experience and individual identity, they could also reshape threatened perceptions of the social body. Faced with powerful and often interconnected arguments about the degeneration of the Anglo-European physique, the fragmentation of social and class structures, and the decline of imperial authority, many writers in the latter decades of the nineteenth century expressed fears about racial and cultural progress through narratives of health and disease. In particular, they constructed stories that involved exaggerated, often precarious confrontations with superior examples of racial health and fitness. These narratives, which paralleled those produced by sociobiologists, appeared most frequently in the form of imperialist adventure stories, science fiction, and fantasy. Some of the most popular ones include H. Rider Haggard's *She* (1887) and the Allan Quatermain novels, Bram Stoker's *Dracula* (1897), and H. G. Wells's *War of the Worlds* (1898).[17] Together, they functioned as a form of collective reimagining, constructing new and improved images of the social body engaged in contests for survival. The very popularity of these narratives, which was often tremendous, consolidated their role as communal social fantasies. In the Martian invasion of Wells's *War of the Worlds*, for example, we are confronted with a vision of the collapsed infrastructure of civilization, a world "losing coherency, losing shape and efficiency, guttering, softening, running at last in that swift liquefaction of the social body" (150). Invoking the rhetoric of putrefaction, contagious disease, miasma, and the sewer, Wells captured the imagination of a culture preoccupied with degeneration and uncertain of its own fitness to survive in the modern world. Yet it is not technology that ultimately triumphs in the Martian war, but evolutionary biology. Civilization is saved by the carefully developed power of the human immune system; the superior weaponry of the Martian forces is useless in the face of their vulnerability to disease. Wells thus charts the tensions between degenerationist pessimism and evolutionary optimism, providing his readers with a set of interpretive codes designed to negotiate their collective relationship to modernity.

Although Wells's fantasy envisions cultural otherness as radically alien, his representations of Martian bodies refigure the same concerns about physical, social, and racial vulnerability (both at home and abroad) that we find in studies like those of Galton, Broca, Nordau, and Lombroso. These concerns did not take a single narrative form or arise from a clearly articulated set of social motives; rather, we can see a diverse group of cultural practices expressed through a pattern of late-nineteenth-century fitness narratives. Apprehensions about imperial decline, urban poverty, or the effects of feminism on middle-class reproductivity could occupy the same conceptual space and share a vocabulary of comparative fitness with Wells's fantasy of Martian invasion. Without ignoring the important differences between these issues, it is nevertheless important to recognize the frequency with which they shared a symbolic territory in the popular imagination.

The translation of categories of racial difference into assumptions about the lower classes—in both scientific and literary narratives of fitness—marked an important ideological leap from questions of foreign savagery to those of domestic politics. As both Greta Jones and Anita Levy have pointed out, the representation of difference as inferiority drew upon an interconnected and often interchangeable set of ideas about the nature of colonial or "primitive" peoples and the lower classes (Jones, 144–45; Levy, 55). Lower-class bodies rarely fulfilled popular ideals of national identity; rather, the urban poor, laborers, and criminals—particularly prostitutes—were associated with the physical, moral, or intellectual signs of racial and cultural otherness. The vocabulary of foreign savagery routinely emerges in the midst of urban landscapes. In *London Labour and the London Poor*, for example, Henry Mayhew describes "the uneducated portion of the street-people" in terms of their resemblance to a potpourri of primitive tribes:

Men whom, for the most part, are allowed to remain in nearly the same primitive and brutish state as the savage—creatures with nothing but their appetites, instincts, and passions to move them, and made up of the same crude combination of virtue and vice—the same generosity combined with the same predatory tendencies as the Bedouins of the desert—the same love of revenge and disregard of pain, and often the same gratitude and susceptibility to kindness as the Red Indian. (Vol. 1: 227)

Similarly, Lombroso described European criminals as those whose "physical insensibility well recalls that of savage peoples who can

bear in rites of puberty, tortures that a white man could never endure. All travellers know the indifference of Negroes and American
savages to pain: the former cut their hands and laugh in order to
avoid work; the latter, tied to the torture post, gaily sing the praises
of their tribe while they are slowly burnt" (from *L'homme criminel*,
translated by Gould, 126). Mayhew's and Lombroso's references to
foreign savagery demonstrate the imaginative link between poverty,
criminality, and racial inferiority. It is not only their behavior that
marks the poor and criminal classes as savage; their very physiology
manifests their primitive character. Focusing on diminished sensory
awareness as a crucial mark of otherness, Mayhew and Lombroso
identify feeling—in this case primarily physical sensibility—as one
of the defining characteristics of civilization. Not only could the pain
thresholds of savage peoples teach scientists about the behavior of
the lower classes, criminals, or slaves, but studies of primitive body
types both at home and abroad implied that there was a physiological basis for both class structure and colonial domination that de-
valued the pain and mortality of those with a perceived inferiority
of bodily construction.

Scientific interpretations of physical differences, though certainly
not new to the nineteenth century, were encouraged by evolutionary theory, which emphasized the trajectory from savagery to civilization through the scrutiny of minute bodily details. If a detail as
seemingly insignificant as a foreshortened earlobe—what came to be
known as "Darwin's ear"—could reveal our residual savagery,
wasn't the entire human body a system of signs that might predict
the future of the species as well as record its past?[18] Evolution provided a compelling framework within which to conceptualize the
historical and social meanings of human anatomy and physiology.
This conceptualization, in turn, served the interests of imperialism
in at least two widely recognized ways. First, by naturalizing hierarchies of physical and cultural difference, one could interpret military and economic aggression in terms of biological imperative. Second, by identifying dominant cultures as more highly evolved, one
could superimpose a moral argument about responsibility upon a
sociobiological one about differential development.

Both of these rationales depended on the assumption that the dominant culture was, in fact, more highly evolved and would continue to demonstrate its essential fitness in the cultural and biological arenas. But many Victorians were confused about what constituted fitness: should one read the social and political consequences of evolution as an optimistic promise of future growth or a pessimistic prediction of moral and intellectual atavism? Degenerationists writing in the 1880's and 1890's argued that the human species was becoming increasingly enfeebled—through everything from syphilis, insanity, feminism, radicalism, crime, and immigration to the stresses of modern civilization. This vision of a steady decline toward racial suicide contradicted popular correlations between evolution and progress. Debates about fitness reproduced this hermeneutic uncertainty. Like Mayhew and Lombroso, many Victorians believed in the physical insensitivity of the lower classes, "savages," and nonwhite races, whether through hereditary factors or repeated exposure to hardship and deprivation. Such powers of resiliency, some argued, suited the lower classes to the physical labors they performed. Yet physical resiliency was also a positive quality that seemed necessary for evolutionary success and racial survival. As Martin Pernick has argued, resistance to suffering could signify traditionally masculine powers of endurance, enabling soldiers, for example, to withstand the rigors of combat (118, 150). How, then, could dominant cultures assess the value of pain or the meaning of fitness and gauge their own continuing potential for progress and survival? Was fitness measured through physical strength and endurance or through intelligence? Was it embodied in muscles or nerves? Many suspected, as Weir Mitchell did, that "in our process of being civilized we have won . . . intensified capacity to suffer" (*Characteristics*, 13). Alternately fascinated and worried by what they saw as the greater physical and emotional sensitivity of the educated classes, and the greater strength and reproductive powers of what Marx called the lumpenproletariat, Victorians came to contradictory conclusions about the evolutionary state of the human species.[19]

It is precisely in negotiating these areas of intradisciplinary debate that we can see the process of cultural displacement and collective anxiety at work. For example, we find competing arguments about the physical construction, reproductive capacity, sensitivity, and comparative health of laborers, immigrants, the poor, criminals, savages, and women of various classes and races. Unquestionably, the common ideological assumptions behind these arguments included a belief in the existence and measurability of physical and mental hierarchies, and in the need for middle- and upper-class white Europeans to maintain their position at the top of those hierarchies. It is equally clear that such assumptions shaped not only the interpretation of scientific data but also the methodology and data collection itself.[20] Yet it is in determining what constituted fitness, whether and why certain bodies were more disposed to health than others, and what role the nervous system might play in negotiating the human relationship to modernity, that we find some of the most revealing somatic fictions at work.

Throughout the latter decades of the nineteenth century we find scientists relying on arguments precariously poised between an apocalyptic rhetoric about "racial suicide" and an evolutionary optimism about intellectual and technological progress. For example, in defining neurasthenia—a nervous condition that involved subtle interpretations of the relationship between pain and culture—George Miller Beard associated the illness with the world's "brainworkers," those with "fine, soft skin, fine hair, delicately-cut features, and tapering extremities" (*Practical Treatise*, 95). Linking fine northern European features with intellectual development and neurasthenic tendencies, Beard saw nervous sensitivity as a harbinger of social progress, a sign that the human race was steadily evolving toward greater mental and physical refinement. Yet the prevalence of neurasthenia could also mark a process of degeneration in which those same oversensitive brainworkers might lose the battle for survival to physically fit but nevertheless more primitive peoples. Tom Lutz has noted the "discursive heterogeneity and semiotic vagrancy" of neurasthenia as a cultural and medical concept at the turn of the century. A trope for the modern condition, neurasthenia provided a sensitive register of social, cultural, moral, and religious differences (23). It was employed, at least in part, as a way of explaining male nervousness without invoking the feminizing stigma of hysteria, and like hysteria, neurasthenia could account for a dazzling array of symptoms. Although the symptoms of neurasthenia arose from diverse, often untraceable causes, they invariably marked the inability of the nervous system to keep pace with the stresses of technological and intellectual progress. Beard argued that it was the very ability to suffer—an ability not granted to all races and cultures equally—that marked both the progress and the precarious health of modern civilization.

In Beard's attempts to distinguish between those at the forefront of civilization and those lingering at its rear, we find a familiar emphasis on the physical components of cultural progress. The British eugenicist Francis Galton used composite photography to identify the normative features of "health, disease and criminality" (14). As in the World's Fair statuary exhibit, his "types" for health included both classical and contemporary ideals. In order to determine the physiognomic components of physical fitness, he used a composite portrait of Alexander the Great taken from antique coinage and a contemporary military composite that blended the faces of twenty-three members of the Royal Engineers. Attempting to provide a transhistorical register of fitness, Galton envisioned health, masculinity, and militarism as conceptually interchangeable. Perhaps because of this, we find no images of female health. For disease, on the other hand, Galton produced composites of fifty-six consumptive women, nine tubercular men, and more than a hundred patients suffering from various "other maladies." By superimposing these photographs to produce visual averages, Galton sought to identify the most essential genetic features of the healthy and the diseased. He not only charted the current state of the social body but also provided a blueprint for its future reconstruction.

During the same period, we find Cesare Lombroso using physiognomy and anthropometry to provide catalogues of criminal atavism. Less sanguine than Beard about the progress of evolution, Lombroso's studies of physical anomalies in the criminal classes insisted upon their links to primitive physiology, identifying male and female "born criminals" through the anatomical stigmata of their residual savagery. Lombroso statistically dissected the criminal body measurement by measurement with a fetishistic enthusiasm for obscure detail. He claimed to find more physical and pathological anomalies in criminal men and women than in what he classified as "normal" men and women of moral rectitude. These anomalies ranged from the size, weight, and position of brain, jaw, ears, nose, neck, cheekbones, and lips to the abundance and waviness of hair. Although both Lombroso and Galton employed the relatively new and scientifically popular medium of photography, they emphasized opposing strategies. Galton created carefully blended composites, which sought a common physiognomic denominator; in contrast, Lombroso emphasized minute fluctuations in form. Ultimately, in their attempts to find a predictive external register of internal identity, Beard, Galton, and Lombroso transformed eighteenth-century theories of physiognomy from a science of individual character to a measure of evolutionary progress (or degeneration) that could be widely applied to social groups. Seeking information about entire populations, they eventually extended the interpretation of facial features to detailed mappings of the body as a whole, thereby identifying the components of difference and affirming that norms existed on the most basic and measurable physiological levels.[21]

External signs of physical fitness, however, were only one small part of the comparative calculations of the social body. As I have already indicated, sensitivity to pain became an important area of definitional conflict, providing criteria for assessing biological, social, and intellectual development. To feel pain acutely implied that one's nerves were finely constructed and thus had evolved to a more advanced degree than those who were less sensitive. Traditionally, women were assumed to have the most delicate nerves; they could be, in the words of physician and novelist Oliver Wendell Holmes, "more fertile in capacities of suffering than a man" (*Elsie Venner*, 51).[22] Yet this ideal of sensitive bourgeois womanhood could also imply that women were more evolutionarily advanced than men. The interpretation of female sensitivity thus became an area of medico-ideological conflict for doctors and sociobiologists alike. If the nervous system was the seat of intellectual and evolutionary development, then it was a "reasonable expectation," in Galton's words, that "sensitivity . . . would on the whole be highest among the intellectually ablest" (29). According to Galton, men's advanced intellect should be accompanied by an advanced sensitivity to external stimuli, including sensations of pain. Yet the greater number of nervously sensitive women seemed to challenge any correlation between intelligence and sensitivity. Galton attempted to solve this dilemma by arguing for a distinction between sensitivity and irritability: "women of delicate nerves" (29) who were distressed by the smallest of stimuli were not necessarily as sensitive or discriminating in their sensory perceptions as men; they were merely more irritable. Other researchers challenged traditional assumptions about female sensitivity by arguing that women's pain thresholds were actually higher than men's: Lombroso concluded that the physical trials of childbirth, like the hardships of poverty, diminished women's sensitivity: women "are more frequently exposed to physical pain—are physiologically bound to endure it" by virtue of their reproductive systems (*Female Offender*, 270–71). More elusively, Richard von Krafft-Ebing argued that woman's higher pain threshold came from her "voluntary subjection to the opposite sex," which he claimed was not a cultural but rather a "physiological phenomenon" (137).

Working by analogy, Lombroso translated his theories about pain and sexual identity into theories encompassing class and race. He concluded that since lower classes and races were, like women, naturally more exposed to pain and hardship than middle- and upper-class men, they too must have nervous systems designed along more primitive lines. Consequently, prostitutes and female criminals were even less conscious of pain than "normal" women, and criminal men were similarly inured to acute physical hardship. This diminished sensitivity was responsible, in turn, for an increased longevity in women and in both male and female criminals. Although Lombroso's interpretation of longevity as a sign of evolutionary inferiority departed from the thinking of many of his contemporaries—in particular those who used census statistics to chart the comparative relationship between birth and mortality rates in different classes and races—he developed similar strategies for denying the importance of longevity to evolutionary progress and survival.[23] Lombroso argued that longevity was an abnormality or anomaly peculiar to the criminal classes, which served to separate them from the general population. Because it was combined with other anomalies that marked out the "born criminal," longevity was not, in itself, indicative of evolutionary success. By attributing inferior mental capacities to criminals, Lombroso sought to diminish the evolutionary importance of qualities such as health and longevity. In Lombroso's reasoning, it did not matter if criminals and people of different races were physically robust, sexually prolific, or long-lived as long as their brains were less developed.

Though he did not develop a systematic theory like Lombroso's, Henry Mayhew had made some similar assumptions about the physical invulnerability and longevity of career prostitutes, closely linking a hardened immorality with a hardened immune system. Distinguishing between recently fallen young women and habitual offenders, Mayhew observed that career prostitutes were notable for both their "remarkable freedom from disease" and "their mental and physical elasticity." In their case,

Syphilis is rarely fatal. It is an entirely distinct race that suffer from the ravages of the insidious diseases that the licence given to the passions and promiscuous intercourse engender. Young girls, innocent and inexperienced, whose devotion has not yet bereft them of their innate modesty and sense of shame, will allow their systems to be so shocked, and their constitutions so impaired, before the aid of the surgeon is sought for, that when he does arrive his assistance is almost useless. (Vol. 4: 213)

Attempting to negotiate the ambiguous territory of feminine sensibility, Mayhew divides prostitutes into two classes based on their capacity to suffer moral and physical pain. Assuming an interrelated etiology of body (pain) and mind (shame), he concludes that to feel pain signals the retention of moral fitness: to die from syphilis marks the triumph of sensibility by declaring one's capacity to feel remorse. Alternatively, to lose one's morals is to lose one's humanity and thus one's capacity for both moral and physical suffering. It is thus the career prostitute who inhabits the bottom of the social and moral hierarchy; an urban savage, she embodies both the threat of contagion and the paradox of immunity.[24]

The importance placed upon pain as an index of nervous development and human worth had significant implications for perceptions about overall health. Regardless of the validity of the data, which were usually anecdotal, the means of interpreting comparative studies of sensory awareness produced confusion in the medical community. These studies could imply that people who felt pain less would feel correspondingly less debilitated by and would recover more rapidly from any illnesses they might develop; they would thus appear healthier than people whose bodies were less resistant to pain. This would mean that people of seemingly inferior nervous construction were actually healthier and better suited to physical survival. Such a view, while challenging the physical fitness of the dominant culture, was nevertheless consistent with myths about the rugged health of peasants and vagrants and the virtual indestructibility of criminals and savages. But insensitivity to pain could also mean that the body was being progressively weakened by injury and disease without any consciousness of such deterioration: sensitivity to pain ensured that people took care of their bodies; insensitivity to pain could lead to indifference and neglect. This view corresponded to images of the urban poor as inherently diseased, disabled, or indifferent to the squalor of their surroundings.

These competing interpretations of the physiological and cultural meaning of pain were embraced by nineteenth-century scientists and doctors according to the extent to which they correlated robust health (including fertility and longevity) with evolutionary superiority. If fitness involved primarily a state of physical well-being, then the population must be proved or made physically fit. If fitness involved moral or intellectual superiority, then health became a less pressing evolutionary concern. Doctors and scientists writing about pain, health, or longevity in the second half of the nineteenth century usually subscribed to one of these two positions or adopted an uneasy compromise between them.

Ultimately, what is most interesting about studies like Lombroso's, Beard's, and Galton's are their conflicting and often contradictory attempts to define the meaning of fitness as a unified tool for measuring comparative social progress. Their inconsistencies in definition, and the competing narrative models they construct, suggest the symbolic importance of fitness (as well as sensitivity) to Victorian culture. In their pressing need to define a differential theory of sensory perception that would conform to an evolutionary narrative about the future of the species, many working in the human sciences found themselves entangled in an ideological quagmire of competing beliefs about racial progress, reproductive health, and corporeal immunity. If fitness was the predictive register of human development, it was also the most elusive of concepts when applied to human bodies and minds. In trying to create an organic, comprehensive story about the health of the human body and its relation to the future of society, Victorian science created not one but many competing narratives of fitness. Each either implicitly or explicitly re-envisioned the relationship between individual bodies and national destinies, tracing the outlines of a collective identity and constructing a model of the social body that was triumphantly, and frighteningly, larger than life.

Physical Immunity and Racial Destiny: Stoker and Haggard

Much of the literature of imperialism written in the latter half of the nineteenth century provided a forum for and put into practice the conflicting medical and social theories I have outlined. Just as ideas about biological inferiority and evolutionary hierarchies of gender, class, and race extended beyond the medical and scientific communities into the educational system, they also appeared in literary portrayals of health and fitness, in adventure stories of exploration and invasion, and in metaphors of military conquest. The heroes of literature were, as Wendy R. Katz has written, "imaginary reflections of a society interested in soldiers, athletes, and sheer physical power" (59). As the state of the body came to be perceived in terms of national destiny, the figurative potential of health and disease was invoked with increasing regularity. In the discourses of empire, representations of physical health provided symbolic affirmations of national and racial identity, while disease connoted a threat to corporeal borderlands—an impediment to both imperial domination and evolutionary progress.

Yet as the problems of administering and maintaining a huge empire became increasingly evident toward the end of the century, the moral values of health and disease became progressively destabilized. Suffering from what Martin Green has called "the anxiety of possession" (234), a number of late Victorian writers demonstrated discomfort with the implications of imperialist practice, simultaneously participating in the rhetoric of health and complicating that rhetoric—on the one hand celebrating imperialist adventure and subscribing to the precepts of social Darwinism, and on the other hand questioning the moral and social value of either absolute health or absolute power. Thus in texts such as *She* and *Dracula* we are confronted with what Stephen Arata has described as a process of "reverse colonization." These fictions offer nightmare versions of imperialist expansion that contemplate the specter of invulnerable health and racial superiority. They fall into the category of imperialist fiction that Patrick Brantlinger has identified as "Imperial Gothic"—a combination of "the seemingly scientific, progressive, often Darwinian ideology of imperialism with an antithetical interest in the occult" (227). This link with occultism is, according to Brantlinger, "especially symptomatic of the anxieties that attended the climax of the British Empire. No form of cultural expression reveals more clearly the contradictions within that climax than imperial Gothic" (227–28). My interest here is in the contradiction between spiritualism and science in Haggard's and Stoker's fictions and in the way they use the gothic genre to reveal the implications of imperialist ideology. Haggard and Stoker legitimize their use of the occult by combining scientific theories of criminality, sexuality, race, and fitness with the discourse of spirituality I discussed in Chapter 2.[25] By merging these genres, Haggard and Stoker disrupt the boundaries between science and supernaturalism, critiquing each as an adequate account of reality. Definitions of health and fitness become ungrounded from their materialist moorings, allowing Haggard and Stoker to explore the consequences of somatic fictions when taken to fantastic extremes.

Their contradictory definitions of fitness make Dracula and Ayesha appropriate symbols for an era obsessed with bodily measurement and evolutionary survival. Both display the stigmata of racial, sexual, or criminal otherness, while at the same time they demonstrate advanced physiological and intellectual development. Each combines physical health, strength, and longevity with either superior intelligence (Ayesha) or reproductive power (Dracula), and the economic authority to pursue their imperial aspirations. By offering spectacles of natural and supernatural selection, *Dracula* and *She* highlight the uncertain outcome of evolutionary progress. And by allying the pursuit of health and longevity with their gothic anti-heroes and the empires they seek to conquer, Stoker and Haggard provided Victorian readers with a means of confronting doubts about racial, cultural, and physical fitness in the modern world.

The signifying power of the healthy body in Stoker's and Haggard's fictions reveals the imaginative link between individual strength and cultural progress. Like Gibb's celebration of chest capacity as a mark of racial superiority or Minchin's tribute to athletic ability as a sign of world hegemony, both Stoker and Haggard link bodily ideals to racial and national destiny.[26] In *Allan Quatermain* (1887), Haggard's eponymous hero and narrator routinely compares male chest sizes, providing hegemonic and homoerotic meditations on male musculature. As if collecting examples for one of Galton's composites of military health, Quatermain claims he has "never seen wider shoulders or a deeper chest" than in his friend Sir Henry Curtis, who is "altogether a magnificent specimen of the higher type of humanity" (495). In *Dracula*, Stoker's Dr. Seward interprets Quincey's courage and physique as symbols of national progress: "If America can go on breeding men like that, she will be a power in the world indeed" (209). Yet even the fittest of fictional heroes cannot compete with the supernatural fitness of Dracula or Ayesha. The healthiest characters in Stoker's and Haggard's novels have crossed over into an abnormal state of corporeal immunity that threatens, variously, to feminize, criminalize, or racially alter the worlds they rule. In *She*, Ayesha's health and longevity provide a means for achieving absolute power: "As she could not die . . . what was there to stop her? . . . I could only conclude that this marvellous creature . . . [would] change the order of the world" (170). Dracula's health is similarly threatening, for it derives from his unnatural relationship to death and decay (*Dracula*, 68). Like the savage insensibility of Lombroso's "born criminal," Dracula's body demonstrates its essential otherness. Relying on an infinitely renewable physical strength and longevity, Dracula seeks to transform the course of evolutionary history and become "the father or furtherer of a new order of beings" (360)—his own version of Lord Rosebury's "imperial race."

Although both *Dracula* and *She* envision physical health as a prelude to imperialist aggression, Haggard's fiction, because of its explicitly imperialist settings, demonstrates the extent to which the healthy body served as a semiotic register of national and racial superiority. Haggard's African adventure narratives offer fantasies of racial health that position savagery and antiquity as parallel sites for the measurement of modern fitness. They posit imperialist adventure not so much as a pursuit of new territory (though this is their stated goal) as a pursuit of human biological history. This relationship between history and imperialism is highlighted most obviously in *She*, where the narrative framework includes a series of family documents dating back to the ancient Greeks and Egyptians, which nevertheless locate the recovery of this history in the heart of the African continent. For Haggard, the embodiment of history has two primary (and paradoxically related) sources: savagery and classicism. Both can be recovered in their purest form in Africa; both are essential for the comparative measurement of modern fitness. They function as transhistorical registers of the human past, for the African native is presumed to remain unevolved and the classical statue (or woman) is preserved through the ages. Each, in turn, has the capacity to affirm white hegemony, though in carefully distinguished (and ultimately gendered) ways: the first through martial conquest, the second through reproductive selection.

In Haggard's fiction, the characters with the most perfect physiques and the most noble bearings, both black and white, are almost always of pure racial lines. The racial pedigrees Haggard gives his idealized male heroes—Sir Henry Curtis's Viking ancestors and Leo Vincy's Hellenic ones—link contemporary England to a history of masculine fitness and imperial power. Thus in *She* we learn that Leo's physique, despite its Hellenic pedigree, is quintessentially English:

Though he is half a Greek in blood, Leo is, with the exception of his hair, one of the most English-looking men I ever saw. He has nothing of the supple form or slippery manner of the modern Greek about him. . . . He is very tall and big-chested, and yet not awkward, as so many big men are, and his head is set upon him in such a fashion as to give him a proud and vigorous air. (142)

The model of an English gentleman, Leo provides visible proof that classical ideals of male beauty and health are reborn in the British physique. Described as "a vigorous young athlete" (44) replete with martial prowess (he slays three natives outright when first attacked), he is a veritable composite of Greek statuary, Galton's Alexander, and the Royal Engineers.

For Haggard, as for Darwin, corporeal details encode history; they are forms of knowledge that, properly interpreted, provide access to scientific and social truths. The bodies of Haggard's characters inevitably reveal the secrets of their lineage. In *King Solomon's Mines*, when Allan Quatermain first appraises his servant Umbopa's physique, he is struck by this "magnificent looking man" who "seemed different from the ordinary run of Zulus" (373). Ultimately he finds the proof of Umbopa's difference etched upon his body in the form of a tattoo, which marks the Kukuana king. Similarly, upon first meeting Sir Henry Curtis, who has the white equivalent of Umbopa's physique, Quatermain is struck by his resemblance to "an ancient Dane . . . a kind of white Zulu." He subsequently discovers that Curtis is indeed "of Danish blood," which "just shows how the blood will show out" (356–57).[27]

Quatermain's use of the Zulus as symbols of physical health and martial ferocity indicates the imaginative function of black physicality in the imperialist imagination. Interchangeable representatives of that powerful scientific and cultural construct—the Negro body—Haggard's Zulu warriors represent nature and fitness, and particularly masculine fitness, in its purest, primitive state.[28] His descriptions invoke popular stereotypes about the health and stamina of Africans, whose blood (unlike that of their American counterparts) was believed to be essentially untainted by racial crossbreeding. Although Brantlinger has dismissed Haggard's representations of Zulus as exceptions in Victorian imperialist literature and throwbacks to Rousseau's ideal of the noble savage (38–39), nobility is not, I would argue, the central issue at stake in Haggard's engagement with the concept of savagery. The function of the Zulu warrior in Haggard's text is more ideologically complex than a mere celebration of the primitive. Haggard's use of black physicality resembles Meredith's use of the healthy female body as a homosocial proving ground for British manhood. The stature of the Zulu warrior is a yardstick by which to measure the masculinity of Haggard's white heroes. Haggard, in turn, equates masculinity with evolutionary superiority through both physical fitness and martial arts. Thus the strength and health of Haggard's black characters serve not as independent expressions of racial development, as the same attributes do for his British heroes, but rather as foils for the expression of Anglo-Saxon hegemony. Insofar as the attributes of black bodies are appropriated into a physical economy that exalts the superiority of white bodies, those attributes are transferred to and reified in Haggard's white heroes. Thus, he frequently pairs and compares the idealized white protagonist with a black warrior of equivalent stature, translating the mythic energy of black physicality into a signifier of white domination. Upon introducing Curtis to the fierce Zulu Umslopogaas in *Allan Quatermain*, Quatermain assures the African that the white lord " 'also is a warrior as great as thou, and strong as thou art; he could throw thee over his shoulder' " (501). In this way, the strength of Haggard's black characters is subsumed into his white ones in a gesture that mirrors the process of imperial conquest.

The journey to Africa thus functions for Haggard's heroes in the same way that the courtship ritual functions for Meredith's Egoist—both afford opportunities for determining who is the "best man." But Haggard's contest is always already a battle of unequals, for his rhetoric of fitness reveals the powerful subtext of racial difference: whereas at the beginning of *King Solomon's Mines* (1885), Quatermain exclaims upon meeting Curtis, "I never saw a finer-looking man" (356), he remarks upon meeting Umbopa, "I never saw a finer native" (373). Haggard leaves no doubt that the finest native can serve only to measure, never to represent, the finest man.[29]

Haggard's fiction further transcribes the imaginative power and collective scale of black bodies onto the African landscape. His vision of Africa is replete with towering images of its natives: "Sheba's Breasts"—the twin mountains that mark the road to King Solomon's Mines—and the "Ethiopian's Head"—a colossal land mass carved by man or nature into the cliffs that mark Ayesha's kingdom—are

examples of how Africa and the Negro body—most often female—
become interchangeable myths in the imperial imagination. The
metaphoric links between imperial conquest and sexual conquest
(implicit in terms like "motherland") are thus crudely literalized in
Haggard's Africa as his white heroes struggle to scale Sheba's breasts
and penetrate the diamond mines that lie beyond them. This corporeal topography forms both the impetus and the object of conquest
for Haggard's white heroes, suggesting that much of the imaginative
energy invested in the Dark Continent arose from an erotic fascination with the physiology of sexual and racial difference.

If racial purity forms the basis of health and strength in Haggard's texts, racial impurity is associated with disease, degeneration,
and decay. The perceived dangers (and potential attractions) of miscegenation can be measured by the frequency with which Haggard's
characters, black and white, need to remind us (and themselves) that
"the sun may not mate with the moon, nor the white with the black"
(*King Solomon's Mines*, 476). As we can see in nineteenth-century
studies of black physiology, the rhetoric of miscegenation was often
synonymous with the rhetoric of disease. The theory that "all negroes are not equally black—the blacker, the healthier and stronger;
any deviation from the black color, in the pure race, is a mark of feebleness or ill health," proposed by the southern physician Samuel A.
Cartwright in 1851, provided an easy formula and immediately visible measure of racial health (310). It simultaneously naturalized and
neutralized the volatile sociosexual issue of miscegenation by equat-
ing it with disease. However, the dis-ease with which Haggard's heroes view the racially impure body suggests, more than feebleness,
the potential for physical contagion. In *She*, the cannibalistic Amahagger tribe, whose name and features "indicate a curious mingling
of races" (121), lead the narrator to question: "Of what race could
these people be? Their language was a bastard Arabic, and yet they
were not Arabs; I was quite sure of that. For one thing they were too
dark, or rather yellow. I could not say why, but I know that their appearance filled me with a sick fear of which I felt ashamed" (55).
Here the physiological effects of racial uncertainty are sublimated in
the narrator's body. The need to establish and adhere to rigid racial
classifications constructs Holly's perceptions of and reactions to the

tribe. His inability to define skin color, to determine whether the Amahagger are too dark or too light, too black or too yellow, produces a fissure in the narrative, a moment when rational categories dissolve into an inexplicable "sick fear." For Holly, the realization that pale-skinned natives could be akin to himself provokes a direct, visceral reaction. At this moment his perception of racial difference shifts from the recognition of difference between races to a recognition of difference within. By associating the Amahagger with feelings of "shame," "revulsion," a "sick fear," and a sense of the "uncanny" (55), Holly translates social discomfort with evidence of miscegenation into a more personal and immediate sense of physical disorientation. The lack of racial clarity in the Amahagger challenges his own sense of racial definition, and Holly experiences the contagion of their ambiguity.[30]

Perhaps as a consequence of these racial anxieties, Haggard's African adventure fictions are filled with examples of suitable, indeed physically perfect, matings between white British heroes and white African queens.[31] As if to stabilize the encounter between an eroticized African landscape and the barely sublimated sexual energy of his virile adventurers, as well as the homoerotic tensions evoked through male martial bonding, Haggard's modern Africa is populated with both the ruins and the survivors of ancient civilizations. Strategically positioned in relation to the tribes of black Africans who surround them, these mystical pockets of classicism provide an alternative standard of comparison and a competing vision of African history. Through these civilizations, Haggard appropriates the cultural heritage of Africa in order to celebrate the glory of European history, following a pattern of cultural "caucasianization" that Martin Bernal has outlined in *Black Athena*. Haggard not only rewrites African cultural history, he appropriates the signifying power of black female sexuality for his white heroines. In his fiction white African women play a role just slightly less vital than Zulu warriors in determining and validating white male fitness. In turn, their own fitness is measured against the ideal of classical statuary. Unlike nineteenth-century women, who could only collectively approximate the contours of antiquity, Haggard's heroines are genuine antiques. Ayesha's body, which has been preserved for centuries, is of a rich "imperial shape . . . more perfect than ever sculptor dreamed of" (*She*, 105), and the veil she drapes over her face is modeled on a veiled female statue of Truth in the ancient city of Kor. In *Allan Quatermain*, the twin white Zu-Vendis queens Nylepta and Sorais surpass the beauty of anything the British explorers have ever seen. The direct descendants of an ancient civilization, which Quatermain speculates dates from ancient Babylon, these queens are members of a dynasty that is directly linked to the classical ideal. Founded by "one of the finest sculptors who ever lived" (577), this civilization's highest accomplishment is its statuary and architecture. Much like Ayesha's resemblance to the statue of Truth, the fairer of the sisters, Nylepta, is compared to her ancestor's most famous female statue—an inspiring angel who revealed to the sculptor his greatest architectural vision. In effect, what we find here is a process of comparative measurement that parallels the function of black masculinity in Haggard's novels. It is the classical female body—both as statue and as flesh—against which modern femininity must be measured and to which modern (British) masculinity must be mated. Although this plot is not ultimately fulfilled in *She* (Ayesha identifies Leo Vincy as the reincarnation of her lost lover but is unable to consummate their union), in *Allan Quatermain* Haggard charts the narrative of natural selection to its logical conclusion. Like Ayesha, Nylepta immediately recognizes the modern British explorer as her masculine equivalent and natural mate. By the end of the novel we find Sir Henry Curtis remaining in Africa to become the king-consort of Nylepta, who bears him "a son and heir . . . a regular curly-haired, blue-eyed young Englishman" (670). Thus, at a time when the collective health of British and American womanhood was in a perceived state of deterioration, the location of the ideal female body in Africa provided a means of transferring stereotypes of savage health, stamina, and fertility onto a racially and sexually purified female body.[32] Primitive vigor and classical form are thus merged in the recovery of African history. Through this return to ancient bloodlines, Haggard imaginatively recuperates western civilization from the degeneration of modernity, offering a purified future for the Anglo-Saxon race.[33]

Unlike Haggard, whose portrayals of physical strength function as overt expressions of British imperial destiny, Stoker examines the conflation of health and empire by displacing it onto a foreign invader. Nevertheless, *Dracula* demonstrates many of the same correlations between racial fitness and imperialist aggression that we see in *King Solomon's Mines, Allan Quatermain,* and *She.* Like both Leo Vincy and Ayesha, Dracula is the last surviving member of "a great and noble race"; in his "veins flows the blood of many brave races who fought as the lion fights, for lordship" (*Dracula*, 288, 41). A hereditary representative of imperial domination, he traces his lineage back to Attila the Hun. Furthermore, during his lifetime Dracula was, as his pursuer Van Helsing tells us, a representative of the highest ideals of civilization, a "soldier, statesman, and alchemist. . . . He had a mighty brain, a learning beyond compare, and a heart that knew no fear and no remorse" (359–60). Dracula's perception of his own fitness to rule is thus substantiated by his intellectual development, military prowess, and racial history. Furthermore, Dracula's physical strength, health, and longevity directly correspond to scientific and cultural anxieties about the racially superior body. Leonard Wolf describes Dracula as "our eidolon. . . . He is huge, and we admire size; strong, and we admire strength. He moves with the confidence of a creature that has energy, power and will" (302). Van Helsing notes that Dracula has "the strength in his hand of twenty men" (*Dracula*, 244). But it is the vampire's capacity to reverse the process of aging—to regain health and youth at will—that most impresses and frightens his pursuers because it suggests that the vampire may indeed represent a superior species, a better version of man. During the course of the novel the Count grows steadily younger: in his coffin in Transylvania, Dracula looks "as if his youth had been half-renewed" (67), and by the time he reaches London Dracula "has grown young" (208).

The correlation Stoker draws between the healthy body, racial heritage, and imperial conquest is literalized in Dracula's relationship to his native soil. Dracula derives his strength from the earth of his ancestors, and only by transporting this dirt from Castle Dracula to London is the vampire able to sustain his supernatural powers. His arrival in England is figured as an invasion of British soil by foreign soil, and the success of his attack depends on distributing and protecting his own ancestral earth from counterinvasion.[34] As his pursuers systematically destroy the boxes of mold, they weaken Dracula's body, thereby forcing his retreat to Transylvania. In this direct correlation between body and soil (which resembles, though in a very different fashion, Haggard's corporealizing of the African landscape), Dracula's physical strength is drained in direct proportion to his loss of native ground. By the end of the novel his mobility and vitality are limited to the dimensions of a single container of earth. And in their anxiety quite literally to contain the vampire, Dracula's pursuers express more general anxieties about uncontainability. Like Lucy Snowe's obsessive bottling and boxing, or Gwendolen Harleth's locking of cabinets and chests, Van Helsing, Seward, Morris, and Quincey channel their anxieties about uncontainable forces—racial and sexual otherness, contagion, reproduction, the supernatural—into the contents of Dracula's coffins.

If soil is one extension of Dracula's protean body, women become another. In Stoker's text women function as the determining instruments of imperial expansion. Dracula literalizes the use of the female body as an expression of male generative authority as Dracula's "health" is spread as a disease through women's bodies. The ultimate egoist, Dracula replicates his own body on those he conquers. The vampire thereby appropriates the female function of reproducing the species. Jonathan Harker concedes that "if we find out that Mina must be a vampire in the end, then she shall not go into that unknown and terrible land alone. I suppose it is thus that in old times one vampire meant many . . . love was the recruiting sergeant for their ghastly ranks" (354). Like the mythic power of the Dark Continent, vampirism represents an "unknown and terrible land" whose topography encompasses the darkest recesses of the imagination.[35] But in Stoker's version of imperial fantasy, the Dark Continent—that jungle of primitive, atavistic drives—has become the colonizer.[36] The function of women within the economy of species reproduction is revealed as the tool by which races and empires are expanded; women now form the army's "ranks" and "recruiting sergeant[s]" in the battle for survival. And in this mingling of military and reproductive metaphors, Stoker signals the fluid gender boundaries of the vampire as yet another transgressive force that his pursuers seek to contain. Ultimately, it is the reproductively empowered, racially other male and the intellectually empowered female (as embodied in Ayesha) that constitute the greatest threat to traditional sources of authority and provide the most fearful spectacle of evolution gone astray.

It is not only the fact of Dracula's reproductivity but also its form that indicates the vampire's invasive potential. The exchange of bodily fluids that constitutes the vampire's reproductive process is also an act of nutritional aggression, exploring how the body ingests the world and how that process defines its relation to a natural world order. For Stoker, the ideology of fitness and the achievement of empire are predicated on the notion that there is a direct correspondence between what we eat and who we are. The act of feeding not only maintains the body's health but perpetuates power through the act of consumption and assimilation. In *Dracula*, consumption functions as a metaphor for imperial expansion. As Dracula drinks his way through the British population, his victims' bodies exhibit the symptoms of consumption because they are, quite literally, being consumed. Their blood is assimilated into the vampire, whose appetite is as excessive as his health and who can colonize and reproduce in a single alimentary gesture.

This nutritional economy of *Dracula* runs parallel to a theory of nutrition articulated (though not exclusively) by Beard, which extended paradigms of evolutionary development to the very food a person consumed. Pointing to the fact that primitive peoples frequently subsisted on a diet of rice or grains, Beard argued that in order to support their greater nervous development, civilized men *"should diminish the quantity of cereals and fruits, which are far below him on the scale of evolution, and increase the quantity of animal food, which is nearly related to him in the scale of evolution, and therefore more easily assimilated"* (*Sexual Neurasthenia*, 258; Beard's emphasis). Ultimately, this constituted more than just nutritional and health advice, for Beard extended his theory to make judgments about the evolutionary developments of foreign cultures. Beard claimed that "savages," by subsisting on roots, berries, and grains, were "much nearer to the forms of life from which they feed" (262), although he refrained from recommending one of the logical implications of this argument—that cannibalism might constitute the highest proof of evolutionary superiority.

This is, of course, the premise entertained by Stoker's novel, and we can see Beard's influence in the lunatic Renfield's desire "to absorb as many lives as he can" (90)—from the lowest flies, to spiders that eat flies, to birds that eat spiders that eat flies, and so on in a kind of phylogenetic fantasy of cumulative life. This nutritional hierarchy makes him recognize the vampire as the "master" carnivore, feeding on the essential component of the highest form of life—human blood. Renfield systematically climbs up the food chain through the lives he consumes, defining his zoological ranking by sheer numbers of lives each species feeds upon for its survival and asserting that this system "was very good and very wholesome; that it was life, strong life, and gave life to him" (88). Ultimately, by absorbing and digesting so many lives, Renfield believes he can perpetuate his own life beyond its normal course. And although these convictions lead to his diagnosis and incarceration as a "zoophagus (life-eating) maniac" (90), his theory is validated in Stoker's text through the vampire's own sanguinary longevity. Van Helsing notes that the vampire's "vital faculties grow strenuous, and seem as though they refresh themselves when his special pabulum is plenty. But he cannot flourish without this diet; he eat not as others" (286).[37] Ultimately, Renfield's correlation between longevity and the food chain reproduces Beard's correlation between diet and evolution in nightmare form. Stoker thus extends Beard's theory to its logical conclusion—that the consumption of human life constitutes the highest proof of evolutionary progress.

The link between nutritional aggression and evolutionary fitness was assimilated into health advice manuals and educational textbooks, thereby helping to shape popular conceptions of culture and race. Pye Henry Chavasse urged mothers to feed their sons meat daily in order for them to be "healthy, strong, and courageous," because " 'all courageous animals are carnivorous, and greater courage is to be expected in a people, such as the English, whose food is strong and hearty, than in the half-starved commonality of other countries' " (287). The nutritional inferiority of other countries was described in more detail in school textbooks both before and after the influence of Darwin. An early-nineteenth-century history book that was used at least through mid-century described the Hindus as "an innocent race of men, whose only food is rice, and who are maintained for three half pence a day per man" (quoted in Chancellor, 122). In a later, particularly severe textbook co-authored by C. R. L. Fletcher and Rudyard Kipling, black West Indians were described as "lazy, vicious and incapable of serious improvement, or of work except under compulsion. In such a climate a few bananas will sustain the life of a negro quite sufficiently" (240). The transmission of an imperialist nutritional theory from medical literature to grammar school textbooks indicates one way in which narratives of health and fitness came to have a widespread cultural influence. Popular fiction provided an alternative route of transmission. In linking the attainment of perfect health to practical questions of diet—however fantastically—Stoker demonstrated Beard's nutritional dictum: "If we know what a nation eats, we know what a nation is or may become" (*Sexual Neurasthenia*, 268).

The correlation between ingestion and identity takes a different form in *She*, where Haggard juxtaposes the specter of African cannibalism with Ayesha's carefully prepared vegetarian diet. Drawing upon a competing nutritional theory, Haggard associates the refinement of Ayesha's physical and intellectual powers with her alimentary asceticism. A number of nineteenth-century health reformers advocated natural grains and vegetarianism as a means of curbing sexual license and masturbation, believing that the consumption of meat fostered primitive animal drives. Invoking a widespread correlation between rich, meaty foods and male sexual appetite, they concluded that eating cereals and grains could promote the health and advancement of civilization by substituting intellectual for sexual energy.[38] Haggard seems to embrace this argument in outlining the dietary requirements for Ayesha's longevity. Espousing the rhetoric of homeopathy and vegetarianism, Ayesha calls attention to her eating habits and their life-preserving qualities: "Behold my food. . . . Naught but fruit doth ever pass my lips—fruit and cakes of flour, and a little water" (104). An earthly replica of nectar and ambrosia, Ayesha's diet prolongs her life, as if by eating like a goddess she can become one. For Ayesha, food is a form of living embalmment, a means of cleansing and perpetuating the body as shrine. It is not accidental that Ayesha's palace is located in the burial chambers of an ancient civilization, where the embalming room and the eating room are one. Ayesha's nutritional asceticism marks her physical and intellectual superiority. More important, it distances her from the passionate energy of the Amahagger tribe she rules, who "place pots upon the heads of strangers" (22) and thereby demonstrate their nutritional and moral barbarity. By linking the attainment of perfect health to practical questions of diet, both Stoker and Haggard suggest the extent to which nutritional theories (albeit competing ones) had entered the popular imagination as signs of both moral behavior and racial identity.

Of all Haggard's fictions, *She* reveals the most ambivalence about both science and imperialism, an ambivalence that results in what seem to be textual contradictions. For example, despite the physiological imperative that seems to necessitate Ayesha's mating with Leo Vincy, we are told that their romance constitutes a challenge to evolutionary theory, an unexpected twist in Darwin's plot. In Haggard's introduction, the editorial persona claims that the story he is about to present to us provides a surprising conclusion to the drama of natural selection. He claims that Ayesha's intellectual superiority should have led her to choose the ugly, but intellectually gifted, Horace Holly over the handsome, but intellectually shallow, Leo Vincy for her perfect mate. He further notes:

There appears to be nothing in the character of Leo Vincy which . . . would have been likely to attract an intellect so powerful as that of Ayesha. . . . Indeed we might imagine that Mr. Holly would under ordinary circumstances have easily outstripped him in the favor of She. Can it be that extremes meet, and that the very excess and splendour of her mind led her by means of some strange physical reaction to worship at the shrine of matter? (6)

Through this opening speculation, Haggard addresses one of the central controversies of social Darwinism, questioning whether it is the healthy body or the active brain that constitutes the real measure of fitness. Do we conclude from Ayesha's choice that the superior body is destined to triumph over the superior mind? This is, in effect, the conclusion we are asked to reach in most of Haggard's fiction, but *She* is the text that most actively questions Haggard's own tendency "to worship at the shrine of matter" and to valorize physical health as a sign of imperial destiny. Haggard's narrator and philosopher, Holly, is an evolutionary throwback, "Short, thick-set, and deep-chested almost to deformity, with long, sinewy arms, heavy features, deep-set grey eyes, a low brow half overgrown with a mop of thick black hair." His features correspond almost exactly to Lombroso's catalogue of criminal atavism. Holly claims, "Only a week before I had heard one [woman] call me a 'monster' . . . and say I had converted her to the monkey theory" (7). Holly's simian physique and well-developed intellect are contrasted with his ward Leo's "tall, athletic form and clear-cut Grecian face" (57). But Leo, despite his careful tutoring and command of languages, exhibits no particular mental gifts. We are thus faced with an interpretive dilemma: How do we read the text of Holly's body? What is the significance of this apparent disjunction between body and brain? Haggard does not provide an answer, but the very terms of the question framed by the text suggest the cultural anxiety that surrounded fitness as a category of cultural definition. Here, as in so many fictions of health and disease, we can see Haggard working out questions of scientific and medical theory on the symbolic terrain of the human body. In this, Haggard resembles those physicians who were so carefully measuring the body's dimensions and grappling with the evolutionary implications of health and disease, for Haggard is similarly unable to find a fully coherent solution to the dilemma he proposes.

The confusion Haggard reveals about the implications of evolutionary theory becomes a source of anxiety by the end of the text, an anxiety that is played out upon the female body. Ayesha functions as both physician and scientist in *She*; her medicine miraculously brings Leo back from the brink of death, and her breeding experiments test the limits of nature. But the use to which science is put in Ayesha's empire ultimately demonstrates the dangerous implications of absolute power. Her systematic pursuit of eugenics, much like the experiments of Wells's Dr. Moreau, demonstrates the consequences of tampering with the course of evolution. Ayesha claims she has manipulated natural selection so as to breed a race of deaf-mutes whose bodies conform to her precise physical and aesthetic needs, and whose lives are dedicated to the perpetuation of her authority.

She claims of these slaves: "I bred them so—it hath taken many centuries and much trouble; but at last I triumphed. Once I succeeded before, but the race was too ugly, so I let it die away; but now, as thou seest, they are otherwise" (104). Within Haggard's moral universe, Ayesha demonstrates that the subordination of scientific knowledge to imperial authority does not necessarily lead, as the biological programs of Victorian eugenicists would have their audience believe, to the elimination of inferior races and the careful breeding of superior ones; rather, it contributes to the perpetuation of inferiority as an economic and political tool. Ayesha reserves the privilege of a perfect health like her own for the ruling elite, condemning her slaves to political and corporeal domination by manipulating the course of their evolution.[39]

Whether discussing her scientific experiments, her harsh punishments of the Amahagger, or her plans for imperialist expansion, Ayesha justifies her actions in the rhetoric of social Darwinism. She asks Holly, "Is it, then, a crime, oh foolish man, to put away that which stands between us and our ends? Then is our life one long crime, my Holly; for day by day we destroy that we may live, since in this world none save the strongest can endure" (136). Declaring herself a moral criminal, Ayesha refuses to be ruled by any laws other than nature's. Like Marlowe's recognition that "the conquest of the earth, which mostly means the taking it away from those who have a different complexion or slightly flatter noses than ourselves, is not a pretty thing when you look into it too much" (Conrad, 10), Ayesha's declaration accepts the inevitability of domination.

The correlations between scientific discourse and imperialist practice are even more fully developed in *Dracula*, but in Stoker's text science prevails over the forces of nature. From almost the beginning of *Dracula* we are presented with a scientific community that works together to combat the vampire by studying his symptoms, developing hypotheses, diagnosing his "disease," and effecting a cure. Two of Stoker's central characters are specialists in neurology and psychology, and their attempts to study the vampire take place either within or near a private lunatic asylum. Stoker emphasizes his doctors' scientific authority through their familiarity with and incorporation of contemporary research. In the course of his discussions of medical and psychological theory, Dr. Van Helsing refers to Charcot, Nordau, and Lombroso, outlining their theories and applying them to the pursuit of vampires. Consulted in Lucy Westenra's case because of his expertise in "obscure diseases" and his European reputation, Van Helsing represents the various continental schools whose research wielded considerable influence in the latter decades of the nineteenth century. In addition to his medical knowledge, Van Helsing is a "philosopher and a metaphysician" (137) who advocates a link between scientific inquiry and spiritualism:

"I suppose now you do not believe in corporeal transference. No? Nor in materialization. No? Nor in astral bodies? No? Nor in the reading of thought. No? Nor in hypnotism—"

"Yes," I said, "Charcot has proved that pretty well." . . .

"Then tell me—for I am student of the brain—how you accept the hypnotism and reject the thought-reading. Let me tell you, my friend, that there are things done to-day in electrical science which would have been deemed unholy by the very men who discovered electricity—who would themselves not so long before have been burned as wizards. There are always mysteries in life." (229–30)

Van Helsing proposes a hypothesis to explain the scientific basis for the existence of vampires, and other instances of abnormal longevity, that echoes Haggard's explanation of Ayesha's immortality in *She*:

The very place where he have been alive, Un-Dead for all these centuries, is full of strangeness of the geologic and chemical world. There are deep caverns and fissures that reach none know whither. There have been volcanoes, some of whose openings still send out waters of strange properties, and gases that kill or make to vivify. Doubtless, there is something magnetic or electric in some of these combinations of occult forces which work for physical life in strange way. (380)

Van Helsing's forays into the mysteries of nature reflect the imaginative energy with which the medical and scientific communities approached the subjects of mind and body, health and disease, as well as the interest they generated in the culture at large. A kind of medical Dark Continent, the human body and brain seemed to offer boundless territory for exploration, a physiological empire to be conquered by the boldest scientific minds. And while Van Helsing's arguments never fully explain the phenomenon of vampires, they reveal Stoker's serious attempt to reconcile the scientific and gothic elements of his text.

Science is also crucial to the pursuit of the vampire, for despite Dracula's racial and intellectual ascendancy in life, Stoker portrays the undead Dracula as an evolutionary throwback, a version of Lombroso's born criminal.[40] This contradiction is convenient for Stoker because it allows him to stress the correlation between Dracula's racial superiority and his imperial project, while providing an explanation for his final defeat. Van Helsing explains that the superior brain of the historic Count Dracula survived only partially after death, leaving the undead vampire, like the born criminal, with a "child-brain." He claims: "In some faculties of mind he has been, and is, only a child; but he is growing, and some things that were childish at the first are now of man's stature" (360). Van Helsing explicitly applies Lombroso's theories to Dracula, claiming:

There is this peculiarity in criminals. It is so constant, in all countries and at all times. . . . The criminal always work at one crime—that is the true criminal who seems predestinate to crime, and who will of none other. This criminal has not full man-brain. . . . The Count is a criminal and of criminal type. Nordau and Lombroso would so classify him, and *qua* criminal he is of imperfectly formed mind. (405–6)

On the basis of this diagnosis, Van Helsing predicts their ultimate victory. He asserts that "our man-brains . . . will come higher than his child-brain . . . that do only work selfish and therefore small" (404). In this way, Van Helsing believes they can defeat the vampire's superior physical strength. However, we can see in Van Helsing's explanation some of the same rationalizations that we observed in Lombroso's discussion of criminals. In each case, the evolutionary status of health is called into question. Just as diagnoses of criminal imbecility counteracted the effects of perceived physical strength, fecundity, or longevity, Van Helsing's diagnosis of Dracula's "child-brain" counteracts the effect of the vampire's superior power, health, and reproductive energy. In both of these formulas, the first set of myths allows the second set of myths to stand intact, thereby reassuring the dominant culture of its evolutionary fitness. Dracula's health thus reveals the vulnerability of Victorian racial theory, for it is only by diagnosing the count as a born criminal of inferior intellect that Van Helsing can oppose the threat raised by the vampire's superior fitness and avoid concluding that he is, indeed, "the better man."

In the final pages of *She* and *Dracula*, Haggard and Stoker retreat from the evolutionary imperatives they have constructed, manipulating and reversing the logical conclusion to Darwin's plot: Ayesha does not go on to fulfill her imperial destiny but shrivels into a "hideous little monkey frame" (*She*, 237) and dies ignominiously; Dracula is defeated by men of inferior physical power, whose cure for the "disease" of vampirism consists of returning and disintegrating Dracula's body into the dust of his homeland. Ultimately, Haggard and Stoker can no more face the consequences of their creations than Victor Frankenstein can his monster. They cannot sustain the spectacle of a superior species in the process of achieving world domination. Thus, by reasserting the primacy of physical vulnerability—subjecting their titular characters to degeneration and decay—Haggard and Stoker repair the imaginative violence effected by their fictions of absolute health.[41]

Nevertheless, Haggard's and Stoker's endings suggest more than the need for happy resolutions to gothic fantasies. The fact that neither Ayesha nor Dracula is able to translate superior health into the conquest of an empire seems to challenge the political and ideological imperatives of Victorian fitness programs and health reforms. The healthy body is not, by the end of these texts, a simple analog of world hegemony; rather, it reflects the problematic status of mind and body in Victorian medical discourse. Ayesha and Dracula combine the attributes of intellectual superiority and criminal degeneracy; they are both geniuses and psychopaths. Having attained perfect physical health, they are seemingly invulnerable; yet their bodies are also profoundly abnormal. They are racial and biological anomalies, and as such they invoke the spectacle of difference—the threat of otherness. This threat is only partially resolved by the endings of *Dracula* and *She*. Like those scientists who reassured themselves and their audiences that regardless of longevity or fecundity, resistance to pain or disease, degenerate populations would pose no threat to the continued predominance of the social and biological norm, Stoker and Haggard never fully resolve the physiological implications of their fictions. Are Dracula and Ayesha prototypes of an advanced species, or are they subhuman specters of a criminal past? Does their health constitute a successful evolutionary adaptation or a sign of moral atavism? Each text poses these questions but fails to answer them, exposing the ideological fissures that marked questions of health and disease.

Ultimately, *Dracula* and *She* reveal that all empires are, like Ayesha's, "empire[s] . . . of the imagination" (*She*, 118) insofar as they are built upon and perpetuate cultural myths. Despite the imaginative energy they expend on health, neither Haggard nor Stoker provides a sustained critique of scientific theory or imperialist practice. Both are deeply invested in the ideologies they sometimes appear to challenge. Whereas Meredith demonstrates the extent to which English domestic culture was built upon a system of imperialist values, sustained by an imperialist economy, and preoccupied with hollow ideals of fitness, Haggard and Stoker never fully confront the imperialist assumptions that their culture, and their fictions, depend upon. While demonstrating many of the troublesome implications of social Darwinism, Stoker's use of science legitimizes more than it attacks, and Haggard's critique of evolution and eugenics is belied by his continued idealizations of British bodies and African adventures. The implicit contradictions in these texts suggest that their authors, like the culture in which they lived, were deeply divided about the politics of empire and the morality of science. Ultimately, the opposition they propose is not between imperialism and anti-imperialism but between different forms and uses of imperialism. Like Conrad's *Heart of Darkness*, the politics of which has long baffled critics because of its ability to be, at once, an exposé of imperialist evils, an apology for imperialist ideals, and a repository of racist stereotypes, *Dracula* and *She* are unclear about the implications of either health or empire.[42] Haggard and Stoker recuperate imperialist ideology while subverting it, sustaining their faith in the British Empire (rather like Marlowe's continued faith in the red sections of the African map), while nevertheless questioning its biological right to power. The very popularity of their fictions, like Wells's *War of the Worlds*, suggests that Haggard and Stoker articulated a widespread concern about comparative fitness and modern capacities for survival. By allowing the human body to triumph over the violence of supernatural immunity, their narratives imaginatively reshape a threatened social body. And in much the same ways that Victorian anthropometry provided a collective and comparative vision of the national health, popular fictions like Haggard's and Stoker's enacted a confrontation between the contemporary social body and the legacies of both primitive and classical history. Africa and Transylvania become the testing grounds for evolutionary superiority, providing cross-cultural and transhistorical opportunities for measuring the fitness of Lord Rosebury's declining "imperial race."

Ultimately, by locating the source of racial and national identity in the health of the body, by measuring its dimensions and charting its norms, Victorian scientists, physicians, anthropologists, politicians, and educators transformed health into a form of national spectacle, thereby displacing issues of political and economic policy onto more immediate questions of physiology. As a validation of both self and social identity, the spectacle of national health seemed to demand increasingly wider geographical horizons and a progressively larger world audience. Imperialist aggression thus became a means of demonstrating the essential fitness of dominant cultures at a time when that fitness seemed most in question. And insofar as imperialism enacted the drama of racial and cultural superiority on the bodies of its foreign subjects, those subjects were subsumed into the signifying systems of their conquerors. The rhetorics of racial difference, evolutionary fitness, and physical health thus became the rhetoric of empire, and imperial expansion became not just an economic, but a biological imperative. By devoting so much attention to the meaning of the body—by tracing its dimensions and defining its norms, assessing its health and categorizing its diseases, measuring its pain and predicting its degeneration—Victorian science helped to define the body as a hermeneutic category signifying cultural and racial destiny. At the same time, Victorian science had produced so many accounts of the body's meaning that moral and ideological distinctions between sickness and health became less and less clear. Thus, by the end of the nineteenth century we see fictions of health that signify moral disease and fictions of disease that challenge cultural norms. This sense of moral and biological relativism extends into the twentieth century, when sickness becomes one of the prevailing metaphors for modernism. From the illness that is both a product and a symbol of Kurtz's visionary imperialism in *Heart of Darkness* to the assertions of health that signal the narrator's neurosis in Ford Maddox Ford's *The Good Soldier*; from the cultural disease that afflicts the residents of T. S. Eliot's *The Wasteland* to the real and philosophical diseases that populate Thomas Mann's *Magic Mountain*; from the shell shock that intrudes upon the world of Virginia Woolf's *Mrs. Dalloway* to the bubonic plague that is assimilated into the routine of daily existence in Albert Camus's *The Plague*, modernist fiction takes disease as emblematic of the modern condition. Shaped by a view of the body as a space for individual and cultural definition, and by a rhetoric of illness that was codified in Victorian medicine and literature, these texts confront the spectacle of disease after its moment of explosion into popular consciousness. They examine, in effect, the scattered remains of Krook's spontaneous combustion.

Conclusion

In charting the historical meanings and ideological functions of illness as an imaginative construct, it has been a central concern of this book to demonstrate first, the process through which Victorian culture tended to manage diffuse and chaotic social issues by displacing them onto more immediate matters of physiology, and second, how this displacement resulted not in the stabilizing of social tensions but rather in a destabilizing of the perceived boundaries of human embodiment, through fears of psychic and somatic permeability, sympathetic identification with another's pain, or conflicting measures of racial and cultural fitness. For example, when we examine medical attempts to explain disturbingly intense spiritual experiences by redefining them as products of nervous illness, we find not the successful management of religious enthusiasm but rather the conceptual collapse of spirituality and nervousness in Victorian culture. This twin gesture of management and collapse appears both within and between medical and literary narratives. In appropriating and reframing the ideas, languages, or narratives produced by other disciplines, literary texts routinely dismantle the very paradigms they employ to legitimate their aims. These discursive conjunctions and disruptions, in turn, helped to shape and express the unruly social imaginary of the Victorian middle classes.

The methodology I have employed—overlapping readings of cultural, medical, and literary narratives—reveals the symbolic density that characterized illness, and particularly psychosomatic illness, in the nineteenth century. It is through this kind of interdisciplinary and intertextual analysis that we can best understand the complexity of cultural processes: that is, structures of belief, patterns of perception, ideological tensions, consistencies, and contradictions. When we look at narrative production across disciplines, what emerges is not so much a sense of underlying uniformity, either formal or ideological, as the capacity of imaginative practices to negotiate conflicting tensions in the cultural field. For example, when studied in the wider context of Victorian cultural history, a concept such as contagion could provide an explanatory model for competing social concerns. Contagion signified not only the passage of disease between bodies but also the transmission of ideas, impressions, feelings, and influences between minds; it could reveal the dangers of class contiguity or interracial contact and chart the powerful relationship between vision and pain. It was used to express anxieties about theatrical spectacle, medical objectivity, and the gendering of sympathy, as well as to explore complex interactive relationships between readers and texts.

The ubiquity of contagion as a master narrative in Victorian culture can be attributed to its conceptual fluidity and its capacity to express and embody ideological conflicts, investing them with the imaginative immediacy of physical threat. However, the process through which such narratives develop relies not so much on an author's directly addressing issues from another discipline as it does on cross-fertilizations of ideas and overlapping ways of thinking about problems of individual and social embodiment. That is, while there are clearly moments in which an author takes up a prominent medical or scientific subject (du Maurier's representation of hypnosis; Meredith's application of evolutionary theory; Stoker's invocation of the "born criminal"), there are many more instances in which contested psychosomatic categories move between disciplinary boundaries through shared acts of imagining. Thus when we look at the interpretation of "natural" languages or the consequences of affective excess, the spiritual ambiguity of nervousness or the politics of comparative health, what we find are not merely instances of parallel rhetoric, but interactive patterns of thought that signal points of conceptual blockage, social transformation, or cultural obsession. Somatic fictions are not the unified products of a coherent cultural logic; rather, they are emblematic of the promiscuous interaction and semiotic drift of cultural forms.

This indeterminacy in the cultural field has, of course, a destabilizing effect on how individual subjects imagine themselves. The process of narrative production takes place both singly and collectively, marking a site of overlap between self- and social definition. The stories we tell of ourselves help to shape the stories we tell of our society, and the stories we receive from our culture become internalized (though not necessarily intact or unedited) as narratives about the self. What I have identified as Victorian cultural narratives about sickness and health were not produced according to a monolithic conception of gender, power, or embodiment, nor were they received and processed uniformly. Insofar as they performed what Mary Poovey has called "ideological work," that work did not always adopt a consistent form or produce consistent results. The role that gender played in discussions of neuromimetic sympathies, for example, while validating arguments opposing female physicians, was also reappropriated (however unevenly) in the service of women's medical education. And while Victorian doctors and critics generally derided the overidentified female reader, her neuromimetic sympathies could provide Harriet Beecher Stowe with a model of a powerful feminine hermeneutic or offer Henry James a strategy for (and theory of) critical cross-dressing. This capacity of somatic fictions to multiply and transform, as well as to repeat themselves obsessively, collapses the very distinctions they seem to assert and makes them apt models for understanding the indirect routes of cultural and narrative transmission as well as subject formation. This flexible system of representational practices and experiences is characteristic of the workings of ideology in the modern period. The very plasticity of somatic fictions reveals wider cultural patterns in which conflict and accommodation exist in a dynamic relation to each other. The contradictions I have discussed are not inherently disruptive or consistent signs of cultural instability. They have the capacity to challenge as well as to secure dominant cultural values, often in the same representational gesture.[1]

My focus on the plural and often conflicting ideological functions of somatic fictions runs the risk, of course, of reducing cultural practices exclusively to the sphere of the imaginary. By only tangentially examining the question of disease's material consequences, this emphasis weights my study toward the representational power of illness. Only fleetingly, in the voices of Louisa May Alcott's wounded soldiers or in Alice James's descriptions of pain, have we heard the accounts of suffering patients. This omission is not meant to imply that such accounts are either unavailable or unimportant for historical study; in fact, many Victorians wrote compellingly about their personal experiences of illness, using a variety of genres. My point, rather, is that the process of *imagining* illness (or health) took on its own peculiar resonance for Victorian culture. And although psychosomatic illness provided the central instance of such imagining, this does not necessarily mean that the Victorian middle classes were hypochondriacs or valetudinarians. The pervasive representations of illness and health in nineteenth-century literature denoted an equally important area of imaginative production. That is, envisioning illness in one's own body and reading or writing about illness in another's became parallel forms of self-projection. The idealized nurse who interprets her patient's physical and emotional feelings and learns to ventriloquize them participates in an economy of illness and imagination that seeks to translate and alleviate the subjective experience of another's physical suffering by projecting it into one's own receptive consciousness. This transference could grant an oblique form of authority to the careful interpreter of pain, an authority distinguished from, though not unconnected to, that held by doctors. We see variations of this self-authorizing process when Lucy Snowe gains narrative authority by accurately imagining the neurotic pain of others through the medium of her own illness, or when the slaves of *Uncle Tom's Cabin* imagine Eva's pain, which is, in turn, a sustained imaginative projection of their own suffering. In each of these cases, the management of another's distress necessitates the collapse of intersubjective boundaries, in a process that indirectly legitimates the sympathetic interpreter.

We find a quite different model of imagining illness, one that displays far more ambivalence about the self-transformative potential of shared suffering, in the practice of the Victorian doctor. The anxiety many doctors felt about maintaining a critical distance from their patients' symptoms in order to prevent their own imaginative contagion can be seen as an exaggerated psychosomatic parallel of the daily process of imagining illness that every physician undertakes when theorizing internal bodily processes, translating symptoms into diagnoses, or making a scientific breakthrough in reconceptualizing a disease. In a society that was self-conscious about the breakdown of gender roles and the feminization of illness, the physician's acts of imaginative projection were subject to a process of self-scrutiny intended to reinforce the boundaries between doctor and patient, masculine and feminine, at the very moment of envisioning their collapse. Thus, to adopt the position of the effective physician meant to recognize the transmissive potential, and curtail the somatic consequences, of one's own self-dividing sympathies.

In this economy of self and other, body and mind, imagining health could be as compelling (or dangerous) as imagining illness, for each involved the transformation of psychic activity into somatic meaning. We have seen how the cultural significance of health became so pathologized by its association with non-European races and the criminal classes that it sometimes functioned as a sign of social disorder. When Stoker and Haggard envision the uncanny health of Dracula and Ayesha as a challenge to British national fitness and a threat to imperial dominance, they participate in a process of cultural imagining similar to more traditional fictions of illness. The symbolic relationship between body and text that allows Lucy Snowe and Gwendolen Harleth to reconceptualize their nervous illnesses as narratives is structurally reproduced in the attempts by Stoker and Haggard to contain and reshape a perceived threat to Britain's national physique through encounters with the supernatural fitness of a criminalized vampire or an immortal African queen. The obsessive interest in the measurement, comparison, and differentiation of bodies that appears in both Victorian science and popular fiction provided a means of imagining the trajectory of reproduction, racial development, and evolutionary progress (or decline), thereby enlarging the symbolic dimensions of human anatomy into a prediction of future survival.

The structures through which Victorian culture imagined illness and health, as the above instances suggest, provided a means of transforming bodies into narratives. Those same narratives, in turn, instructed many Victorians (and perhaps us) in methods of close reading. Narrative theory has maintained that stories project their own relationship to an implied reader, creating and identifying the position(s) from which they are to be viewed. As we have seen, these positions were routinely and at times transgressively gendered in nineteenth-century fiction and culture, suggesting that the operative categories of self-definition were not necessarily as stable as the Victorian rhetoric of sexual difference would imply. The models of somatic legibility and illegibility that the preceding chapters have examined presume that reading is a performative process of gender identification. This is most obvious in the protean narrative alliances established in Eliot and James, but we find it as well in the many cultural narratives that sought to link gender, illness, and interpretation. When Gabriel Tarde identifies popular fiction as a managed form of moral contagion, providing protohysterical women with a communal experience that prevents more dangerous congregations and further epidemics, he invokes the same assumptions about mental and physical permeability as did doctors and critics who argued *against* popular fiction because of its pathological effects on suggestible, usually female, readers. Similarly, Alcott's meditation on the different ways in which doctors and nurses read wounded bodies makes distinctions about gender and professionalism that echo those Weir Mitchell or William Osler assert when they argue for the necessary emotional distance of the successful doctor and the dangers of a feminizing sensibility. The structural similarities in these often opposing arguments suggest a common framework of belief about the imbrication of reading, writing, and illness. Yet even the most essentializing correlations between masculinity and objectivity, or femininity and overidentification, posited a world in which those positions were in imminent danger of collapse. This structural instability, whether ideologically embraced or deplored, informed Victorian conceptions of reading and associated it (however unevenly) with the transmissibility of disease.

Ultimately, the preoccupation of Victorian writers with illness epitomizes the ways that narratives of embodiment complicated, more than clarified, the issues they were invoked to resolve. Illness became a powerful symbol of cultural discord because of its ability to relocate the abstractions of social disorder onto a narrative of physical distress, thereby demanding explanation, diagnosis, and cure. To imagine a healthy social body was to complete this process of self-transformation, but such a transformation involved understanding what constituted health. And defining the meaning of health proved as conceptually slippery as defining nervous disease or moral contagion. Victorian culture was left, then, attempting to tell coherent stories about itself, to manage its anxieties, and to define its place in the modern world. The various and overlapping narratives of illness, as William Osler seemed to caution in his invocation of Scheherazade, could distract and displace, even as they sought to explain the mind, the body, and the world.

REFERENCE MATTER

Notes

Introduction

1. Foucault discusses the function of discursive restriction as a form of controlled incitement in *The History of Sexuality*. Susan Sontag's pioneering study *Illness as Metaphor* and her more recent *AIDS and Its Metaphors* offer analyses of what happens when illness enters into language. Sontag has identified how the use of illness as a cultural and literary metaphor has perpetuated debilitating social stereotypes that condition our attitudes toward the sick. She demonstrates how the idea that individual human behavior, character, and morality influence the body's health has been used to mystify the workings of disease. Sontag's gesture of protest, which was directed primarily at stereotypes of tuberculosis in the nineteenth century and cancer in the twentieth, has become particularly resonant in the face of AIDS and the myths that surround it, as *AIDS and Its Metaphors* testifies. Yet Sontag's assumptions about the workings of metaphor and its relationship to illness oversimplify the process through which the body enters into language. Her project of separating the reality of disease from its various figurations tends to produce rigid categories of good and bad metaphors (or mythicized and demythicized diseases) that seek to counteract the inevitable role that language plays in shaping and transforming physical experience.

2. For a discussion of recent theories of cultural history see Lynn Hunt's *New Cultural History*.

3. Helena Michie's *Flesh Made Word* discusses the relationship between illness, language, and the construction of female identity in Victorian literature. In her opening chapter on anorexia, Michie argues that heroines' bodies conform to the anorectic ideal of Victorian womanhood, denied the ap-

petite for food because of its association with forbidden sexual appetite and original sin. In her more recent article on *Bleak House* and *Our Mutual Friend*, Michie reads pain as a privileged channel for the construction of female subjectivity.

4. My interest in the nineteenth-century understandings of body and mind as ways of structuring identity has been influenced by Cameron's studies of bodily allegories in Hawthorne and Melville as methods of identic definition and violation.

5. In charting the historical permutations of psychosomatic illnesses, medical historian Edward Shorter has noted the power of cultural narratives and beliefs about illness to affect how individuals experience symptoms. Shorter uses the concept of a "symptom pool" to explain the process through which a given culture provides "templates, or models, of illness." Both collective and constantly changing, these models constitute the possible ways of interpreting physical experience at a given moment in history (*Paralysis to Fatigue*, 2–3). Shorter sees the symptom pool as relatively stable in the case of organic diseases and relatively unstable in the case of psychosomatic ones. Where I differ with Shorter is in locating the sources of symptom pools and the trajectory of their influence. Although he claims that a culture shapes its own symptom pool, Shorter emphasizes the role of the doctor as, in most cases, the primary agent of this cultural shaping. Doctors, Shorter argues, create a patient's experience of psychosomatic symptoms through suggestion and improper diagnostic technique. Charcot's shaping of hysterical symptoms through hypnosis provides an example of this process at work. Although I agree with Shorter that the doctor may constitute an avenue of transmission to the individual patient, I am interested in the interaction between medical paradigms and other cultural influences such as literature, religion, evolutionary theory, and popular advice manuals in producing cultural narratives about illness.

6. Jameson argues that both literary and nonliterary narratives constitute cultural artifacts; they can be read as socially symbolic acts in response to particular historical dilemmas (*The Political Unconscious*, chapter 1). Peter Brooks also has discussed the function of narrative in the nineteenth century in terms that are useful for my analysis. Brooks speculates that "the enormous narrative production of the nineteenth century may suggest an anxiety at the loss of providential plots: the plotting of the individual or social or institutional life story takes on new urgency when one no longer can look to a sacred masterplot that organizes and explains the world" (6). In anthropological terms, Victor Turner's analysis of narrative has seen it as a "metagenre . . . a universal cultural activity, embedded in the very center of the social drama," with the capacity to "motivate human conduct into situational structures of 'meaning' " (163). See also Hayden White's *Metahistory*.

7. Foucault has noted the careful shaping and surveillance of disciplinary boundaries, particularly in the medical sciences, during this period. Following these lines, much recent criticism of nineteenth-century literature and culture has emphasized forms of self- and social policing (*History of Sexuality*, 17, 18, 44).

8. Much recent scholarship by medical and cultural historians has dealt with the history of the human body. The journal *Representations* has devoted at least two full volumes and numerous related articles to the subject over the past few years, and the three-volume *Zone* series, *Fragments for a History of the Human Body*, covers an extensive, if necessarily incomplete, range of cultural and corporeal histories. In addition to Laqueur, Schiebinger, and Jordanova, critics and historians such as Elaine Scarry, Catherine Gallagher, Peter Stallybrass and Allon White, D. A. Miller, Mary Poovey, Sander Gilman, and most recently Barbara Maria Stafford and Peter Brooks have theorized problems of embodiment and provided wide-ranging and extremely important cultural analyses. In addition to her tremendously influential *Body in Pain*, Elaine Scarry's edited collection *Literature and the Body* has provided a theoretical model for conceiving the relationship between language and the material world (xi). The essays collected in Jacobus, Keller, and Shuttleworth's *Body/Politics: Women and the Discourses of Science* have further theorized the importance of interpreting gender in the context of scientific paradigms.

9. See Ruth Richardson's discussion of the 1832 Anatomy Act, which authorized the use of the unclaimed corpses of the poor for medical dissection, thereby incorporating dissection as a punishment for poverty (145).

10. The physician Axel Munthe describes Charcot's performances as "a hopeless muddle of truth and cheating" (302) that nevertheless fascinated him enough to attend for years. In his semi-autobiographical narrative, *The Story of San Michele*, Munthe describes how he carried out his own experiments in posthypnotic suggestion and telepathy on a Salpêtrière patient, though he subscribed to Bernheim's and the Nancy school's theories about hypnosis, not to Charcot's. For an excellent discussion of competing French theories of hypnosis, see Ruth Harris, *Murders and Madness*, chapter 5. See also Drinka, 88.

11. In *The Politics and Poetics of Transgression*, Stallybrass and White trace the images and symbols of traditional European carnival practices through the symptoms of bourgeois hysteria in the late nineteenth century. They demonstrate how "Freud's patients can be seen as enacting desperate ritual fragments salvaged from a festive tradition, *the self-exclusion from which* had been one of the identifying features of their social class" (176). In a study of the Salpêtrière photographs, Mary Russo has specifically linked Charcot's hysterics to carnivalesque inversion and spectacle (223).

12. Judith Fryer has discussed the nineteenth-century equation of

surgery and spectacle in " 'The Body in Pain' in Thomas Eakins' Agnew Clinic," 195–96.

13. In *Body Criticism*, Barbara Maria Stafford has noted the important relationship between exterior visual signs and interior meanings in the eighteenth-century development of physiognomy and other "dissective" sciences. These theories formed the foundation upon which nineteenth-century sciences sought meaning in external bodily signs. See also Foucault's *Birth of the Clinic*.

14. Thomas Laqueur has made this point in his study of early-nineteenth-century autopsy reports, "Bodies, Details and the Humanitarian Narrative."

15. For a discussion of Foucault's blindness to issues of gender, as well as his many points of convergence with feminist criticism, see Irene Diamond and Lee Quinby's *Feminism and Foucault*, ix–xx. See also Nancy Hartsock's "Foucault on Power: A Theory for Women?" in *Feminism/Postmodernism*.

16. Newton and Rosenfelt go on to discuss how the materialist-feminist critic seeks "to locate in the same situation the forces of oppression and the seeds of resistance; to construct women in a given moment in history simultaneously as victims and as agents" (xxii). See also Kuhn and Wolpe, eds., *Feminism and Materialism*.

17. In *The Female Malady*, Showalter extends this discussion to argue that ideas about proper feminine behavior shaped diagnoses of women's mental illnesses, and both Showalter and Herndl discuss the role of literature in forming nineteenth-century stereotypes of feminine illness. Cynthia Eagle Russett's *Sexual Science* and the medical chapters of Carroll Smith Rosenberg's *Disorderly Conduct* also provide important feminist perspectives on views of women and biological essentialism in nineteenth-century medicine and science. While their work, like Showalter's, tends to view gender ideology as a coherent set of practices, they also place considerable emphasis on the specific terms of debates within the Victorian sciences.

18. Anita Levy has identified this process in the nineteenth-century human sciences, noting the common ideological underpinnings of apparently contradictory arguments within the field of anthropology. According to Levy, these contradictions reveal "a strategy whereby intellectuals agree to disagree on issues within a framework, so that the framework itself remains the more firmly in place and far-reaching in scope" (56). Although Levy's emphasis on strategic disagreement implicitly grants more agency and awareness to the historical participants in intradisciplinary feuds than her examples support, and more than I think it is possible to claim, her analysis of the effect of such disagreements in consolidating institutional frameworks of belief seems to me one important way of thinking about the po-

tential function of disagreement within academic and scientific disciplines. The danger in this argument, however, is its tendency to collapse all disagreement and contradiction into a monolithic conception of ideology.

19. A number of studies of nervous illnesses in the nineteenth century provide important reference points for this project. See in particular George Frederick Drinka's *Birth of Neurosis*, Janet Oppenheim's *Shattered Nerves*, Edward Shorter's *From Paralysis to Fatigue*, John Haller and Robin Haller's *Physician and Sexuality in Victorian America*, and in the field of cultural criticism, Tom Lutz's *American Nervousness, 1903*. More generally, Charles Rosenberg's extensive work in medical history and Carroll Smith-Rosenberg's work in medical and social history have provided crucial background on a variety of issues related to illness.

20. Lawrence Rothfield's recent study of nineteenth-century medical realism, *Vital Signs*, is the only book-length work to address the extensive relationship between British literature and medicine in the nineteenth century. Rothfield argues that nineteenth-century clinical medicine provided a central model for the development and expression of realism in the French and British novels, and that the attraction of clinical medicine for novelists arose out of a desire to legitimize literary authorship according to the model of medical professionalization. Bruce Haley's *Healthy Body and Victorian Culture* has charted the close relationship between Victorian literature and cultural discourses about health, including an introductory chapter on Victorian medicine. Haley's recognition of health and fitness as powerful cultural preoccupations that helped to shape Victorian conceptions of masculinity provides an important historical context for understanding the symbolic significance of health in the nineteenth century, though Haley ignores women's roles in the Victorian fitness movement. Diane Price Herndl's recent *Invalid Women* studies representations of female invalidism in nineteenth-century American literature, combining previous feminist arguments about the medical profession's definition of women as inherently sick, popular views of female invalidism as fashionable, and interpretations of the female invalid as a transgressive heroine. I go on to discuss Herndl's and other feminist approaches to reading feminine illness more extensively in Chapter 1.

21. I am influenced here by what Elaine Scarry has termed "consentual materialism"—the acceptance of the material world on one's own terms by "lifting the body into language" (*Literature and the Body*, xvi, xv). See also *The Body in Pain*.

Chapter 1

1. In his 1895 essay "The Psychology of Women," the American psychologist George T. W. Patrick extended Spencer's emphasis on linguistic indirection to claim the naturalness of feminine duplicity: "Deception and ruse

in woman, far more than in man, have become a habit of thought and speech. A series of conditions, social, intellectual, and physiological, have forced this habit upon her as a means of self-defense" (217–18). See also Haller and Haller, 73–74. Another American, the physician and novelist Oliver Wendell Holmes, described women's capacity for unspoken communication in his 1867 novel about hysteria, *The Guardian Angel*. Holmes writes, "Talk without words is half their conversation, just as it is all the conversation of the lower animals. Only the dull senses of men are dead to it as to the music of the spheres" (9–10).

2. For example, see Henry Maudsley's discussion of reading human emotions through bodily signs in *The Physiology of Mind*, 379–89. Although I am primarily interested in how nineteenth-century culture understood the relationship between gender, language, and illness on its own (pre-Freudian) terms, there is a substantial amount of feminist scholarship, particularly in debates between feminist and psychoanalytic theorists, that has discussed the relationship between women and language through bodily symptoms. In particular, the interest in hysteria as a form of female communication through the body in the works of feminists such as Hélène Cixous, Catherine Clément, Luce Irigaray, Dianne Hunter, and Mary Jacobus (to name just a few) has provided models for reinterpreting psychoanalytic discourse, as well as literary and historical accounts of women's illnesses. Cixous writes, "Silence: silence is the mark of hysteria. The great hysterics have lost speech. . . . Their tongues are cut off and what talks isn't heard because it's the body that talks, and man doesn't hear the body" (49). While Cixous contends that women's—and particularly hysterics'—body language went unheard, I argue that Victorians were deeply interested in "hearing" the body, though only according to their own paradigms of somatic meaning.

3. There have been many recent studies of women's use of and relationship to language. Broadly defined, this issue has been at the center of feminist criticism, particularly in France. Toril Moi's *Sexual/Textual Politics* provides a useful discussion of Hélène Cixous's, Luce Irigaray's, and Julia Kristeva's theories. See also Margaret Homans's *Bearing the Word*; Deborah Cameron's *Feminist Critique of Language* and *Feminism and Linguistic Theory*; Jennifer Coates's *Women, Men, and Language*; Robin Lakoff's *Language and Woman's Place* and *Talking Power*.

4. These readings of the hysteric are not necessarily mutually exclusive. Cixous and Clément's interpretation of Dora and other hysterics in "the role of a resistant heroine: the one whom psychoanalytic treatment would never be able to *reduce*" (*Newly Born Woman*, 9) are perhaps the best (though certainly not the only) examples of this first model. Clément argues that we must look to figures defined as culturally "other"—in particular sorceresses

and hysterics—for all that which society has suppressed. It is in studying these most transgressive, deviant, or delinquent figures that we may begin to find a new language of female sexuality, an *écriture féminine*. The hysteric, in particular, becomes a privileged figure of transgression for Cixous and Clément because, in Freudian terms, she relives the (collective) repressed past, "resum[ing] and assum[ing] the memories of the others" (5). Clément notes, however, the ambiguity of the hysteric's position, its essential conservatism, insofar as the hysteric ultimately ends up "inuring others to her symptoms." Ultimately, "the family closes around her again, whether she is curable or incurable" (5). Elaine Showalter's study of women and madness combines the first and second models, as does Diane Price Herndl's *Invalid Women*. Drawing on the work of Cixous, Clément, and Hunter, she identifies the madwoman and the female hysteric as rebellious heroines within her larger account of women's role as passive victim of a patriarchal and misogynist psychiatric history. Herndl, even more explicitly than Showalter, subscribes to both feminist models for interpreting women's illnesses, arguing that illness can be read as both a resistance to male medical authority and a product of it, a means of power and a form of victimization (5).

5. Although the feminist critics and theorists I have discussed focus primarily on hysteria, I have chosen in this chapter to discuss a number of conditions other than hysteria that were sometimes perceived as indirect forms of communication—anorexia, chlorosis, consumption, brain fever—and to examine their function in Victorian literature. In the following chapter I examine two Victorian fictions of hysteria that seek to reconnect women, and the disease that has been used most often to represent their silence, with the control of language and the act of narrative expression. For a reading of female suicide as a form of body language, see Margaret Higonnet's "Speaking Silences: Women's Suicide."

6. See, for example, the discussion of sexual difference and the applications of energy conservation in Cynthia Eagle Russett's *Sexual Science*, chapter 4.

7. See Foucault, *Madness and Civilization*, 219; Mullan, *Sentiment and Sociability*, 223–24. Connections between reading and illness are also the subject of Chapter 3, where I focus on audience responses to sentimental deathbed scenes.

8. In addition to the novels I analyze here, representations of illness in *Wuthering Heights*, *Scenes of Clerical Life*, *Uncle Tom's Cabin*, *Bleak House*, and *Diana of the Crossways*, as well as the nursing scenes in *Our Mutual Friend*, demonstrate many of the emphases I have discussed. I have chosen the texts I examine in this chapter because of the way they highlight the linguistic and interpretive implications of illness. In *The Madwoman in the Attic*, Sandra Gilbert and Susan Gubar read fictional illnesses as ex-

pressions of female "dis-ease" with patriarchal power structures. Helena Michie has also discussed the communicative power of the heroine's body in *The Flesh Made Word*. Michie argues that both real women and fictional heroines used anorexia as a proof of virginity (16), denying their sexual "appetite" (13).

9. Alcott's division between the nurse's interpretation of spirit and the doctor's concern with flesh corresponds to what Martha Vicinus has identified as a specifically female vision of the nurse's role in medical care. In *Independent Women*, Vicinus argues that nursing ideology, at least in the early stages of the nursing reform movement, provided an alternative to the "narrow medical model of the doctors, who increasingly limited themselves to the care of bodies" (93). The nurse could potentially reform the moral and spiritual life of the patient, as well as tend to physical needs. This "unique mission," Vicinus claims, drew in part upon the ancient tradition of nursing as a religious vocation, but eventually "could not survive the growing power of the scientific approach" (93). While this idealistic "mission" may not have survived the professionalization of nursing and, as Vicinus makes clear, hardly corresponded to the actual expectations placed upon women who chose nursing as a career, it remained, nevertheless, an important component of Victorian ideals of the selfless nurse. Vicinus notes that "nurses captured the public imagination; they were surrogates for those who could not or would not give up their own lives for others. . . . Nurses were as close to saints as a Protestant country could have" (112).

10. For an excellent discussion of the relationship between shell shock and hysteria in World War I, see Showalter's *Female Malady*, chapter 7.

11. I take up this distinction between the proper role of feminine sympathy and the blunting of sensibilities in the medical profession in Chapter 3, where I outline the ways that women's association with sympathy was used to prevent them from entering the field of medicine.

12. Alcott's assessment of surgical value is in conflict with the standard qualifications for a surgeon in this (and earlier) periods. Albert D. Hutter has noted that "the primary qualifications of a good surgeon were speed, nerve, manual dexterity, and great strength: surgeons who could hold down a patient with one hand while sawing off a limb with the other, requiring only one, or, at the most, two other assistants, were greatly admired" (167). See also M. Jeanne Peterson, *The Medical Profession in Mid-Victorian London*.

13. Paul's role as narrative interpreter of Phillis's emotional life and bodily symptoms marks his ambiguously "feminine" role in the text, which is partly a product of his youth. Gaskell repeatedly describes Paul in terms of his liminal manhood; apprenticed to an engineer and in his first stay away from home, Paul is only at the stage where he is "beginning to think of whiskers" (222).

14. Gaskell notes that Holdsworth's body has itself been made more acutely readable by a recent illness—a "low fever" that infected him while on a surveying job (255). Holdsworth declares to Paul, "Since my illness I am almost like a girl, and turn hot and cold with shyness, as they do, I fancy" (256).

15. Gaskell's account of this illness is structurally similar to the analysis of anorexia nervosa in contemporary family systems therapy. Self-starvation becomes the adolescent daughter's only means of control over dysfunctional family behaviors, bringing tensions within the family network to a somatic crisis that is nearly impossible to ignore. For a discussion of this process see Joan Jacobs Brumberg's *Fasting Girls: The History of Anorexia Nervosa*.

16. In Paul's case, as in Holdsworth's, the "effect" of language is to produce Phillis's illness.

17. It is interesting to note that while Spencer associated women's body language with layered, encoded, and indeterminate meaning—i.e., with a way of hiding the "truth" of their emotions—Gaskell associates it with univocality and the adherence to a materially grounded emotional "truth."

18. For other interpretations of illness in *Shirley*, see Sandra Gilbert and Susan Gubar, *The Madwoman in the Attic*, 372–98; Miriam Bailin, " 'Varieties of Pain': The Victorian Sickroom and Brontë's *Shirley*"; and Linda Hunt, "Charlotte Brontë and the Suffering Sisterhood."

19. See Armstrong's discussion of how the domestic female body is expected to disappear "into the woodwork to watch over the household" (80).

20. Audrey C. Peterson's study of brain fever in nineteenth-century medicine and literature stresses the unusual combination of mental and emotional causes with severe physical effects. Possibly corresponding to modern conditions such as encephalitis or meningitis, brain fever was consistently linked to mental shock or strain in nineteenth-century medical textbooks, and its symptoms always included delirium. Fictional accounts of the disease, as Peterson has shown, go even further in assigning emotional causality, though less often fatality (448–49).

21. It is interesting to note that as an heiress in charge of a large family estate, Shirley is able to enter the masculine domains that are closed to Caroline. Throughout the novel Shirley jokes about her masculine characteristics and her androgynous name and behavior. Shirley's ability to cross gender boundaries indicates Brontë's interest in the way that distinctions of class often intersected with distinctions of gender.

22. Although Brontë's representation of Caroline's decline is the most extended exploration of illness in the novel, it is important to note that the four central characters in *Shirley*—Robert and Louis Moore, Shirley Keeldar, and Caroline—all become ill or wounded during the course of the narrative. For a discussion of Louis's illness and its parallel with Caroline's, see

Margaret Smith's "Introduction" to the Oxford edition of *Shirley*. Smith argues that Louis's dependent position and unfulfilled love make him a "masculine version" of Caroline (xxi). Robert and Shirley, in contrast, are both wounded by external forces. The forms and causes of their illnesses thus correspond to their more active, masculine roles in the novel. For a discussion of Shirley's anxiety about hydrophobia and its parallels in *Jane Eyre*, see Gilbert and Gubar, *Madwoman in the Attic*, 392–93.

23. This idealized connection between nursing and motherhood became an important justification for the nursing profession later in the century. As Martha Vicinus has pointed out, late Victorian nursing journals emphasized "maternal instincts" as one of the most essential qualities for effective nursing. "Endless changes were rung on the metaphor of the nurturing, motherly nurse," influencing even Florence Nightingale's rhetoric, which had previously described nursing through military metaphors (*Independent Women*, 108). For another discussion of the rhetoric surrounding Nightingale's nursing career, see Mary Poovey's chapter in *Uneven Developments*, "A Housewifely Woman: The Social Construction of Florence Nightingale." Poovey argues that these two narratives about the "patriotic service" of nursing, "a domestic narrative of maternal nurturing and self-sacrifice and a military narrative of individual assertion and will," actually converged. "The military narrative," Poovey claims, "was always at least compatible with—if not implicit in—the domestic narrative" (169).

24. Helena Michie has argued that Esther Summerson's illness helps her to construct a position of subjectivity in *Bleak House*, in part through the scarring of Esther's facial features from smallpox and the consequent distinction between her mother's face and her own. See " 'Who Is This in Pain?' Scarring, Disfigurement, and Female Identity in *Bleak House* and *Our Mutual Friend*."

25. Brontë's emphasis on the healing powers of maternity and the integration of maternal and romantic love has interesting parallels with a pattern of developmental figurations that Nancy Chodorow has proposed in *The Reproduction of Mothering*. Emphasizing the role of the pre-oedipal phase of development in the construction of female desire, Chodorow argues that "the mother remains a primary internal object to the girl" (198) and thus forms the basis of her later search for affection. "As a result of being parented by a woman, both sexes look for a return to this emotional and physical union" (199).

26. The attending physician suggests that William's death is from consumption, a hereditary predisposition to which, predictably, traces back to Lady Isabel's side of the family. Her own death combines the symptoms of hysteria, consumption, and emotional exhaustion.

Chapter 2

1. I would make a distinction here between these three nervous illnesses and some of the conditions mentioned in Chapter 1. Although illnesses such as anorexia nervosa, chlorosis (a form of anemia popularly associated with adolescent love sickness), brain fever, and consumption were often associated with subjective emotional states, they were also recognized as producing visible signs of illness (and, in the case of consumption, organic causes) that were more recognizably "real" and potentially life-threatening (as well as potentially more treatable) than the vague, mobile, and often invisible (i.e., subjective) symptoms of hysteria, hypochondria, and neurasthenia.

2. My discussion of the discrepancy between the immediacy of pain and the absence of public crediting is indebted to Elaine Scarry's work in *The Body in Pain*. See her introduction, 3–11, where this is listed as the first of three major premises of the book, as well as 13, 29, 44, 56–57, 66. See also Helena Michie's *Flesh Made Word: Female Figures and Women's Bodies* for a discussion of the relationship between language and the female body that differs from mine.

3. I do not mean to suggest that Alice James's diary was solely or even primarily a record of her illness. Much of it constituted an outpouring of her rich intellectual life and a vehicle of expression comparable to Henry James's novels or William James's philosophy. However, frustration with her illness in many ways shaped the form of her writing, and the secret diary expressed Alice's sense of a private self that was substantially different from public (and even familial) perceptions of her. For an interpretation of Alice's diary as "an excessive staging of the body as a death-inscribed entity," see Elisabeth Bronfen's *Over Her Dead Body: Death, Femininity and the Aesthetic* (384–92). I take up the issues of gender and the staging of death in more detail in Chapter 3.

4. My use of the term "hysteria" to describe Lucy's and Gwendolen's nervous conditions is intended to be taken loosely, as it often was in the nineteenth century, and is certainly open to debate. Although both Brontë and Eliot occasionally use the word "hysterical" to describe their heroines' behavior, both heroines exhibit vague nervous symptoms that are never formally diagnosed as hysteria in the text. Furthermore, their mixture of symptoms correspond to a variety of different conditions rather than any specific functional disorder. We can see the effect of this ambiguity in critical studies of *Villette* and *Daniel Deronda*, which have tended to view Lucy and Gwendolen according to modern diagnostic categories and to see their illnesses as exclusively mental. In *The Female Malady*, Elaine Showalter suggests that Lucy Snowe "comes close to madness" (70). Similarly, Sandra Gilbert and Susan Gubar view Lucy's "buried life" as akin to "schizophrenia" (*The Madwoman in the Attic*, 114–15). The one exception to this pat-

tern is Sally Shuttleworth's excellent recent study of neurosis in *Villette*, which demonstrates Brontë's familiarity with mid-nineteenth-century psychological theory. Shuttleworth's argument focuses primarily on issues of surveillance from nineteenth-century theories of insanity and new techniques of moral management. She stresses the different forms of surveillance to which Lucy Snowe is subject in the novel and argues that Lucy "employs physiological explanations of mental life and appropriates to herself theories of a female predisposition to neurosis and monomania" (332). Shuttleworth's emphasis, like Showalter's, is primarily on the mental components of neurosis and the role of sexual repression in the construction of Lucy's symptoms. In a feminist-Freudian reading of *Daniel Deronda*, Deirdre David has diagnosed Gwendolen as suffering from "pre-Oedipal sexual arrest" (178). More recently, Simon During has noted the similarities between Gwendolen's fantasies of drowning her husband and cases of "monomania" that were identified and categorized (rather elusively) by the medical profession in the nineteenth century. Although During ultimately determines that Gwendolen's fantasies are random enough to be diagnosed as monomania, he suggests that Eliot uses Gwendolen's character to explore a variety of cultural and psychological issues raised by this particular form of mental illness. See "The Strange Case of Monomania: Patriarchy in Literature, Murder in *Middlemarch*, Drowning in *Daniel Deronda*," 99. For a more comprehensive discussion of female nervous diseases during the Victorian period, see Oppenheim's excellent chapter "Neurotic Women" in *Shattered Nerves*.

5. For a discussion of nineteenth-century attitudes toward tuberculosis and cancer, see Susan Sontag's *Illness as Metaphor*.

6. For example, J. T. McGillicuddy's 1896 study *Functional Disorders of the Nervous System in Women* included charts of exhausted nerves to women's facial blood vessels, which were considered a result of excessive blushing, and drawings of women's distended and discolored abdomens, thought to be caused by nervous exhaustion, at a time when both psychological and hereditary theories of nervous illness predominated.

7. It is interesting to note that the title of George Henry Lewes's *Physical Basis of Mind*, from his multivolume study *Problems of Life and Mind*, participated in this general conflation of terminology. See also Drinka's discussion of Jackson, chapter 4.

8. For a discussion of the relationship between Spencer's 1881 theory of evolution as a cause of nervous exhaustion and a similar theory of Beard's that appeared just after Spencer's, see Drinka, 192–93. For hereditary theories of neurosis, see Bénédict Auguste Morel, who developed the degenerate myth of neurosis in *Traité des dégénérescences* (1857); J. M. Charcot, who linked hysteria and heredity in *Lectures on the Diseases of the Ner-*

vous System (1879); Cesare Lombroso, who developed a theory of criminal degeneracy in *L'uomo delinquente* (1876); and Richard von Krafft-Ebing, who linked heredity to various sexual "disorders," including homosexuality, in *Psychopathia Sexualis* (1882).

9. The British physician and proto-psychologist Henry Maudsley later expanded on Clarke's thesis in an article entitled "Sex in Mind and Education," which first appeared in *Fortnightly Review* in 1874. For a discussion of this debate see Showalter, *The Female Malady*, 125–26.

10. For an extended discussion of various theories that connected neurosis and spirituality, see Drinka, chapters 6 and 11.

11. See also Isaac Ray's discussion of "religious fanaticism" (165), hysteria, and nervous susceptibility from the fifteenth through the nineteenth centuries in chapter 3 of *Mental Hygiene*.

12. See Désiré Bourneville and Paul Regnard, *Iconographie photographique de la Salpêtrière*.

13. Janet Oppenheim discusses the often tense and entangled relationship between the emerging field of psychology in the latter decades of the nineteenth century and the study of spiritualism and other psychical phenomena by the Society for Psychical Research (founded in 1882) in her excellent book *The Other World*, pp. 236–48.

14. Williams has explained how "the different interpretations of conditions of altered consciousness illustrate how the mind became a disputed subject in late-Victorian Britain, as the intellectual world ceased to have a shared complex of religious and philosophical ideas, and words such as 'mind' and 'soul' were used in incompatible ways by different groups with different purposes in increasingly specialized and isolated disciplines" (234). See also W. F. Bynum, "The Nervous Patient in Eighteenth- and Nineteenth-Century Britain: The Psychiatric Origins of British Neurology," 94–99.

15. Although the terms mesmerism and hypnosis refer to the same process, the word hypnosis was coined by the surgeon James Braid (1780–1860), who was the first to posit that trance states were an effect of the nervous system rather than a product of the "fluid" Anton Mesmer had termed "animal magnetism" (Drinka, 133). The term "hypnosis" later came to be associated with medical applications of trance states, such as those of Charcot. For a discussion of the historical role of mesmerism and hypnosis in the diagnosis and treatment of hysteria, see Ilza Veith, *Hysteria: The History of a Disease*, 221–56.

16. See, for example, Mary S. Hartman's *Victorian Murderesses* on the case of Constance Kent (126), and Ruth Harris's discussion of the cases of Gabrielle Bompard and Gabrielle Fenayrou (*Murders and Madness*, chapter 5). Harris claims that "it is no exaggeration to say that hypnosis in the 1880s and early 1890s was at the confluence of almost every major cultural

trend, forming an important aspect of the 'revolt against rationalism' and providing experimental proof for the need to revise social and political thinking in line with new discoveries about the human mind" (157–58).

17. Mary Douglas traces this relationship between the symbolic boundaries of the individual and the social body more broadly in *Purity and Danger*.

18. See Freud, *Dora: An Analysis of a Case of Hysteria*, 71.

19. Records from the George Eliot–George Henry Lewes library show an extensive collection of medical and psychological treatises, some of which contain marginal notations in Eliot's handwriting. According to William Baker's *George Eliot–George Henry Lewes Library: An Annotated Catalogue of their Books at Dr. Williams's Library, London,* Eliot and Lewes owned copies of Robert Brudenell Carter's and Jean-Martin Charcot's works on hysteria and nervous disease, some of George Miller Beard's treatises on "brainworkers," early studies by Thomas Laycock on mental disease, Henry Maudsley's *Body and Mind*, and numerous books by Herbert Spencer, John Hughlings Jackson, and Alexander Bain. In addition, marginal notes and underlinings in Eliot's handwriting appear in Henry Maudsley's *The Physiology of Mind*, in James Sully's *Sensation and Intuition: Studies in Psychology and Aesthetics*, and in the chapters on emotion in Spencer's *First Principles*.

20. For a fuller discussion of Lewes's work in relation to Eliot's fiction, see Chase, 145–50.

21. For an excellent discussion of the somatic effects of sensation fiction, see D. A. Miller, *The Novel and the Police*, 146–48. Miller claims that the sensation novel "offers us one of the first instances of modern literature to address itself primarily to the sympathetic nervous system" (146). For a discussion of the development of sensation fiction as a genre, see Winifred Hughes, *The Maniac in the Cellar: Sensation Novels of the 1860s*.

22. Although Chase focuses primarily on Brontë's use of containers, attics, and houses in *Jane Eyre*, she claims that in Brontë's novels "psychic life, spiritual life, domestic life, all appear as matters of arrangement, of architecture, of spatial relation" (65; see also 60–65).

23. John Kucich recently has challenged the application of psychoanalytic conceptions of repression to the complex matrix of psychological responses—repression, renunciation, self-denial—that formed a part of Victorian culture. Kucich argues that as it appears in Victorian fiction, repression "heightens and vitalizes emotional autonomy, rather than threatening or suppressing it" (*Repression in Victorian Fiction*, 2–3).

24. Eliot's use of the term "dynamic" to describe Gwendolen's glance, as Simon During has noted, came out of her readings in the mental sciences and confused many of her early reviewers (98). Jacqueline Rose has also dis-

cussed the relationship between vision, science, and narrative authority in this scene. She identifies it as a moment when the male narrator faces "a crisis in the act of telling" and "a panic about the meaning of the woman," and she sees it as part of the more general "hysterisation of the body of the woman in the second half of the nineteenth-century" (117, 116, 115). Although Rose's reading of this scene differs from mine, she places a similar emphasis on the relationship between hysteria and specularity.

25. It is interesting to note that Simon During qualifies his diagnosis of Gwendolen's disease as monomania precisely because of the divided narrative mode of her outbursts and visions (99–100). He claims, "No causal nexus, no narrative could explain acts emerging from monomania," because monomania is "the absence of structure" (87, 100).

26. I don't mean by this to suggest that Gwendolen's hysteria functions as a form of rebellion in the feminist terms that Cixous and Clément have outlined (see Chapter 1, note 2). Rather, I read her challenge to the dominant narrative voice as a means of complicating the interpretation of spirituality in the text. Gwendolen's illness confuses the perceived ways in which body and mind interact, but it remains a cause of personal suffering. At no point does Eliot suggest that Gwendolen interprets her own "narrative" as a form of feminist resistance. Instead, Gwendolen remains deeply confused by her symptoms, searching for ways to contain their disruptive potential rather than exploiting it.

27. Gilbert and Gubar argue that "the ambiguous ending of *Villette* reflects Lucy's ambivalence, her love for Paul and her recognition that it is only in his absence that she can exert herself fully to exercise her own powers" (*The Madwoman in the Attic*, 438). Similarly, Elaine Showalter claims that "only when she finds the assurance that she is loved—along with rewarding work—is Lucy no longer sick" (*Female Malady*, 71). Nina Auerbach emphasizes the "Amazonian" nature of Lucy's final economic authority and her entrance into a female world "all regnant" (*Communities of Women*, 113). Auerbach further claims that "as seen through Lucy's eyes, the end of the novel can be regarded as a triumph of decent and orderly deviousness" (112).

28. Karen Chase has discussed this storm scene in terms quite different from mine. In an attempt to read Lucy as psychologically cured, Chase argues that M. Paul's withdrawal enlarges Lucy's view and that the ocean provides a healthy and expansive vista for Lucy's newfound independence (90).

29. Alan Krohn's 1978 monograph on the history and definition of hysteria points out the hysteric's "high sensitivity to the [cultural] environment." Krohn claims that "the facility with which the hysteric can utilize roles considered acceptable by his culture attests to his sensitivity to the norms of the culture, the limits of acceptability . . . and interpersonal sensitivity"

(161–62). What this suggests is the possibility of reading Victorian culture through the symptoms and interpretations of its hysterics.

Chapter 3

1. Translation by Kathleen Marien. See also a discussion of this incident in Drinka, 152. Although Drinka mistakenly dates the Bernhardt performance as 1861, on the basis of a misprinted number in a footnote from his source, Paul Aubry's *Contagion du meurtre*, Bernhardt's Moscow tour was actually in 1881, and the first published account of the Bernhardt story appeared in Gabriel Tarde's 1893 article. Tarde proposed the incident as a confirmation of Aubry's theory of nervous suggestion and Tarde's own theory of imitation and crowd behavior. Subsequently, in the 1894 and 1896 editions of his *Contagion du meurtre*, Aubry referred to the *Deux mondes* article and used the incident as an example of how suggestion could provoke involuntary behavior on a large scale.

2. Although my central concern in this chapter is to locate questions of visual contagion in their historical context, it is impossible to ignore the extensive and compelling debates about "the gaze" in recent feminist film criticism, which has examined the psychology of spectatorship as it relates to representations of women in film. Much of this criticism, in turn, has been influenced by Jacques Lacan's analysis of phallic empowerment as a form of looking. See Laura Mulvey's "Visual Pleasure and Narrative Cinema"; E. Ann Kaplan's "Is the Gaze Male?" in *Women and Film*; Mary Ann Doane's chapter "Clinical Eyes: The Medical Discourse" in *The Desire to Desire: The Woman's Film of the 1940s*; and Larysa Mykyta, "Lacan, Literature, and the Look: Woman in the Eye of Psychoanalysis." Ludmilla Jordanova's *Sexual Visions: Images of Gender in Science and Medicine Between the Eighteenth and Twentieth Centuries* also provides an important analysis of medical and scientific metaphors of vision.

3. My interest in the structure of medical authority has been influenced by Foucault's *Birth of the Clinic: An Archaeology of Medical Perception*. Foucault makes a distinction between the medical "gaze" and the medical "glance," claiming that "the gaze implies an open field . . . it records and totalizes; it gradually reconstitutes immanent organizations. . . . The glance, on the other hand, does not scan a field: it strikes at one point, which is central or decisive; the gaze is endlessly modulated, the glance goes straight to its object" (121). Although this distinction is not important for the purposes of my argument, my use of the term "gaze" inevitably draws on the work of Foucault.

4. Although the phenomenon of nervous mimicry had been medically recognized at least as early as 1818 in Sir Benjamin Brodie's *Pathological and Surgical Observations on Diseases of the Joints*, it did not receive the

name "neuromimesis" until Paget's 1875 article. Paget used the terms "nervous mimicry" and "neuromimesis" interchangeably (172–73). More general medical discussions of the imitative etiology of nervous disease date back to the eighteenth century, and James Turner has pointed out to me that the Renaissance essayist Michel de Montaigne described this same phenomenon in an essay titled "Of the Power of the Imagination." Montaigne gives numerous examples of the power of imagination over the body, including some from his own experience: "I am one of those who are very much influenced by the imagination. . . . The sight of other people's anguish causes very real anguish to me, and my feelings have often usurped the feelings of others. A continual cougher irritates my lungs and throat. . . . I catch the disease that I study, and lodge it in me" (68). What was unique about the emphasis on neuromimesis in the nineteenth century, however, was the way it became part of a widespread cultural narrative that linked (and gendered) concerns about contagion, imitation, visual authority, and collective or crowd behavior.

5. For example, in one medical encyclopedia published in 1886 (Buck, *A Reference Handbook of the Medical Sciences*), neuromimesis received a longer entry than either hysteria or neurasthenia. Twenty years and two editions later, it had lost its status as a separate disease and was incorporated in the category of hysterical joint diseases.

6. Nye, 68; Rothman, 286. See also Terry Castle's "Contagious Folly: An Adventure and Its Skeptics."

7. This incipient theory of group psychology and mental contagion was most fully articulated by Le Bon in his 1895 *Psychologie des foules*, which formed the starting point for Freud's 1921 study *Group Psychology and the Analysis of the Ego*. Freud devoted his first chapter to Le Bon's theory, the essential points of which were, according to Freud, that "in a group every sentiment and act is contagious, and contagious to such a degree that an individual readily sacrifices his personal interest to the collective interest"; that "an individual immersed for some length of time in a group in action soon finds himself—either in consequence of the magnetic influence given out by the group, or from some other cause of which we are ignorant—in a special state, which much resembles the state of 'fascination' in which the hypnotized individual finds himself in the hands of the hypnotizer. . . . The conscious personality has entirely vanished; will and discernment are lost"; and finally that "by the mere fact that he forms part of an organized group, a man descends several rungs in the ladder of civilization" (quoted in Freud, *Group Psychology*, 7–9). Freud claimed that he used Le Bon's description as an introduction to his study because "it fits in so well with our own psychology in the emphasis which it lays upon unconscious mental life" (14).

8. The most influential proponents of these theories included Tarde,

Sieghele, Le Bon, and Freud. For a more detailed discussion of their contributions to crowd theory and group psychology, see McClelland, chapters 6–8, and Barrows, chapter 6. For more recent debates about crowd behavior and group psychology, see Helen MacGill Hughes, ed., *Crowd and Mass Behavior*. For discussions of crowd behavior in history, see George Rudé, *The Crowd in History: A Study of Popular Disturbances in France and England, 1730–1848*, and Mark Harrison, *Crowds and History: Mass Phenomena in English Towns, 1790–1835*. In addition, Elias Canetti's *Crowds and Power* provides an important theoretical and cross-cultural discussion of crowd phenomena.

9. For example, Gabriel Tarde's theories of imitation and consciousness were first translated and explained in the British journal *Mind* in 1894; subsequently, his book *The Laws of Imitation* was translated into English in 1903; Le Bon, whom Robert Nye has called "the supreme scientific vulgarizer of his generation" (3), had his book *Psychologie des foules* translated into English in 1896. It was later translated into 16 languages. From the other direction, Le Bon drew upon the work of both Herbert Spencer and Walter Bagehot in developing his concept of imitation (Nye, 68). Even American presidential elections, according to Isaac Ray, could foster an unhealthy transmission of nervous excitement. Ray warned "people of keen sensibilities" to "avoid participating in those great social movements, whether moral, political, or religious, which frequently agitate modern communities" (179).

10. In an echo of Bain, we find the American physician Sarah MacNutt warning in 1908 against the effects of dance performances. A 1908 article entitled "The Vulgarization of Salomé" cites MacNutt as asserting that "the intense abnormal passion simulated by the dancers must reach across the footlights and take hold of the nervous system of the hysterical women in the audience" (439). I am indebted to David Black for bringing this passage to my attention.

11. See also Lewes's discussion of mental contagion, which cites cases of sympathetic convulsions, as well as suicides, criminal acts, and revolutionary fervor, as examples of the "influence of Imagination" (459–60). For a discussion of the evolutionary implications of sympathy to pain, see Spencer, *Principles of Psychology*, 570. Spencer argues that torturers must have less highly evolved powers of imaginative representation to be able to inflict pain without sympathetically feeling it. In general, Spencer notes "the relatively-slow development of sympathy during civilization" (ibid., 569). See also Chapter 4 for a more extended discussion of the relationship between pain and evolution.

12. The psychologist Henry Maudsley extended this distinction to claim that there were "two different classes of mind among mankind,—a subjec-

tive class marked by the tendency to feel intensely rather than to see clearly . . . more often met with amongst women than men; and an objective class, more able to look at things in the dry light of reason" (*Physiology of Mind*, 377).

13. For a discussion of the necessary "moral callousness" produced by surgeons' repeated need to inflict pain on their patients, as well as their effective directing of sympathy into appropriate channels, see Spencer, *Principles*, 572.

14. One can only speculate about the personal significance of this dilemma for Mitchell, but one way of viewing his extraordinary fictional output during his years as a practicing physician is as a rechanneling of his own sympathetic energies into narrative creation. We might think of this as a counterpart to the process of transference from neurosis to narrative that we saw in Alice James's diary and Brontë's and Eliot's novels.

15. To complicate my argument about the medical gaze and gender, it should be noted that Jacques Donzelot points out that in the late eighteenth century the medical establishment aligned itself with the bourgeois family, and particularly in a "privileged alliance with the mother" in order to displace the traditional authority of women healers and midwives in the home (18). Donzelot describes this strategy as an appropriation by the doctor of "the notion of observation (in favor of a discreet but ubiquitous mother's gaze)" (19). Here Donzelot views the mother's gaze as empowered and authorized, though only in relation to her children, by the cultural status of the family. However, this alliance between doctors and mothers enhanced the authority of the medical establishment (rather than mothers) over the family and was part of a larger movement to discredit female healers and to exclude women from the medical profession.

16. The one exception to the doctor's command of visual authority was in the practice of gynecology and obstetrics, in which doctors held divided opinions about the propriety of ocular inspection and medical students often were taught how to perform digital explorations and to introduce instruments such as the forceps into the vagina without the benefit of sight. Judith Leavitt has suggested that this practice, in addition to other factors, may have created more risks to women in childbirth than traditional female midwifery, which was not impeded by visual restrictions between women. See " 'Science' Enters the Birthing Room," 83–84. One could also argue that this one scopic prohibition simply emphasized the cultural significance of vision and served to highlight the other forms of visual authority the doctor was routinely granted, as well as the heightened specular authority of those doctors who disregarded issues of female propriety in order to make vaginal examinations. In addition, one should note that issues of class and race often mediated the issue of propriety in medicine, and paying female

patients were granted quite different treatment from poor women, whose access to medical care was in the teaching hospitals.

17. Foucault argues that the Panopticon marks the transition from a society based on a binary system of exclusion, branding and separating those who do not belong (as in the leper colony), to a society whose power is based on the concept of individual surveillance, classification, and control. Here the Panopticon functions as a mechanism to disperse human collectivity (and thus the dangers of the crowd) in order to replace it with a "collection of separated individualities" that better lend themselves to surveillance, whether in the penitentiary, the hospital, the school, the workhouse, or the psychiatric asylum (*Discipline and Punish*, 198–201). The Panopticon further refines the process of visual authority, he says, by "dissociating the see/being seen dyad: in the peripheric ring, one is totally seen, without ever seeing; in the central tower, one sees everything without ever being seen" (202). Foucault's analysis of visual power relations is open to critique, both because it collapses individual forms of cultural and political domination into a generalized model of power and because it ignores the historically specific ways in which visual relations were gendered. Nevertheless, it provides a useful paradigm for analyzing constructions of medical (as well as other forms of scopic) authority.

18. Andrews goes on to argue that the surgeon "must carry in his heart, that abiding kindness which will insure him against exciting a single useless terror in the patient's mind, or a single needless pang of bodily pain" (595). It is thus in negotiating the proper placement and control (rather than absence) of sympathy that the ideal surgeon must excel.

19. For a more extensive discussion of "medical imperialism," see Drinka, chapter 3.

20. I am indebted to Lemuel Johnson for bringing this parallel to my attention. For a discussion of Sims's fantasies of female colonization in relation to imperialist discourse of the late nineteenth century, see Gilbert and Gubar's *No Man's Land: The Place of the Woman Writer in the Twentieth-Century*, volume 2: *Sexchanges*, 33. See Barker-Benfield's chapter "Architect of the Vagina" for a discussion of the race and gender politics of Sims's research.

21. We can see the criticism women doctors were accustomed to facing in the preface to Harriot Hunt's 1855 autobiography, *Glances and Glimpses*. In anticipation of the flaws that would be attributed to a woman doctor by the medical establishment, Hunt addresses this challenge to her imagined critics: "*Critics, satirists!* here is work for you; there are plenty of *defects*, plenty of rough *granite* for your *hard* natures to hammer upon; an overflow of *enthusiasm* for you to brand as mere *impulse;* a confidence in

intuition which will startle your *causality*" (xi). We can see from Hunt's ital-
ics the words that were of special significance in the debate over the role of
women in medicine and science. As a woman, Hunt expected to be considered defective, impulsive, and irrational by her critics.

22. For a further discussion of the development of moral therapy, see
Elaine Showalter, *The Female Malady*, 23–51; David Rothman, *Discovery
of the Asylum*; Andrew Scull, ed., *Madhouses, Mad-Doctors, and Madmen:
Social History of Psychiatry in the Victorian Era*.

23. One might note here the parallel metaphors of mental permeability between Jacobi's sympathy, which apparently enters "into the mind of
the patient" in order to understand, and Mitchell's "magnetizing," which
enters in order to control. However, despite the high value placed on sympathy in Gilman's description of Jacobi, it should be noted that Jacobi herself (unlike her contemporary Elizabeth Blackwell) embraced the values of
the new science, arguing the need for women physicians to prove their scientific objectivity in the male medical arena and against Blackwell's argument for a separate sphere of women's medicine. Jacobi wrote to her mother
from medical school describing her vision of heaven as "the Region of Pure
Thought. In the latter alone is to be found the calm, lofty serenity, that results from . . . an emancipation from the overwhelming dominion of personal emotion and instinct" (*Life and Letters*, 216). In this passage, Jacobi
seems to be rejecting the affective definitions of femininity that Blackwell
embraced. See Morantz-Sanchez, 184–202, for an extended comparison of
the different strategies of medical enfranchisement adopted by Blackwell
and Jacobi. For a discussion of Gilman's relation to issues of gender in nineteenth-century science, see Russett, 84–86.

24. Blackwood, Hunt, and Beecher's assumptions about fallen women
were not necessarily the only cultural models available. As Nina Auerbach
has pointed out, in Victorian iconography the fallen women is a defiant figure rather than a passive victim. See her chapter "The Rise of the Fallen
Woman" in *Woman and the Demon*, 150–84.

25. A recent example that suggests the persistence of this correlation
can be found in a 1971 anatomy textbook (subsequently taken off the mar-
ket) that used outtakes from *Playboy* magazine photographs as its visual
referents in order to appeal to the implied male audience of medical students. See Rosalind A. Coleman and James Rolleston, "Anatomy Lessons:
The Destiny of a Textbook, 1971–72." See also Ludmilla Jordanova's analysis of the veiling and unveiling of women's bodies as metaphors for medical
and scientific knowledge in *Sexual Visions*, 87–110.

26. Paget claims that the morality of the medical profession had improved since the time he was a student and that "such stories, I believe, are

now never told, and the change is among the many I have watched as significant of a vast increase in the habitual decency . . . of students" (51). See also Lansbury, 416.

27. It is interesting to note that Johnson sees an increasing danger of influence from more realistic genres, or what he terms "the universal drama, as may be the lot of any other man," as opposed to romances of the past (21). See also Kendrick's discussion of Johnson, 25.

28. For example, Dickens was censured by critics for his overuse of sensational and sentimental subjects, especially in the later novels, and despite the enormous emotional response to the death of Little Nell and the popularity of *The Old Curiosity Shop*, he was criticized for what some found a "shockingly calculating" repetition of childrens' deathbed scenes in works like *Dombey and Son* and *Bleak House* (Ford, 40, 55–59). Dickens's fiction seems to have been particularly susceptible to audience participation, as exhibited in his public readings. Furthermore, in the common practice of translating popular novels into plays, we can see the tendency of fiction to transform into spectacle and thereby encourage audience involvement in the text. See Kendrick's discussion of Victorian theories of reading and feeling, 25–26. For a discussion of the paradoxes of sentimental culture in Victorian America and the theatricality of sympathetic display, see Karen Halttunen's *Confidence Men and Painted Women*.

29. D. A. Miller's study of sensation and gender in Wilkie Collins's *Woman in White* has emphasized the ways in which sensation fiction positions its readers through exemplary scenes of emotional and somatic response. Miller argues that "in order to make us nervous, nervousness must first be represented" (*The Novel and the Police*, 148). Miller goes on to suggest how these examples have the effect of disrupting gender identity in Collins's novel.

30. For examples of reader response theories that are based on gender, see Judith Fetterley's *Resisting Reader: A Feminist Approach to American Fiction*; Elaine Showalter's "Toward a Feminist Poetics" in *The New Feminist Criticism: Essays on Women, Literature & Theory*, 125–43; Annette Kolodny's "Reply to Commentaries: Women Writers, Literary Historians, and Martian Readers"; and Jonathan Culler's chapter "Reading as a Woman" in *On Deconstruction: Theory and Criticism after Structuralism*, 43–63. Culler's argument examines the idea of readerly role playing (a man reading as a woman) in relation to feminist reader response theories.

31. The relationship between fiction and emotion has continued to be a problem for modern philosophy. Bijoy H. Boruah has discussed the history of this debate in aesthetic theory in *Fiction and Emotion: A Study in Aesthetics and the Philosophy of Mind*.

32. The only deathbed scene to rival Eva's in the nineteenth-century

popular imagination was, of course, that of Little Nell in *The Old Curiosity Shop*. I have chosen not to discuss this scene here because it is curiously devoid of the complex visual structuring that attends so many other deathbeds in nineteenth-century novels. The narrative focus is on those rushing to Nell's bedside, only to find, too late, that she has already died. For a discussion of eighteenth- and nineteenth-century deathbed scenes that includes readings of both *The Old Curiosity Shop* and *Uncle Tom's Cabin*, see Bronfen, 76–94.

33. In her article "Bodily Bonds: The Intersecting Rhetorics of Feminism and Abolition," Karen Sánchez-Eppler asserts the importance of reader response to the conventions of sentimental anti-abolitionist narratives. Sánchez-Eppler identifies the reader's tears as the central mechanism through which these narratives, including *Uncle Tom's Cabin*, propose to rescue the bodies of slaves (36). See also Ann Douglas's *Feminization of American Culture* for a reading of the sentimentality of Eva's deathbed scene. For an argument that challenges the efficacy of sentimental illness in *Uncle Tom's Cabin* and focuses on Eva's mother's hypochondria as a more characteristic representation of female invalidism, see Herndl, *Invalid Women*, 50–55.

34. The comparison that Stowe draws between the sensibilities of the innocent, the powerless, and the disenfranchised challenges Victorian medical dogma that claimed that the bodies of servants, slaves, and workers were duller and more resistant to pain than those of what George Miller Beard called society's "brainworkers." I take up this issue again in the final chapter. However, it should be noted that Stowe still separates black and white bodies by giving Eva a spiritualized death that invokes her body only indirectly, through Christian rhetoric, whereas slaves' bodies in *Uncle Tom's Cabin* are insistent in their physical presence. If Eva dies in the spirit of Christ, Uncle Tom suffers Christ's physical death through the whipping wounds inflicted by Simon Legree.

35. Fisher's claims for the radical politics of sentimental fiction contradict more traditional views of sentimentality that devalue its emphasis on emotional excess in favor of realism or modernist experimentation. See also Jane Tompkins's *Sensational Designs: The Cultural Work of American Fiction* for a reading of *Uncle Tom's Cabin* that reconstructs the literary and political claims of the sentimental novel and challenges historical biases against sentimental fiction. For a discussion of the position of sentimentality within the tradition of philosophical idealism, see Fred Kaplan's *Sacred Tears: Sentimentality in Victorian Literature*.

36. Bompard's case drew considerable attention from the European medical establishment because both prosecution and defense called upon doctors to give medical testimony about the potential effects of and susceptibility to hypnosis. According to Ruth Harris, the trial pitted members

of the Ecole de Nancy, who argued that anyone who was sufficiently susceptible could be forced to act against his or her will under the influence of
hypnosis, against followers of Charcot and the Ecole Salpêtrière, who maintained that hypnosis was possible only among hysterics or those predisposed
to hysteria, thereby providing a public forum for an important and volatile
medical debate ("Murder Under Hypnosis," 159–60). We can see a further
parallel to du Maurier's story in Axel Munthe's autobiography, which describes a dispute between himself and Charcot over one of Charcot's most
spectacular hysterics. According to Munthe, he and Charcot became involved in a battle of wills over a young female patient, Munthe trying to induce her, through hypnosis, to return to her honest peasant parents and
Charcot trying to get her to stay at the Salpêtrière. Eventually Charcot accused Munthe of trying to sexually seduce the girl through hypnosis, and
Munthe accused Charcot of seducing her into acting the part of a hysteric
for his performances (303–13). Each accusation highlights the association
between hypnotic and sexual authority that du Maurier plays upon.

    37. Freedman discussed this issue in a talk presented at the University
of Michigan, "Mania and the Middlebrow: The Case of *Trilby*."

    38. The fact that Richard von Krafft-Ebing, in his 1882 study *Psy-
chopathia Sexualis* (revised and expanded in 1902), had already begun to
catalogue and diagnose many of the era's most sensational sex crimes, linking them to other forms of hereditary criminal degeneracy, insanity, and nervous disease, suggests a correspondence between the preoccupations of late
nineteenth-century neurology and those of *fin-de-siècle* aesthetics. Bram
Dijkstra has catalogued and discussed the "cult of invalidism" and the "cult
of the woman as corpse" as they relate to the art of this period, claiming
that the numerous depictions of dead women "represent a stage of development in which the aesthetic pleasure in female suffering of earlier generations of artists had begun to mingle with a morbid appeal to the viewer's
participatory self-projection into that suffering" (54). Dijkstra quotes Krafft-
Ebing's theory of masochism and Cesare Lombroso's claims for women's
lesser sensitivity to pain to demonstrate how the masochistic and necrophilic
fantasies of *fin-de-siècle* artists were legitimized by the medical community.
He also describes how Sarah Bernhardt exploited this aesthetic and erotic
fascination with dead women by being photographed in a coffin she claimed
to have used as a bed (101, 45–6).

    39. Tarde cites similar examples of "leadership after death" in order to
explain how an apparently leaderless crowd can act in unison upon the influence of a memory or idea (*L'opinion et la foule*, 177–78; trans. in Mc-
Clelland, 191).

    40. One could argue that the representation of audience response in
Trilby necessarily privileges and normalizes the feminized crowd's act of

identification rather than the racially vilified Svengali's gaze. Although this seems to me a potentially useful point to consider, it does not, I believe, counteract the fundamental structure of authority upon which Svengali bases his powers. For a discussion of Svengali as an anti-Semitic stereotype, see Edgar Rosenberg, *From Shylock to Svengali: Jewish Stereotypes in English Fiction.*

41. These issues have an extensive critical history that has involved link-ing the narrative alliances in Eliot's novel to her diverse areas of scientific and philosophical interest. In particular, critics such as J. Hillis Miller, D. A. Miller, and David Carroll have discussed the doubleness of tone in *Mid-dlemarch* (see J. Hillis Miller, "Optic and Semiotic in *Middlemarch*"; D. A. Miller, *Narrative and Its Discontents*; David Carroll, *George Eliot and the Conflict of Interpretations*). For an excellent account of the status of knowl-edge in *Middlemarch* and a review of the critical background on this sub-ject, see Alexander Welsh, *George Eliot and Blackmail*, chapter 11. On Eliot's uses of nineteenth-century science and scientific metaphor, see espe-cially George Levine, "The Scientific Texture of *Middlemarch*"; Michael York Mason, "*Middlemarch* and Science: Problems of Life"; Jeremy Tam-bling, "*Middlemarch*, Realism and the Birth of the Clinic"; Sally Shuttle-worth, *George Eliot and Nineteenth-Century Science*, chapter 7; Gillian Beer, *Darwin's Plots*, chapter 5; and Lawrence Rothfield, *Vital Signs*, chap-ter 4. Shuttleworth specifically allies Eliot's use of nineteenth-century or-ganic theory with her construction of sympathy, arguing that Dorothea's sympathy embodies the "organic ideal" (173). For critical discussions of Eliot's theory of sympathy and her attempts to reconcile feelings and knowl-edge, see especially J. Hillis Miller, *The Form of Victorian Fiction*; Elizabeth Ermarth, "George Eliot's Conception of Sympathy"; K. K. Collins, "G. H. Lewes Revised: George Eliot and the Moral Sense." See also John Kucich's discussion of subjectivity and the internalization of otherness in *Repression in Victorian Fiction*, chapter 2.

42. J. Hillis Miller makes this argument in his seminal essay "Optic and Semiotic in *Middlemarch*." Lawrence Rothfield has argued that Eliot and other nineteenth-century realists employed a "medicalized style" in their writing in order to model their own rising professionalism on that of the medical profession in the first half of the nineteenth century (*Vital Signs*, 44).

43. Although James never names Milly's illness, critics have generally assumed it to be tuberculosis because James's cousin Minny Temple, who was the inspiration for Milly Theale, died of tuberculosis. However, Caro-line G. Mercer and Sarah. D. Wangensteen have made a persuasive case against tuberculosis. They argue that Milly's disease corresponds more closely to the symptoms of chlorosis, or green sickness—a form of anemia

traditionally associated with virgins and unrequited love. See " 'Consumption, Heart-Disease, or Whatever': Chlorosis, a Heroine's Illness in *The Wings of the Dove*," 264–65. Their diagnosis is particularly interesting since it rests, in part, on the scene in which Milly stands beside the Bronzino portrait and compares the green tints of the skin to her own, even more vivid pallor. For another argument against tuberculosis, see Adeline R. Tintner and Henry D. Janowitz, "Inoperable Cancer: An Alternate Diagnosis for Milly Theale's Illness." For two recent and extensive discussions of illness in *The Wings of the Dove*, see Herndl's *Invalid Women*, chapter 6 and Rothfield's *Vital Signs*, chapter 7. Herndl discusses James's focus on economies of illness and the role that money and exchange play in various characters' assessments of Milly's value, including her own. Rothfield focuses on the role of medical authority as the basis of James's realism, arguing that it is the physician's knowledge of death, "whose very domain of discourse is that of the sentient and throbbing body," rather than Milly and her "extravagant flightiness," that James ultimately endorses and that makes *Wings* a realist novel (174). I would argue that James's "endorsement" of the doctor's perspective is far less complete than Rothfield allows, precisely because James is more interested in the multiple angles of vision offered by Milly's illness.

44. Sir Luke Strett apparently was modeled on the renowned London physician Sir Andrew Clark, who had diagnosed Alice James's breast cancer in 1891. According to the entries in Alice's diary, she had become disenchanted with him by 1892, describing his "polished surface, as comforting and nourishing as that of a billiard ball" (226). In a lengthy discussion of Clark, his medical career, and his relation to Alice James, Mercer and Wangensteen have speculated about the effect of Alice's disillusionment with Clark on Henry James's portrayal of Strett, noting that Densher feels Sir Luke "has no more than a professional interest in Milly, is not the great friend and would-be savior that she considers him" (281). As with James's qualification of Susan Stringham's sympathy, I would argue that his portrayal of Strett's objectivity is equally ambivalent.

45. James would have been familiar with Mitchell's methods and ideas through Alice, who, though she never went to Mitchell's Philadelphia clinic for treatment, was interested in the methods and results of his rest cure. Alice had been treated (unsuccessfully) in 1866 by the neurologist Charles Fayette Taylor, who shared some of Mitchell's thinking (Strouse, 114–15), and in 1883 by Dr. Frank Page (also unsuccessfully) at the Adams Nervine Asylum, which offered a version of Mitchell's rest cure (Strouse, 243–44). When William James met Mitchell at a dinner party, he wrote to Alice and referred to the doctor as "your friend Weir Mitchell," indicating, according

to Strouse, not Alice's acquaintance with the physician, but her continued interest in his ideas (Strouse, 246–47).

46. In his excellent article "Sexuality and Visual Terrorism in *The Wings of the Dove*," Michael Moon has noted the tendency of James's narrative to foster "optical illusions" of power. However, Moon's feminist Lacanian reading of the novel emphasizes the illusions of female scopic authority that are ultimately unmasked to reveal and restore a phallic economy of vision. Challenging the dominant critical tendency to see Milly as a "beatific creature, passive and manipulated," Moon argues that Milly participates in her culture's "psychosexual power games," undergoing a process of "phallicization . . . during her initial interview with Strett as a result of his look" (431–32). Although I share Moon's conviction that phallic power transferred remains, in its essential structure, intact, I would argue that James's emphasis on an ambiguously gendered interpretive stance allows for a more fluid interpretation of gender alliances than Moon's argument does.

Chapter 4

1. George F. Shee's 1903 article "The Deterioration in the National Physique," which quoted Rosebury, provided statistics to prove that "a serious deterioration in the national physique has been going on for some years" and had recently come to the attention of numerous prominent doctors, politicians, and military leaders (797). For a discussion of late Victorian anxieties about physical deterioration, see Anthony Wohl's treatment of Shee in *Endangered Lives*, 333.

2. For a reading of nineteenth-century systems of bodily measurement as part of a widespread negotiation between the "natural" body and machine culture, see Mark Seltzer, *Bodies and Machines*, 154.

3. Here one might extend Stallybrass and White's analysis of the "gaze," the body, and the topography of the city to the axis of world geography. Stallybrass and White argue that in the nineteenth century "the fear of differences . . . was articulated above all through the 'body' of the city" (125), producing a scopic economy in which the middle class (associated with the rationality of the upper body and the denial of lower bodily functions) became obsessively preoccupied with the lower classes and urban spaces—slums and sewers, dirt and sexuality—that were then associated with the lower bodily functions (145). I would argue that southern continents and territories such as Africa and India corresponded structurally to the urban slum and the lower body in the nineteenth-century bourgeois imagination.

4. See Janet Oppenheim's chapter "Nervous Degeneration" in *Shattered Nerves* for a discussion of late Victorian anxieties about racial fitness.

5. See Park, 61; Vertinsky, 259; Smith-Rosenberg and Rosenberg, 18, 21.

6. Atkinson's description of the exhibit draws upon a book published in 1894 by Sara Burstall, mistress of the North London Collegiate School for Girls, who had heard about the World's Fair exhibit during a trip to the United States as part of a group of five British women teachers who came to study American methods of secondary education for women. See *The Education of Girls in the United States*. Atkinson uses the exhibit to argue that physical education and measurement became important tools in the feminist educational reform movement.

7. There were a number of medical opinions about the potential dangers and benefits of corsets. Patricia Vertinsky has noted that "corsets were usually recommended for adolescents and women as a necessary support for their internal organs, but many females were criticized for using corsets for modelling rather than support" (263).

8. See also Haller and Haller's chapter, "Body Religion," in *The Physician and Sexuality in Victorian America*.

9. According to Kathleen McCrone, athleticism provided women with a channel through which to express their rebellion against social norms. See *Sport and the Physical Emancipation of English Women, 1870–1914*.

10. J. A. Mangan has discussed the relationship between muscular Christianity and social Darwinism in his article "Social Darwinism and Upper-Class Education in Late Victorian and Edwardian England." He claims that in many cases, muscular Christianity was an acceptable way of packaging what were really the tenets of social Darwinism: "There was an ideology for public consumption and an ideology for personal practice; in a phrase muscular Christianity for the consumer, Social Darwinism for the constrained" (139). See also Oppenheim's chapter "Manly Nerves," especially 147–51, in *Shattered Nerves*.

11. I do not mean to suggest that Victorian educational theory was a fully unified or monolithic body of discourse. Matthew Arnold, for one, had objected to the idea that public schools should be primarily concerned with turning out healthy animals rather than educated young men (Haley, 171). However, the influence of the physical fitness and sports programs on British public schools was, as Mangan has pointed out, extremely widespread. For a discussion of the relationship between organized sports, physical fitness, and Arnold's ideas about education in *Culture and Anarchy*, see "Anarchy and Physical Culture" in Haley's *Healthy Body and Victorian Culture*.

12. Martin Green has a useful discussion of Rhodes and imperialism in *Dreams of Adventure, Deeds of Empire*, 285–89. For a further discussion of public school games and the Victorian preoccupation with health, see "Anarchy and Physical Culture" in Haley's *Healthy Body and Victorian*

Culture, 161–79. See also J. R. De S. Honey's *Tom Brown's Universe: The Development of the Victorian Public School* and David Newsome's *Godliness and Good Learning: Four Studies in a Victorian Ideal*. For a discussion of the Boy Scout movement as a product of late-nineteenth-century anxieties about adolescent masculinity and the development of the social body, see Mark Seltzer, *Bodies and Machines*, 149.

13. Meredith was not alone in his literary fascination with physical culture. In 1870 Wilkie Collins's novel *Man and Wife* parodied male athleticism as a "contagion of barbarism" (147) and exposed physical fitness training as a fraud. In Collins's novel the famous athlete, Geoffrey Delamayn, builds his muscles at the expense of his "vital power" (149), eventually collapsing from overdevelopment.

14. Even after Meredith developed ataxia in his early fifties and became an invalid, he continued to be an avid follower of popular health trends. Bruce Haley points out that "Meredith's life and writings are a kind of synthesis of Victorian attitudes and ideas about health. He kept current on all the latest methods for staying well and tried many of them himself: hydropathy, homeopathy, Change of Climate, vegetarianism, calisthenics" (228).

15. See Haller and Haller, *The Physician and Sexuality in Victorian America*, chapter 3, and Stephen Marcus, *The Other Victorians*, chapter 1. In addition, Sir Austin's system for combating these evils bears a strong resemblance to advice given in the medical and educational literature of the period. See, for example, Ronald G. Walters's *Primers for Prudery: Sexual Advice to Victorian America*. Walters's chapters are divided into many of the same categories of advice as Sir Austin's system. They include: "Woman, Sensuous and Otherwise"; "Marriage"; "Controls and Cures"; and "Perfecting the Race" (ix).

16. Patrick Brantlinger has noted the importance of imperialist ideology to domestic subjects in the Victorian novel: "Imperialism influenced not only the tradition of the adventure tale but the tradition of 'serious' domestic realism as well. Adventure and domesticity, romance and realism, are the seemingly opposite poles of a single system of discourse. . . . In the middle of the most serious domestic concerns, often in the most unlikely texts, the Empire may intrude as a shadowy realm of escape, renewal, banishment, or return" (12). He cites texts such as *Sense and Sensibility*, *Mansfield Park*, *Jane Eyre*, and *Cranford* as examples of domestic fiction that contain intrusions of empire.

17. Judith Wilt has argued that the tremendous output of gothic and science fiction fantasies in the 1880's and 1890's was fueled by anxieties about imperialist decline. Wilt sees these fictions as subverting imperialist ideology. See "The Imperial Mouth: Imperialism, the Gothic, and Science

Fiction." See also Patrick Brantlinger's discussion of imperial gothic fiction in *Rule of Darkness* and Stephen Arata's account of imperialism, tourism, and racial anxiety in the 1890's in "The Occidental Tourist: *Dracula* and the Anxiety of Reverse Colonization."

18. Darwin, *The Descent of Man*, 21–23. For a discussion of how Darwin's observations about the ear were applied to judgments about comparative human development and criminal behavior, see Gilman, *Difference and Pathology*, 95; Sekula, "The Body and the Archive"; and Drinka, chapter 7, especially 158–68.

19. Catherine Gallagher has noted the discrepancy between Victorian ideas about the weak bodies of industrial workers and the strong bodies of more "nomadic" laborers and vagrants in Mayhew. See "The Body Versus the Social Body in the Works of Thomas Malthus and Henry Mayhew," 98–99.

20. See, for example, Stephen J. Gould's *Mismeasure of Man* and Cynthia Eagle Russett's *Sexual Science*.

21. It is important to note that in another sense Lombroso functioned as an apologist for criminal behavior. By introducing the category of the "born criminal" into legal and medical terminology he sought to distance antisocial behavior from approved social interaction through the unassailable barrier of heredity, thereby diminishing the individual's moral responsibility for criminal actions.

22. For a discussion of the relationship between pain and gender difference in nineteenth-century thinking, see Pernick, chapter 7.

23. This technique was particularly prevalent in post-Emancipation discussions of comparative racial health in America. For a discussion of the importance of the ninth and tenth censuses of 1870 and 1880 to theories of racial deterioration and longevity, see Haller, *Outcasts from Evolution*, 40–41. Haller claims that "despite the complexity of the problem and the reservations of many, the belief in the Negro's extinction became one of the most pervasive ideas in American medical and anthropological thought during the late nineteenth century" (41).

24. These class prejudices were perhaps most clearly embodied in (and reinforced by) the highly publicized case of Typhoid Mary, an Irish-American cook and rare disease carrier who spread fifty-two cases of typhoid in her employers' homes before she was diagnosed and quarantined (Ehrenreich and English, *Complaints and Disorders*, 57–59). Mary Mallon's case suggested to the popular imagination that while servants could be dangerous spreaders of disease, their laboring bodies were either insensitive or immune to sickness and animal-like in their capacity to withstand physical hardship.

25. Both Rosemary Jann and John L. Greenway have discussed the relationship between science and spiritualism in *Dracula*. Jann argues that de-

spite its emphasis on the supernatural, *Dracula* is "heavily invested in valorizing the rationalistic authority conventionally associated with scientific thought" (273). See Rosemary Jann, "Saved by Science? The Mixed Messages of Stoker's *Dracula*." Greenway, on the other hand, focuses on the importance of new scientific paradigms in the latter decades of the nineteenth century, paradigms that took investigation into subjects like telepathy and hypnosis seriously and offered physiological explanations of psychical events. See "Seward's Folly: *Dracula* as a Critique of 'Normal Science.' "

26. In a discussion of the health risks of urban living, Haggard claimed that "men and women sound in body and equal even if slow in mind, are of more importance to a country than any material wealth" (*Rural England*, vol. 2, 564). Stoker's emphasis on health grew, like Meredith's, out of a personal experience with childhood illness. Leonard Wolf notes that once Stoker recovered from the semi-invalidism of his childhood and early adolescence, he became a vigorous athlete.

27. As Norman Etherington has pointed out in *The Annotated She*, Haggard believed that he had been reincarnated, having had "visions of previous existences as a savage in stone-age England, a black African warrior, an Egyptian, and a Viking" (228). Haggard discusses these visions in his autobiography, *The Days of My Life* (vol. 2: 167–71).

28. By bracketing the term "Negro body" I do not mean to deny the reality of black physicality, but rather to point out that the only black bodies that appear in imperialist fictions like Haggard's are emblems of the racial myths created by the scientific community and the dominant culture. My bracketing is intended to call into question the idea of race as a classifiable, categorizable set of physical characteristics, and to identify it instead as what Henry Louis Gates has called a "trope of ultimate, irreducible difference" (5).

29. In *Cetywayo and His White Neighbours*, Haggard's nonfictional account of the Zulu king and his relationship to the Boers, Haggard dismisses arguments for the superiority of white races and their destiny to rule as "wicked" because they lead to wholesale slaughter, but he goes on to explain that "nothing is more ridiculous than the length to which the black brother theory is sometimes driven by enthusiasts. A savage is one thing, and a civilised man is another; and though civilised men may and do become savages, I personally doubt if the converse is even possible" (liii). For a further discussion of *Cetywayo*, see Katz, 145–46.

30. Although assumptions about racial difference occasionally translated into advocacy for racial crossbreeding—Anthony Trollope, for one, proposed the plan of mixing white intellectual ability with black stamina to produce people capable of colonizing and civilizing the tropics (Brantlinger, 6)—both the medical community and the authors of imperialist fiction were

far more likely to see the products of such matings as debasing racial purity and causing the degeneration of physical health.

31. See, in particular, *Allan Quatermain* and *She*.

32. Recent critics have tended to read *She* in terms of Victorian anxieties about femininity or the New Woman, as Sandra Gilbert and Susan Gubar propose in *No Man's Land*, or more specifically about Queen Victoria, as Adrienne Auslander Munich has argued in "Queen Victoria, Empire, and Excess." These studies usually ignore the ways in which issues of gender and race intersect in Haggard's novels. One recent study that focuses on this intersection is Laura Chrisman's "The Imperial Unconscious? Representations of Imperial Discourse." Chrisman's work is particularly valuable for identifying the ways in which Haggard's imperialism is constructed through contradictions. Chrisman emphasizes the various forms of "otherness" in Haggard's fictions and the instability of any monolithic reading of imperialist discourse.

33. The trope of purification is made most explicit in Sir Henry Curtis's final intention to devote himself to "the total exclusion of all foreigners from Zu-Vendis" in order to preserve the population from conquest (both martial and implicitly sexual) by modern civilizations (Haggard, *Allan Quatermain*, 669). Through this endeavor, Curtis is able to retain African sources of historical renewal intact from the degenerative trends of modernity, having already proven his own fitness to conquer and revive British racial stock.

34. There also seems to be a metonymic connection between Dracula's boxes of earth and the rats that surround and protect them on the boat from Transylvania and in Castle Carfax. The soil is thus linked with the instruments of disease, suggesting that Dracula's invasion is a modern form of plague that threatens to overwhelm the population of England. This connection is emphasized more explicitly in F. W. Murnau's 1922 film *Nosferatu—Eine Symphonie des Grauens* and Werner Herzog's 1979 *Nosferatu: Phantom der Nacht*.

35. There are repeated references in the text to the darkness and unknown character of Transylvania, culminating in the final chase of Dracula by water: "We seem to be drifting into unknown places and unknown ways; into a whole world of dark and dreadful things" (425). Geoffrey Wall has argued that Transylvania functions as "Europe's unconscious" (20). I would add that Transylvania functions as a substitute for the Dark Continent; both, in turn, function symbolically as Europe's unconscious. Conrad, of course, provides the most extended exploration of this theme in *Heart of Darkness*.

36. This is the central premise of Stephen Arata's excellent argument about tourism and reverse colonization in *Dracula*. Arata is also one of the

few critics writing about Dracula to note Stoker's emphasis on the vampire's health (631).

37. For an excellent interpretation of the gender implications of feeding in *Dracula*, see Christopher Craft's discussion of Lucy's "dietary indiscretions" and the inversion of breastfeeding in Mina's sucking at Dracula's chest in " 'Kiss Me With Those Red Lips': Gender and Inversion in Bram Stoker's *Dracula*," 229.

38. Sylvester Graham and Henry Kellogg were the most prominent spokespersons for this movement. See Stage, 61; Haller and Haller, 97; and Walters, 60–61. See also Helena Michie's discussion of the gendering of eating habits in Victorian fiction and advice literature (*The Flesh Made Word*, 15).

39. Wendy R. Katz has pointed out that there is "some suggestion that Haggard was attracted to theories of eugenics and favoured a eugenic programme to improve the quality of society" (71). *The Times* reported that in a speech he gave to the Church Army at Bungay, Haggard discussed the burden on society of the "degenerates" in the population and he "wondered . . . whether society in self-defense might not adopt measures which would put a stop to the multiplication of the unfit" (July 15, 1911, 11). There is no evidence, however, that Haggard would have believed in the kind of biological manipulations that Ayesha undertakes, and by putting the argument for eugenics in Ayesha's mouth, Haggard seems to question the moral and political implications of such a program.

40. In *The Annotated Dracula*, Leonard Wolf has noted the correlation between Lombroso's descriptions of criminal physiognomy and Stoker's description of the vampire, as recorded by Jonathan Harker:

> Harker writes: "[The Count's] face was . . . aquiline, with high bridge of the thin nose and peculiarly arched nostrils . . . "
> Lombroso: "[The criminal's] nose . . . is often aquiline like the beak of a bird of prey."
> Harker: "His eyebrows were very massive, almost meeting over the nose . . ."
> Lombroso: "The eyebrows are bushy and tend to meet across the nose."
> Harker: " . . . his ears were pale and at the tops extremely pointed . . . "
> Lombroso: "with a protuberance on the upper part of the posterior margin . . . a relic of the pointed ear . . . " (300)

In addition, I would note that the female vampires have "high aquiline noses, like the Count's, and great dark, piercing eyes." Their hair, like Lombroso's female offender's, is in "wavy masses" (*Dracula*, 51). See also Ernest Fontana's "Lombroso's Criminal Man and Stoker's *Dracula*" and Daniel Pick's excellent article " 'Terrors of the Night': *Dracula* and 'Degeneration' in the Late Nineteenth Century." Both Pick and Fontana emphasize the link between degeneration and disease in *Dracula*. Fontana specifically associates Dracula's atavism with epilepsy as a sign of degenerative tendencies. Pick points out that the most literal versions of Lombroso's theories (those emphasizing external physical anomalies) were being challenged by a number of scientists in the 1890's. At the same time a new generation of biological determinists were substituting more obscure, internal anomalies of blood, nerves, and brain for the more physiognomical features Lombroso had emphasized (79).

41. Christopher Craft has described this narrative pattern as a process of "aesthetic management" in which the text "first invites or admits a monster, then entertains and is entertained by monstrosity . . . [and finally] expels or repudiates the monster and all the disruption that he/she/it brings" (217). Here, health becomes part of the monstrosity that the text must repudiate.

42. For a discussion of critical responses to *Heart of Darkness* and Conrad's imperialist fiction in general, see Martin Green's *Dreams of Adventure: Deeds of Empire*, chapter 10, and Patrick Brantlinger's *Rule of Darkness*, chapter 9. Brantlinger's work is particularly useful on the question of racial politics, examining the arguments of both Conrad's apologists and those who, like the Nigerian novelist Chinua Achebe, have sought to drop *Heart of Darkness* from the teaching curriculum.

Conclusion

1. I am indebted to Marjorie Levinson for clarifying many of my ideas about the flexibility of ideology in the modern period.

Bibliography

Abell, Mrs. L. G. *Woman in Her Various Relations: Containing Practical Rules for American Females.* New York: R. T. Young, 1853.

"Addresses at the Unveiling of a Memorial Tablet in Honor of Mary Putnam Jacobi." *Women's Medical College of Pennsylvania Alumnae Transactions* (1907): 56–71.

Alcott, Louisa May. *Hospital Sketches* [1863]. Boston: Applewood Books, 1986.

———. *Little Women* [1868]. Boston: Little, Brown, 1968.

Almond, Hely Hutchinson. "The Breed of Man." *Nineteenth Century* 48 (1900): 656–69.

Andrews, Edmund. "The Surgeon." *The Chicago Medical Examiner* 2 (Nov. 1861): 587–98.

Arata, Stephen D. "The Occidental Tourist: *Dracula* and the Anxiety of Reverse Colonization." *Victorian Studies* 33 (Summer 1990): 621–45.

Armstrong, Nancy. *Desire and Domestic Fiction: A Political History of the Novel.* New York: Oxford University Press, 1987.

Ashbee, Henry. *Index Librorum Prohibitorum, Being Notes Bio: Biblio: Icono: Graphical and Critical, on Curious and Uncommon Books, by Pisanus Fraxi.* London, 1877.

Atkinson, Paul. "The Feminist Physique: Physical Education and the Medicalization of Women's Education." In Mangan and Park, eds., *From 'Fair Sex' to Feminism*, 38–57.

Aubry, Paul. *La contagion du meurtre: Etude d'anthropologie criminelle.* Paris: Felix Alcan, 1896.

Auchard, John. *Silence in Henry James: The Heritage of Symbolism and Decadence*. University Park, Pa.: Pennsylvania State University Press, 1986.

Auerbach, Nina. "Afterword." In Louisa May Alcott, *Little Women*. New York: Bantam, 1983.

———. *Communities of Women: An Idea in Fiction*. Cambridge, Mass.: Harvard University Press, 1978.

———. *Woman and the Demon: The Life of a Victorian Myth*. Cambridge, Mass.: Harvard University Press, 1982.

Bailin, Miriam. " 'Varieties of Pain': The Victorian Sickroom and Brontë's *Shirley*." *Modern Language Quarterly* 48 (Sept. 1987): 254–78.

Bain, Alexander. *The Emotions and the Will*. London: John W. Parker, 1859.

Baker, William. *The George Eliot–George Henry Lewes Library: An Annotated Catalogue of Their Books at Dr. Williams's Library, London*. New York: Garland, 1977.

Barker-Benfield, G. J. *The Horrors of the Half-Known Life: Male Attitudes Toward Women and Sexuality in Nineteenth-Century America*. New York: Harper & Row, 1976.

Barrows, Susanna. *Distorting Mirrors: Visions of the Crowd in Late Nineteenth-Century France*. New Haven, Conn.: Yale University Press, 1981.

Bassuk, Ellen L. "The Rest Cure: Repetition or Resolution of Victorian Women's Conflicts?" In Suleiman, ed., *The Female Body in Western Culture*, 139–51.

Beard, George Miller, M.D. *American Nervousness, Its Causes and Consequences, a Supplement to Nervous Exhaustion (Neurasthenia)*. New York: G. P. Putnam's Sons, 1881.

———. *A Practical Treatise on Nervous Exhaustion (Neurasthenia), Its Symptoms, Nature, Sequences, Treatment*. New York: W. Wood, 1880.

———. *Sexual Neurasthenia (Nervous Exhaustion): Its Hygiene, Causes, Symptoms, and Treatment, with a Chapter on Diet for the Nervous*. 3rd ed. New York: E. B. Treat, 1891.

Beer, Gillian. *Darwin's Plots: Evolutionary Narrative in Darwin, George Eliot, and Nineteenth-Century Fiction*. Boston: Routledge & Kegan Paul, 1983.

Benstock, Shari, ed. *Feminist Issues in Literary Scholarship*. Bloomington: Indiana University Press, 1987.

Bernal, Martin. *Black Athena: The Afroasiatic Roots of Classical Civilization*. London: Free Association Press, 1987.

Bernheimer, Charles, and Claire Kahane, eds. *In Dora's Case: Freud—Hysteria—Feminism*. New York: Columbia University Press, 1985.

Bissell, Mary T., M.D. "Emotions *Versus* Health in Women." *Popular Science Monthly* 32 (Feb. 1888): 504–10.

Blackwell, Elizabeth. *Pioneer Work in Opening the Medical Profession to Women*. London: Longmans, Green, 1895.

Blaikie, William. *How to Get Strong and How to Stay So*. New York: Harper, 1879.

Boruah, Bijoy H. *Fiction and Emotion: A Study in Aesthetics and the Philosophy of Mind*. Oxford, Eng.: Clarendon Press, 1988.

Bourneville, Désiré, and Paul Regnard. *Iconographie photographique de la Salpêtrière*. 3 vols. Paris: Progrès Médical, 1876–80.

Brantlinger, Patrick. *Rule of Darkness: British Literature and Imperialism, 1830–1914*. Ithaca, N.Y.: Cornell University Press, 1988.

Breuer, Josef, and Sigmund Freud. *Studies on Hysteria* [1895]. Trans. James Strachey. New York: Basic Books, 1957.

Brodie, Sir Benjamin. *Pathological and Surgical Observations on Diseases of the Joints*. 2nd ed. Philadelphia: B. Warner, 1821.

Bronfen, Elisabeth. *Over Her Dead Body: Death, Femininity and the Aesthetic*. New York: Routledge, 1992.

Brontë, Charlotte. *Shirley* [1849]. Oxford, Eng.: Oxford University Press, 1981.

———. *Villette* [1853]. Harmondsworth, Eng.: Penguin, 1982.

Brooks, Peter. *Body Work, Objects of Desire in Modern Narrative*. Cambridge, Mass.: Harvard University Press, 1993.

———. *Reading for the Plot: Design and Intention in Narrative*. New York: Vintage Books, 1985.

Brown, Gillian. "The Empire of Agoraphobia." *Representations* 20 (Fall 1987): 134–57.

Brumberg, Joan Jacobs. *Fasting Girls: The History of Anorexia Nervosa*. New York: New American Library, 1988.

Buck, Albert H., M.D., ed. *A Reference Handbook of the Medical Sciences, Embracing the Entire Range of Scientific and Practical Medicine and Allied Science*. 9 vols. New York: W. Wood, 1885–93.

Burstall, Sara A. *The Education of Girls in the United States*. London: Swan Sonnenschein, 1894.

Bynum, W. F. "The Nervous Patient in Eighteenth- and Nineteenth-Century Britain: The Psychiatric Origins of British Neurology." In Bynum, Porter, and Shepherd, eds., *The Anatomy of Madness*, vol. 1, 89–102.

Bynum, W. F., and Roy Porter, eds. *Medical Fringe & Medical Orthodoxy, 1750–1850*. London: Croom Helm, 1987.

Bynum, W. F., Roy Porter, and Michael Shepherd, eds. *The Anatomy of Madness: Essays in the History of Psychiatry*. 2 vols. London: Tavistock, 1985.

Cameron, Deborah. *Feminism and Linguistic Theory*. New York: St. Martin's Press, 1985.

————, ed. *The Feminist Critique of Language: A Reader*. London: Routledge, 1990.

Cameron, Sharon. *The Corporeal Self: Allegories of the Body in Melville and Hawthorne*. Baltimore, Md.: Johns Hopkins University Press, 1981.

Canetti, Elias. *Crowds and Power*. Trans. Carol Stewart. New York: Viking Press, 1962.

Caplan, Arthur L., H. Tristram Engelhardt, Jr., and James J. McCartney, eds. *Concepts of Health and Disease: Interdisciplinary Perspectives*. Reading, Mass.: Addison-Wesley Advanced Book Program, 1981.

Carroll, David. *George Eliot and the Conflict of Interpretations*. Cambridge, Eng.: Cambridge University Press, 1992.

Carter, Robert Brudenell. *On the Influence of Education and Training in Preventing Diseases of the Nervous System*. London: Churchill, 1855.

Cartwright, Samuel A., M.D. "Report on the Diseases and Physical Peculiarities of the Negro Race" [1851]. In Caplan, Engelhardt, Jr., and McCartney, eds., *Concepts of Health and Disease*, 305–25.

Castle, Terry. "Contagious Folly: *An Adventure* and Its Skeptics." *Critical Inquiry* 17, no. 4 (Summer 1991): 741–72.

————. "Phantasmagoria: Spectral Technology and the Metaphorics of Modern Reverie." *Critical Inquiry* 15, no. 1 (Autumn 1988): 26–61.

Cecil, Mirabel. *Heroines in Love, 1750–1974*. London: Michael Joseph, 1974.

Chancellor, Valerie. E. *History for Their Masters: Opinion in the English History Textbook: 1800–1914*. New York: A. M. Kelley, 1970.

Charcot, J. M. *Lectures on the Diseases of the Nervous System*. Trans. George Sigerson, M.D. Philadelphia, Pa.: H. C. Lea, 1879.

Chase, Karen. *Eros and Psyche: The Representation of Personality in Charlotte Brontë, Charles Dickens, George Eliot*. New York: Methuen, 1984.

Chavasse, Pye Henry. *The Physical Training of Children, with a Preliminary Dissertation*. Philadelphia, Pa.: New-World, 1872.

Child, Lydia Maria. *The Mother's Book*. Boston: Carter, Hender and Babcock, 1831.

Chodorow, Nancy. *The Reproduction of Mothering: Psychoanalysis and the Sociology of Gender*. Berkeley: University of California Press, 1978.

Chrisman, Laura. "The Imperial Unconscious? Representations of Imperial Discourse." *Critical Quarterly* 32, no. 3 (Autumn 1990): 38–58.

Christ, Carol. "Aggression and Providential Death in George Eliot's Fiction." *Novel* 9 (1976): 130–40.

Cixous, Hélène. "Castration or Decapitation?" Trans. Annette Kuhn. *Signs* 7, no. 1 (1981): 41–55.

Cixous, Hélène, and Catherine Clément. *The Newly Born Woman*. Trans. Betsy Wing. Minneapolis: University of Minnesota Press, 1986.

Clarke, Edward H., M.D. *Sex in Education; Or, A Fair Chance for the Girls.* Boston: J. R. Osgood, 1873.

Clouston, Thomas Smith, M.D. *The Hygiene of Mind.* 4th ed. New York: E. P. Dutton, 1906.

Coates, Jennifer. *Women, Men, and Language: A Sociolinguistic Account of Sex Differences in Language.* London: Longman, 1986.

Coleman, Rosalind A., and James Rolleston. "Anatomy Lessons: The Destiny of a Textbook, 1971–72." *South Atlantic Quarterly* 90, no. 1 (Winter 1991): 153–75.

Collins, K. K. "G. H. Lewes Revised: George Eliot and the Moral Sense." *Victorian Studies* 21 (1978): 463–92.

Collins, Wilkie. *The Dead Secret* [1857]. New York: Dover, 1979.

———. *Man and Wife* [1870]. London: Chatto and Windus, 1871.

Combe, Andrew, M.D. *The Principles of Physiology Applied to the Preservation of Health, and to the Improvement of Physical and Mental Education.* 14th ed. Edinburgh: Maclachlan and Stewart, 1852.

Conrad, Joseph. *Heart of Darkness* [1899]. New York: W. W. Norton, 1988.

Craft, Christopher. " 'Kiss Me with Those Red Lips': Gender and Inversion in Bram Stoker's *Dracula.*" In Showalter, ed., *Speaking of Gender,* 216–42.

Culler, Jonathan. *On Deconstruction: Theory and Criticism After Structuralism.* Ithaca, N.Y.: Cornell University Press, 1982.

Darwin, Charles. *The Descent of Man, and Selection in Relation to Sex* [1871]. Princeton, N.J.: Princeton University Press, 1981.

———. *Origin of Species* [1859]. Cambridge, Eng.: Cambridge University Press, 1981.

David, Deirdre. *Fictions of Resolution in Three Victorian Novels: North and South, Our Mutual Friend, Daniel Deronda.* New York: Columbia University Press, 1981.

de Lauretis, Teresa, ed. *Feminist Studies/Critical Studies.* Bloomington: Indiana University Press, 1986.

Dendy, Walter Cooper. *The Philosophy of Mystery.* New York: Harper, 1845.

Diamond, Irene, and Lee Quinby, eds. *Feminism & Foucault: Reflections on Resistance.* Boston: Northeastern University Press, 1988.

Dijkstra, Bram. *Idols of Perversity: Fantasies of Feminine Evil in Fin-de-Siècle Culture.* New York: Oxford University Press, 1986.

Doane, Mary Ann. *The Desire to Desire: The Woman's Film of the 1940s.* Bloomington: Indiana University Press, 1987.

Donzelot, Jacques. *The Policing of Families* [1977]. Trans. Robert Hurley. New York: Pantheon, 1979.

Douglas, Ann. *The Feminization of American Culture.* New York: Doubleday, Anchor Books, 1977.

Douglas, Mary. *Purity and Danger: An Analysis of the Concepts of Pollution and Taboo* [1966]. London: Routledge, 1991.

Drinka, George Frederick, M.D. *The Birth of Neurosis: Myth, Malady and the Victorians*. New York: Simon & Schuster, 1984.

du Maurier, George. *Trilby* [1894]. London: J. M. Dent, 1992.

During, Simon. "The Strange Case of Monomania: Patriarchy in Literature, Murder in *Middlemarch*, Drowning in *Daniel Deronda*." *Representations* 23 (Summer 1988): 86–104.

Ehrenreich, Barbara, and Deirdre English. *Complaints and Disorders: The Sexual Politics of Sickness*. New York: The Feminist Press, 1973.

———. *For Her Own Good: 150 Years of the Experts' Advice to Women*. New York: Doubleday, Anchor Books, 1978.

Eliot, George. *Daniel Deronda* [1876]. Harmondsworth, Eng.: Penguin, 1979.

———. *Middlemarch* [1871–72]. Harmondsworth, Eng.: Penguin, 1979.

Ermarth, Elizabeth. "George Eliot's Conception of Sympathy." *Nineteenth Century Fiction* 40 (June 1985): 23–42.

Fellman, Anita Clair, and Michael Fellman. *Making Sense of Self: Medical Advice Literature in Late Nineteenth-Century America*. Philadelphia, Pa.: University of Pennsylvania Press, 1981.

Felman, Shoshana. *Writing and Madness (Literature/Philosophy/Psychoanalysis)*. Ithaca, N.Y.: Cornell University Press, 1985.

———. "Women and Madness: The Critical Phallacy." *Diacritics* 5, no. 4 (Winter 1975): 2–10.

Fetterley, Judith. *The Resisting Reader: A Feminist Approach to American Fiction*. Bloomington: Indiana University Press, 1978.

Fisher, Philip. *Hard Facts: Setting and Form in the American Novel*. New York: Oxford University Press, 1987.

Fletcher, C. R. L., and Rudyard Kipling. *A History of England*. Oxford, Eng.: Clarendon Press, 1911.

Fontana, Ernest. "Lombroso's Criminal Man and Stoker's *Dracula*." *The Victorian Newsletter* 66 (Fall 1984): 25–27.

Ford, George H. *Dickens and His Readers: Aspects of Novel-Criticism Since 1836*. Princeton, N.J.: Princeton University Press, 1955.

Forster, E. M. *A Passage to India* [1924]. San Diego, Calif.: Harcourt, Brace, Jovanovich, 1984.

Foucault, Michel. *The Birth of the Clinic: An Archaeology of Medical Perception* [1963]. Trans. A. M. Sheridan Smith. New York: Random House, Vintage Books, 1975.

———. *Discipline and Punish: The Birth of the Prison* [1975]. Trans. Alan Sheridan. New York: Random House, Vintage Books, 1977.

———. *The History of Sexuality*. Volume 1: *An Introduction* [1976]. Trans. Robert Hurley. New York: Random House, Vintage Books, 1980.

———. *Madness and Civilization: A History of Insanity in the Age of Reason* [1961]. Trans. Richard Howard. New York: Random House, Vintage Books, 1988.

Freedman, Jonathan. "Mania and the Middlebrow: The Case of *Trilby*." Paper presented at the University of Michigan, February 1991.

Freud, Sigmund. *Dora: An Analysis of a Case of Hysteria* [1905]. Trans. James Strachey. New York: Macmillan, 1963.

———. *Group Psychology and the Analysis of the Ego* [1921]. Trans. James Strachey. New York: Norton, 1975.

Fryer, Judith. " 'The Body in Pain' in Thomas Eakins' *Agnew Clinic*." *Michigan Quarterly Review* 30, no. 1 (Winter 1991): 191–209.

Gallagher, Catherine. "The Body Versus the Social Body in the Works of Thomas Malthus and Henry Mayhew." *Representations* 14 (Spring 1986): 83–106.

———. "George Eliot and *Daniel Deronda*: The Prostitute and the Jewish Question." In Yeazell, ed., *Sex, Politics, and Science in the Nineteenth-Century Novel*, 39–62.

———. *The Industrial Reformation of English Fiction: Social Discourse and Narrative Form, 1832–1867*. Chicago: University of Chicago Press, 1985.

Gallagher, Catherine, and Thomas Laqueur, eds. *The Making of the Modern Body: Sexuality and Society in the Nineteenth Century*. Berkeley: University of California Press, 1987.

Galton, Sir Francis. *Inquiries into Human Faculty and Its Development*. London: Macmillan, 1883.

Gardner, Augustus Kinsley. "New York Medical College for Women." *Frank Leslie's Illustrated Newspaper* 30, no. 759 (April 10, 1879): 71.

Gaskell, Elizabeth. *Cousin Phillis* [1863–64]. In *Cranford/Cousin Phillis*. Harmondsworth, Eng.: Penguin, 1982.

———. *The Life of Charlotte Brontë* [1857]. Harmondsworth, Eng.: Penguin, 1985.

Gates, Henry Louis, Jr. "Writing 'Race' and the Difference It Makes." *Critical Inquiry* 12 (Autumn 1985): 1–20.

Gilbert, Sandra, and Susan Gubar. *The Madwoman in the Attic: The Woman Writer and the Nineteenth-Century Literary Imagination*. New Haven, Conn.: Yale University Press, 1979.

———. *No Man's Land: The Place of the Woman Writer in the Twentieth Century*. Volume 2: *Sexchanges*. New Haven, Conn.: Yale University Press, 1988.

Gilman, Sander L. *Difference and Pathology: Stereotypes of Sexuality, Race, and Madness.* Ithaca, N.Y.: Cornell University Press, 1985.

———. *Disease and Representation: Images of Illness from Madness to AIDS.* Ithaca, N.Y.: Cornell University Press, 1988.

Goldfarb, Russel M. *Sexual Repression and Victorian Literature.* Lewisburg, Pa.: Bucknell University Press, 1970.

Gould, Stephen Jay. *The Mismeasure of Man.* New York: W. W. Norton, 1981.

Grand, Sarah. *The Heavenly Twins* [1893]. Ann Arbor: University of Michigan Press, 1992.

Green, Martin Burgess. *Dreams of Adventure, Deeds of Empire.* New York: Basic Books, 1979.

Greenway, John L. "Seward's Folly: *Dracula* as a Critique of 'Normal Science.' " *Stanford Literature Review* 3, no. 2 (Fall 1986): 213–30.

Gwendolen. Boston: Bradley, 1878.

Haggard, H. Rider. *Allan Quatermain* [1887]. In *The Works of H. Rider Haggard.* Roslyn, N.Y.: Walter J. Black, 1928.

———. *The Annotated She: A Critical Edition of H. Rider Haggard's Victorian Romance* [1886]. Ed. Norman Etherington. Bloomington: Indiana University Press, 1991.

———. *Cetywayo and His White Neighbours.* 2nd ed. London: Kegan Paul, Trench, Trübner, 1896.

———. *The Days of My Life.* 2 vols. London: Longmans, Green, 1882.

———. *King Solomon's Mines* [1885]. In *The Works of H. Rider Haggard.* Roslyn, N.Y.: Walter J. Black, 1928.

———. *Rural England: Being an Account of Agricultural and Social Researches Carried Out in the Years 1901 and 1902.* 2 vols. London: Longmans, Green, 1906.

Haight, Gordon S. *George Eliot: A Biography.* London: Clarendon Press, 1968.

Haley, Bruce. *The Healthy Body and Victorian Culture.* Cambridge, Mass.: Harvard University Press, 1978.

Haller, John S. *Outcasts from Evolution: Scientific Attitudes of Racial Inferiority, 1859–1900.* Urbana: University of Illinois Press, 1971.

Haller, John S., and Robin Haller. *The Physician and Sexuality in Victorian America.* Urbana: University of Illinois Press, 1974.

Halttunen, Karen. *Confidence Men and Painted Women: A Study of Middle-Class Culture in America, 1830–1870.* New Haven, Conn.: Yale University Press, 1982.

Harris, Ruth. "Murder Under Hypnosis in the Case of Gabrielle Bompard: Psychiatry in the Courtroom in Belle Epoque Paris." In Bynum, Porter, and Shepherd, eds., *The Anatomy of Madness,* vol. 2, 197–241.

————. *Murders and Madness: Medicine, Law, and Society in the Fin de Siècle.* Oxford, Eng.: Clarendon Press, 1989.

Harrison, Mark. *Crowds and History: Mass Phenomena in English Towns, 1790–1835.* Cambridge, Eng.: Cambridge University Press, 1988.

Hartman, Mary S. *Victorian Murderesses.* New York: Schocken Books, 1977.

Hartman, Mary S., and Lois Banner, eds. *Clio's Consciousness Raised: New Perspectives on the History of Women.* New York: Harper & Row, 1974.

Hartsock, Nancy. "Foucault on Power: A Theory for Women?" In Nicholson, ed., *Feminism/Postmodernism,* 157–75.

Herndl, Diane Price. *Invalid Women: Figuring Feminine Illness in American Fiction and Culture, 1840–1940.* Chapel Hill: University of North Carolina Press, 1993.

Higonnet, Margaret. "Speaking Silences: Women's Suicide." In Suleiman, ed., *The Female Body in Western Culture,* 68–83.

Hoffman, Frederick L. "Race Traits and Tendencies of the American Negro." *Publications,* American Economic Association 11 (August 1896): 1–329.

Holmes, Oliver Wendell. *Elsie Venner: A Romance of Destiny* [1861]. New York: A. L. Burt, 1903.

————. *The Guardian Angel* [1867]. Boston: Houghton Mifflin, 1892.

Homans, Margaret. *Bearing the Word: Language and Female Experience in Nineteenth-Century Women's Writing.* Chicago: University of Chicago Press, 1986.

Honey, John Raymond De Symons. *Tom Brown's Universe: The Development of the Victorian Public School.* London: Millington, 1977.

Hughes, Helen MacGill, ed. *Crowd and Mass Behavior.* Boston: Allyn and Bacon, 1972.

Hughes, Winifred. *The Maniac in the Cellar: Sensation Novels of the 1860s.* Princeton, N.J.: Princeton University Press, 1980.

Hunt, Harriot K., M.D. *Glances and Glimpses; or, Fifty Years Social, Including Twenty Years Professional Life.* Boston: J. P. Jewett, 1856.

Hunt, Linda. "Charlotte Brontë and the Suffering Sisterhood." *Colby Library Quarterly* 19, no. 1 (March 1983): 7–17.

Hunt, Lynn, ed. *The New Cultural History.* Berkeley: University of California Press, 1989.

Hunter, Dianne. "Hysteria, Psychoanalysis, and Feminism: The Case of Anna O." *Feminist Studies* 9 (1983): 465–88.

Hutner, Gordon. *Secrets and Sympathy: Forms of Disclosure in Hawthorne's Novels.* Athens: University of Georgia Press, 1988.

Hutter, Albert D. "Dismemberment and Articulation in *Our Mutual*

Friend." *Dickens Studies Annual: Essays on Victorian Fiction* 11 (1983): 135–75.

Ian, Marcia. "The Elaboration of Privacy in *The Wings of the Dove*." *ELH* 51 (Spring 1984): 107–36.

Irigaray, Luce. *Speculum of the Other Woman*. Trans. Gillian C. Gill. Ithaca, N.Y.: Cornell University Press, 1985.

Jackson, John Hughlings. *Selected Writings of John Hughlings Jackson*. Vol. 1. London: Hodder and Stroughton, 1931–32.

Jacobi, Mary Putnam. *Life and Letters of Mary Putnam Jacobi*. Ed. Ruth Putnam. New York: G. P. Putnam's Sons, 1925.

Jacobus, Mary. *Reading Woman: Essays in Feminist Criticism*. New York: Columbia University Press, 1986.

Jacobus, Mary, Evelyn Fox Keller, and Sally Shuttleworth, eds. *Body/Politics: Women and the Discourses of Science*. New York: Routledge, 1990.

James, Alice. *The Diary of Alice James*. Ed. Leon Edel. Harmondsworth, Eng.: Penguin, 1982.

James, Henry. *The Complete Notebooks of Henry James*. Ed. Leon Edel and Lyall H. Powers. New York: Oxford University Press, 1987.

———. "The Science of Criticism." In Leon Edel, ed., *Literary Criticism: Essays on Literature, American Writers, English Writers*, 95–99. New York: Library of America, 1984.

———. *The Wings of the Dove* [1902]. New York: W. W. Norton, 1978.

Jameson, Fredric. *The Political Unconscious: Narrative as a Socially Symbolic Act*. Ithaca, N.Y.: Cornell University Press, 1981.

Jann, Rosemary. "Saved by Science? The Mixed Messages of Stoker's *Dracula*." *Texas Studies in Literature and Language* 31, no. 2 (Summer 1989): 271–87.

Jennings, Samuel K. *The Married Lady's Companion, or, Poorman's Friend*. New York: Lorenzo Dow, 1808.

Johnson, E. D. H. " 'Daring the Dread Glance': Charlotte Brontë's Treatment of the Supernatural in *Villette*." *Nineteenth-Century Fiction* 20 (March 1966): 325–36.

Johnson, Samuel. *Rambler* no. 4. In W. J. Baite and Albrecht B. Strauss, eds., *Samuel Johnson: The Rambler*, vol. 1, 19–25. New Haven, Conn.: Yale University Press, 1969.

Jones, Greta. *Social Darwinism and English Thought: The Interaction Between Biological and Social Theory*. Atlantic Highlands, N.J.: Humanities Press, 1980.

Jordanova, Ludmilla. *Sexual Visions: Images of Gender in Science and Medicine Between the Eighteenth and Twentieth Centuries*. Madison: University of Wisconsin Press, 1989.

Kaplan, E. Ann. *Women and Film: Both Sides of the Camera*. N.Y.: Methuen, 1983.

Kaplan, Fred. *Sacred Tears: Sentimentality in Victorian Literature*. Princeton, N.J.: Princeton University Press, 1987.

Katz, Wendy R. *Rider Haggard and the Fiction of Empire: A Critical Study of British Imperial Fiction*. Cambridge, Eng.: Cambridge University Press, 1987.

Kendrick, Walter M. *The Novel-Machine: The Theory and Fiction of Anthony Trollope*. Baltimore, Md.: Johns Hopkins University Press, 1980.

Kolodny, Annette. "Reply to Commentaries: Women Writers, Literary Historians, and Martian Readers." *New Literary History* 11, no. 3 (1980): 587–92.

Krafft-Ebing, Richard von. *Psychopathia Sexualis, with Especial Reference to Contrary Sexual Instinct* [1882]. 7th ed. Trans. Gilbert Chaddock, M.D. Philadelphia: F. A. Davis, 1908.

Krohn, Alan. *Hysteria: The Elusive Neurosis*. New York: International Universities Press, 1978.

Kucich, John. *Excess and Restraint in the Novels of Charles Dickens*. Athens: University of Georgia Press, 1981.

———. *Repression in Victorian Fiction: Charlotte Brontë, George Eliot, and Charles Dickens*. Berkeley: University of California Press, 1987.

Kuhn, Annette, and Ann Marie Wolpe, eds. *Feminism and Materialism: Women and Modes of Production*. London: Routledge & Kegan Paul, 1978.

Lakoff, Robin. *Language and Woman's Place*. New York: Harper & Row, 1975.

———. *Talking Power: The Politics of Language in Our Lives*. New York: Basic Books, 1990.

Langbauer, Laurie. *Women and Romance: The Consolations of Gender in the English Novel*. Ithaca, N.Y.: Cornell University Press, 1990.

Lansbury, Coral. "Gynecology, Pornography, and the Antivivisection Movement." *Victorian Studies* 28, no. 3 (Spring 1985): 413–38.

Laqueur, Thomas W. "Bodies, Details, and the Humanitarian Narrative." In Hunt, ed., *The New Cultural History*, 176–204.

———. *Making Sex: Body and Gender from the Greeks to Freud*. Cambridge, Mass.: Harvard University Press, 1990.

Laycock, Thomas, M.D. *Mind and Brain*. [1860]. 2 vols. New York: Arno Press, 1976.

———. *A Treatise on the Nervous Diseases of Women; Comprising an Inquiry in the Nature, Causes, and Treatment of Spinal and Hysterical Disorders*. London: Longmans, 1840.

Leavitt, Judith Walzer. " 'Science' Enters the Birthing Room: Obstetrics in America Since the 18th Century." In Leavitt and Numbers, eds., *Sickness and Health in America*, 81–97.

Leavitt, Judith Walzer, and Ronald L. Numbers, eds. *Sickness and Health in America: Readings in the History of Medicine and Public Health*. Madison: University of Wisconsin Press, 1985.

Le Bon, Gustave. *The Crowd: A Study of the Popular Mind*. Translated from the French. London: Ernest Benn, 1947. Originally published as *Psychologie des foules* (1895).

LeFevre, Sir George, M.D. *An Apology for the Nerves: or, Their Influence and Importance in Health and Disease*. London: Longmans, Brown, Green and Longmans, 1844.

Levine, George, ed. *One Culture: Essays in Science and Literature*. Madison: University of Wisconsin Press, 1987.

———. "The Scientific Texture of *Middlemarch*." In Harold Bloom, ed., *George Eliot*, 187–202. New York: Chelsea House, 1986.

Levy, Anita. *Other Women: The Writing of Class, Race, and Gender, 1832–1898*. Princeton, N.J.: Princeton University Press, 1991.

Lewes, George Henry. *Problems of Life and Mind*. Third series. London: Trübner, 1879.

Loesberg, Jonathan. "The Ideology of Narrative Form in Sensation Fiction." *Representations* 13 (Winter 1986): 115–38.

Lombroso, Cesare. *L'uomo delinquente* [1876]. Rome: Napoleone, 1971.

Lombroso, Cesare, and William Ferrero. *The Female Offender* [1895]. Trans. Frank J. Pirone, M.D. New York: D. Appleton, 1915.

Lombroso-Ferrero, Gina. *Criminal Man, According to the Classification of Cesare Lombroso*. New York: G. P. Putnam's Sons, 1911.

Lutz, Tom. *American Nervousness, 1903: An Anecdotal History*. Ithaca, N.Y.: Cornell University Press, 1991.

McClelland, J. S. *The Crowd and the Mob from Homer to Canetti*. London: Unwin Hyman, 1988.

McCrone, Kathleen E. *Sport and the Physical Emancipation of English Women, 1870–1914*. London: Routledge, 1988.

McGillicuddy, Timothy J. *Functional Disorders of the Nervous System in Women*. New York: W. Wood, 1896.

Mangan, J. A. *The Games Ethic and Imperialism*. New York: Viking Press, 1985.

———. "Social Darwinism and Upper-Class Education in Late Victorian and Edwardian England." In Mangan and Walvin, eds., *Manliness and Morality*, 135–59.

Mangan, J. A., and Roberta J. Park, eds. *From 'Fair Sex' to Feminism: Sport and the Socialization of Women in the Industrial and Post-Industrial Eras*. London: Frank Cass, 1987.

Mangan, J. A., and James Walvin, eds. *Manliness and Morality: Middle-Class Masculinity in Britain and America, 1800–1940*. Manchester, Eng.: Manchester University Press, 1987.

Marcus, Stephen. *The Other Victorians: A Study of Sexuality and Pornography in Mid-Nineteenth-Century England*. New York: Basic Books, 1966.

Martin, Everett Dean. *The Behavior of Crowds: A Psychological Study*. New York: Harper, 1920.

Martineau, Harriet. *Deerbrook* [1839]. London: Virago, 1983.

Mason, Michael York. "*Middlemarch* and Science: Problems of Life." *Review of English Studies* 22 (1971): 151–69.

Maudsley, Henry. *Body and Mind*. London: Macmillan, 1870.

———. *The Physiology of Mind*. New York: D. Appleton, 1878.

———. "Sex in Mind and Education." *Fortnightly Review* 15 (1874): 466–83.

Mayhew, Henry. *London Labour and the London Poor*. 4 vols. London: Griffin, Bohn, 1864.

Maynard, John. *Charlotte Brontë and Sexuality*. Cambridge, Eng.: Cambridge University Press, 1984.

Mercer, Caroline G., and Sarah D. Wangensteen. " 'Consumption, Heart-Disease, or Whatever': Chlorosis, a Heroine's Illness in *The Wings of the Dove*." *Journal of the History of Medicine and Allied Sciences* 40 (1985): 259–85.

Meredith, George. *The Egoist* [1879]. Harmondsworth, Eng.: Penguin, 1978.

———. *The Ordeal of Richard Feverel* [1859]. New York: Random House Modern Library, 1950.

Michie, Helena. *The Flesh Made Word: Female Figures and Women's Bodies*. New York: Oxford University Press, 1987.

———. " 'Who Is This in Pain?' Scarring, Disfigurement, and Female Identity in *Bleak House* and *Our Mutual Friend*." *Novel* 22 (Winter 1989): 199–212.

Miller, D. A. "The Late Jane Austen." *Raritan* (Summer 1990): 55–79.

———. *Narrative and Its Discontents: Problems of Closure in the Traditional Novel*. Princeton, N.J.: Princeton University Press, 1981.

———. *The Novel and the Police*. Berkeley: University California Press, 1988.

Miller, J. Hillis. *The Form of Victorian Fiction*. Notre Dame, Ind.: University of Notre Dame Press, 1968.

———. "Optic and Semiotic in *Middlemarch*." In Jerome Buckley, ed., *The Worlds of Victorian Fiction*, 125–48. Cambridge, Mass.: Harvard University Press.

Mills, Nicolaus. *The Crowd in American Literature*. Baton Rouge: Louisiana State University Press, 1986.

Minchin, James George Cotton. *Our Public Schools: Their Influence on English History*. London: Swan Sonnenschein, 1901.

Mitchell, S. Weir, M.D. *Characteristics: A Novel* [1892]. New York: Century, 1905.

———. *Lectures on Diseases of the Nervous System, Especially in Women*. Philadelphia, Pa.: Lea Brothers, 1885.

Mitchell, W. J. T., ed. *On Narrative*. Chicago: University of Chicago Press, 1981.

Moi, Toril. *Sexual/Textual Politics: Feminist Literary Theory*. London: Routledge, 1985.

Montaigne, Michel de. *The Complete Works of Montaigne*. Trans. Donald M. Frame. Stanford, Calif.: Stanford University Press, 1948.

Moon, Michael. "Sexuality and Visual Terrorism in *The Wings of the Dove*. *Criticism: A Quarterly for Literature and the Arts* 28, no. 4 (Fall 1986): 427–43.

Moore, George. *Esther Waters* [1894]. London: J. M. Dent, 1977.

Morantz-Sanchez, Regina Markell. *Sympathy and Science: Women Physicians in American Medicine*. Oxford, Eng.: Oxford University Press, 1985.

Morel, Bénédict Auguste. *Traité des dégénérescences physiques, intellectuelles et morales de l'espèce humaine et des causes qui produisent les variétés maladives*. Paris: J. B. Baillière, 1857.

Mullan, John. *Sentiment and Sociability: The Language of Feeling in the Eighteenth Century*. Oxford, Eng.: Clarendon Press, 1988.

Mulvey, Laura. "Visual Pleasure and Narrative Cinema." *Screen* 16, no. 3 (Autumn 1975): 6–18.

Munich, Adrienne Auslander. "Queen Victoria, Empire, and Excess." *Tulsa Studies in Women's Literature* 6, no. 2 (Fall 1987): 265–81.

Munthe, Axel. *The Story of San Michele* [1929]. New York: E. P. Dutton, 1932.

Mykyta, Larysa. "Lacan, Literature, and the Look: Woman in the Eye of Psychoanalysis." *Sub Stance* 39 (1983): 49–57.

Newsome, David. *Godliness and Good Learning: Four Studies in a Victorian Ideal*. London: John Murray, 1961.

Newton, Judith, and Deborah Rosenfelt, eds. *Feminist Criticism and Social Change. Sex, Class and Race in Literature and Culture*. New York: Methuen, 1985.

Nicholson, Linda J., ed. *Feminism/Postmodernism*. New York: Routledge, 1990.

Nordau, Max. *Degeneration*. Translated from the German. New York: D. Appleton, 1895.

"Novels and Novelists of the Day." *North British Review* 38 (Feb. 1863): 168–90.

Nye, Robert A. *The Origins of Crowd Psychology: Gustave Le Bon and the Crisis of Mass Democracy in the Third Republic*. London: Sage Publications, 1975.

Oppenheim, Janet. *The Other World: Spiritualism and Psychical Research in England, 1850–1914*. Cambridge, Eng.: Cambridge University Press, 1985.

———. *'Shattered Nerves': Doctors, Patients, and Depression in Victorian England*. New York: Oxford University Press, 1991.

Osler, Sir William. *Counsels and Ideals*. Boston: Houghton Mifflin, 1905.

Paget, Sir James, M.D. *Clinical Lectures and Essays*. London: Longmans, Green, 1875.

———. *Memoirs and Letters of Sir James Paget*. Ed. Stephen Paget. London: Longmans, Green, 1901.

Park, Roberta J. "Sport, Gender and Society in a Transatlantic Victorian Perspective." In Mangan and Park, eds., *From 'Fair Sex' to Feminism*, 58–93.

Patrick, George T. W. "The Psychology of Woman." *Popular Science Monthly* 47 (1895): 209–25.

Pernick, Martin S. *A Calculus of Suffering: Pain, Professionalism, and Anesthesia in 19th-Century America*. New York: Columbia University Press, 1985.

Peterson, Audrey C. "Brain Fever in Nineteenth-Century Literature: Fact and Fiction." *Victorian Studies* 19 (June 1976): 445–64.

Peterson, M. Jeanne. "Dr. Acton's Enemy: Medicine, Sex, and Society in Victorian England." *Victorian Studies* 29 (Summer 1986): 569–90.

———. *The Medical Profession in Mid-Victorian London*. Berkeley: University of California Press, 1978.

Pick, Daniel. " 'Terrors of the Night': *Dracula* and 'Degeneration' in the Late Nineteenth Century." *Critical Quarterly* 30, no. 4 (Winter 1988): 71–88.

Plato. *The Republic and Other Works*. Trans. B. Jowett. Garden City, N.Y.: Anchor Books, 1973.

Poirier, S. "The Weir Mitchell Rest Cure: Doctors and Patients." *Women's Studies* 10 (1983): 15–40.

Poovey, Mary. *Uneven Developments: The Ideological Work of Gender in Mid-Victorian England*. Chicago: University of Chicago Press, 1988.

Ray, Isaac. *Mental Hygiene*. Boston: Ticknor and Fields, 1863.

Richardson, Ruth. *Death, Dissection and the Destitute.* Harmondsworth, Eng.: Penguin, 1988.

Rose, Jacqueline. *Sexuality in the Field of Vision.* London: Verso, 1986.

Rosenberg, Charles. "The Therapeutic Revolution: Medicine, Meaning, and Social Change in 19th-Century America." In Leavitt and Numbers, eds., *Sickness and Health in America,* 39–52.

Rosenberg, Edgar. *From Shylock to Svengali: Jewish Stereotypes in English Fiction.* Stanford, Calif.: Stanford University Press, 1960.

Rothfield, Lawrence. *Vital Signs: Medical Realism in Nineteenth-Century Fiction.* Princeton, N.J.: Princeton University Press, 1992.

Rothman, David J. *The Discovery of the Asylum: Social Order and Disorder in the New Republic.* Boston: Little, Brown, 1971.

Rudé, George. *The Crowd in History: A Study of Popular Disturbances in France and England, 1730–1848.* New York: Wiley, 1964.

Russett, Cynthia Eagle. *Sexual Science: The Victorian Construction of Womanhood.* Cambridge, Mass.: Harvard University Press, 1989.

Russo, Mary. "Female Grotesques: Carnival and Theory." In de Lauretis, ed., *Feminist Studies/Critical Studies.* 213–29.

Sadoff, Dianne F. " 'Experiments Made by Nature': Mapping the Nineteenth-Century Hysterical Body." *Victorian Newsletter* 81 (Spring 1992): 41–44.

Sánchez-Eppler, Karen. "Bodily Bonds: The Intersecting Rhetorics of Feminism and Abolition." *Representations* 24 (Fall 1988): 28–59.

Scarry, Elaine. *The Body in Pain: The Making and Unmaking of the World.* New York: Oxford University Press, 1985.

———, ed. *Literature and the Body: Essays on Populations and Persons. Selected Papers From the English Institute, 1986.* Baltimore, Md.: Johns Hopkins University Press, 1988.

Schiebinger, Londa. *The Mind Has No Sex?: Women in the Origins of Modern Science.* Cambridge, Mass.: Harvard University Press, 1989.

Scull, Andrew, ed. *Madhouses, Mad-Doctors, and Madmen: The Social History of Psychiatry in the Victorian Era.* Philadelphia, Pa.: University of Pennsylvania Press, 1981.

Sekula, Allan. "The Body and the Archive." *October* 39 (Winter 1986): 3–64.

Seltzer, Mark. *Bodies and Machines.* New York: Routledge, 1992.

Shee, George F. "The Deterioration in the National Physique." *The Nineteenth Century* 53 (May 1903): 797–805.

Shorter, Edward. *Bedside Manners: The Troubled History of Doctors and Patients.* New York: Simon & Schuster, 1985.

———. *A History of Women's Bodies.* New York: Basic Books, 1982.

———. *From Paralysis to Fatique: A History of Psychosomatic Illness in the Modern Era.* New York: Free Press, 1992.

Shortt, S. E. D. "Physicians and Psychics: The Anglo-American Medical Response to Spiritualism, 1870–1890." *Journal of the History of Medicine and Allied Sciences* 39 (1984): 339–55.

Showalter, Elaine. *The Female Malady: Women, Madness, and English Culture, 1830–1980.* Harmondsworth, Eng.: Penguin, 1985.

———. "Syphilis, Sexuality, and the Fiction of the Fin de Siècle." In Yeazell, ed., *Sex, Politics, and Science in the Nineteenth-Century Novel,* 88–115.

———, ed. *The New Feminist Criticism: Essays on Women, Literature & Theory.* New York: Pantheon, 1985.

———, ed. *Speaking of Gender.* New York: Routledge, 1989.

Shuttleworth, Sally. *George Eliot and Nineteenth-Century Science: The Make-Believe of a Beginning.* Cambridge, Eng.: Cambridge University Press, 1984.

———. " 'The Surveillance of a Sleepless Eye': The Constitution of Neurosis in *Villette.*" In Levine, ed., *One Culture,* 313–35.

Sidis, Boris. *The Psychology of Suggestion: A Research into the Subconscious Nature of Man and Society.* New York: D. Appleton, 1898.

Sims, J. Marion. *The Story of My Life.* Ed. H. Marion Sims. New York: D. Appleton, 1884.

Smith, Margaret. "Introduction." In Brontë, *Shirley,* vii–xxiii.

Smith-Rosenberg, Carroll. *Disorderly Conduct: Visions of Gender in Victorian America.* New York: Oxford University Press, 1985.

Smith-Rosenberg, Carroll, and Charles Rosenberg. "The Female Animal: Medical and Biological Views of Women and their Role in Nineteenth-Century America." In Mangan and Park, eds., *From 'Fair Sex' to Feminism,* 13–37.

Sontag, Susan. *Illness as Metaphor.* New York: Vintage Books, 1979.

———. *AIDS and Its Metaphors.* New York: Farrar, Straus, and Giroux, 1989.

Spencer, Herbert. *First Principles.* New York: D. Appleton, 1886.

———. *Principles of Psychology.* Vol. 2. 2nd ed. New York: D. Appleton, 1897.

———. *The Study of Sociology.* New York: D. Appleton, 1896.

Stafford, Barbara Maria. *Body Criticism: Imaging the Unseen in Enlightenment Art and Medicine.* Cambridge, Mass.: MIT Press, 1991.

Stage, Sarah. *Female Complaints: Lydia Pinkham and the Business of Women's Medicine.* New York: W. W. Norton, 1979.

Stallybrass, Peter, and Allon White. *The Politics and Poetics of Transgression.* Ithaca, N.Y.: Cornell University Press, 1986.

Stewart, Garrett. *Death Sentences: Styles of Dying in British Fiction*. Cambridge, Mass.: Harvard University Press, 1984.

Stoker, Bram. *Dracula* [1897]. Harmondsworth, Eng.: Penguin, 1979.

———. *The Annotated Dracula*. Ed. Leonard Wolf. New York: Clarkson N. Potter, 1975.

Stowe, Harriet Beecher. *Uncle Tom's Cabin; or, Life Among the Lowly* [1852]. Harmondsworth, Eng.: Penguin, 1986.

Strouse, Jean. *Alice James: A Biography*. New York: Bantam Books, 1982.

Suleiman, Susan Rubin., ed., *The Female Body in Western Culture: Contemporary Perspectives*. Cambridge, Mass.: Harvard University Press, 1986.

Sully, James. *Sensation and Intuition: Studies in Psychology and Aesthetics*. London: H. S. King, 1874.

Talbot, Eugene S., M.D. *Degeneracy: Its Causes, Signs, and Results*. London: W. Scott, 1898.

Tambling, Jeremy. "*Middlemarch*, Realism and the Birth of the Clinic." *ELH* 57 (Winter 1990): 939–60.

Tarde, Gabriel. "Foules et sectes au point de vue criminel." *Revue des deux mondes*, November 15, 1893, 349–87.

———. *The Laws of Imitation* [1890]. Trans. Elsie Clews Parsons. New York: H. Holt, 1903.

———. *L'opinion et la foule*. Paris: Felix Alcan, 1901.

Tintner, Adeline R., and Henry D. Janowitz. "Inoperable Cancer: An Alternate Diagnosis for Milly Theale's Illness." *Journal of the History of Medicine and Allied Sciences* 42 (1987): 73–76.

Tompkins, Jane. *Sensational Designs: The Cultural Work of American Fiction, 1790–1860*. New York: Oxford University Press, 1985.

Trotter, Thomas. *A View of the Nervous Temperament: Being a Practical Enquiry into the Increasing Prevalence, Prevention, and Treatment of Those Diseases Commonly Called Nervous, Bilious, Stomach and Liver Complaints: Digestion; Low Spirits; Gout, &c.* London: Longman, 1807.

Tuke, Daniel Hack, M.D. *Illustrations of the Influence of the Mind upon the Body in Health and Disease, Designed to Elucidate the Action of the Imagination*. London: J. and A. Churchill, 1872.

Turner, Victor. "Social Dramas and Stories About Them." In Mitchell, ed., *On Narrative*, 137–64.

Veith, Ilza. *Hysteria: The History of a Disease*. Chicago: University of Chicago Press, 1965.

Vertinsky, Patricia. "Body Shapes: The Role of the Medical Establishment in Informing Female Exercise and Physical Education in Nineteenth-

Century North America." In Mangan and Park, eds., *From 'Fair Sex' to Feminism*, 256–81.

Vicinus, Martha. *Independent Women: Work and Community for Single Women, 1850–1920.* Chicago: University of Chicago Press, 1985.

———, ed. *Suffer and Be Still: Women in the Victorian Age.* Bloomington: Indiana University Press, 1972.

Vigouroux, Auguste, and Paul Juquelier. *La contagion mentale.* Paris: Doin, 1905.

"The Vulgarization of Salomé." *Current Literature* 45 (1908): 437–40.

Wall, Geoffrey. " 'Different from Writing': *Dracula* in 1897." *Literature and History* 10, no. 1 (1984): 15–23.

Walters, Ronald G., ed. *Primers for Prudery: Sexual Advice to Victorian America.* Englewood Cliffs, N.J.: Prentice-Hall, 1979.

Walvin, James. "Symbols of Moral Superiority: Slavery, Sport and the Changing World Order, 1800–1940." In Mangan and Walvin, eds., *Manliness and Morality*, 242–60.

Warren, Samuel. "Passages from the Diary of a Late Physician." *Blackwood's Edinburgh Magazine* 18 (September 1830): 474–95.

Weatherly, J. S., M.D. "Woman: Her Rights and Her Wrongs." *Transactions of the Medical Association of the State of Alabama* 24 (1872): 63–80.

Wells, H. G. *The War of the Worlds* [1898]. London: William Heinemann, 1930.

Welsh, Alexander. *George Eliot and Blackmail.* Cambridge, Mass.: Harvard University Press, 1985.

White, Hayden. *Metahistory: The Historical Imagination in Nineteenth-Century Europe.* Baltimore, Md.: Johns Hopkins University Press, 1973.

Whitlock, Roger. "The Psychology of Consciousness in *Daniel Deronda.*" *Victorians Institute Journal* 4 (1975): 17–24.

Williams, Carolyn. "Natural Selection and Narrative Form in *The Egoist.*" *Victorian Studies* 27 (Autumn 1983): 53–79.

Williams, J. P. "Psychical Research and Psychiatry in Late Victorian Britain: Trance as Ecstasy or Trance as Insanity." In Bynum, Porter, and Shepherd, eds., *The Anatomy of Madness*, vol. 1, 233–54.

Wilt, Judith. "The Imperial Mouth: Imperialism, the Gothic, and Science Fiction." *Journal of Popular Culture* 14 (Spring 1981): 618–28.

Wohl, Anthony S. *Endangered Lives: Public Health in Victorian Britain.* Cambridge, Mass.: Harvard University Press, 1983.

Wolf, Leonard. *A Dream of Dracula: In Search of the Living Dead.* Boston: Little, Brown; 1972.

Wood, Ann Douglas. " 'The Fashionable Diseases': Women's Complaints and Their Treatment in Nineteenth-Century America." In Hartman and Banner, eds., *Clio's Consciousness Raised*, 1–22.

Wood, Mrs. Henry. *East Lynne* [1861]. New Brunswick, N.J.: Rutgers University Press, 1984.

Yeazell, Ruth Bernard, ed. *Sex, Politics, and Science in the Nineteenth-Century Novel. Selected Papers from the English Institute, 1983–84.* Baltimore, Md.: Johns Hopkins University Press, 1986.

Index

In this index an "f" after a number indicates a separate reference on the next page, and an "ff" indicates separate references on the next two pages. A continuous discussion over two or more pages is indicated by a span of page numbers, e.g., "57–59." *Passim* is used for a cluster of references in close but not consecutive sequence.